Henrietta Maria

QUEEN OF THE CAVALIERS

HENRIETTA MARIA
QUEEN OF THE CAVALIERS

BY QUENTIN BONE

UNIVERSITY OF ILLINOIS PRESS

Urbana, Chicago, London

Queen Henrietta Maria, consort of England's Charles I, has not wanted biographers, but to my knowledge there has been no attempt to tell her life's story from the political standpoint or to explain fully her political role. Only two of her biographers, Henrietta Haynes (London, 1914) and Carola Lenanton Oman (London, 1936), have documented their works. The former emphasized Henrietta's position as a Catholic queen, pointing to her efforts in mitigation of penalties against recusants in England, while the latter was interested in Henrietta as a historical personality. I might also mention Ida Ashworth Taylor's two-volume narrative (London, 1905), which, though more detailed than the two noted above, contains scanty footnote references and lists only a modest bibliography of fewer than three pages of published sources.

This present work is a study of Henrietta's significance in English politics during those years when her position, first as a French princess eligible to become Charles's wife and then as his queen, enabled her to have some bearing upon English affairs. From the queen's time to the present century there has been repeated comment concerning her nefarious influence upon her husband's political actions. To be sure, a wife so loved by her husband was certain to affect his attitudes and behavior, but a closer study of her life appears to reveal that her influence was primarily of a personal and familial sort rather than of a significant political nature. If Charles treated the Catholics with more than accustomed leniency, it was not merely because of the queen's entreaties in their behalf, but also because he personally bore little enmity toward individual Catholics; he was not a religious persecutor. If during the Civil Wars the queen solicited aid from Catholic powers to support the crown, this was not her doing alone; Charles sought aid wherever he could get it and was not reluctant to second his wife's endeavors. In really important matters of state Charles acted independently of his wife's advice. Charles's appointments to top offices rarely coincided with the queen's wishes, as was true when he appointed Bishop Juxon to the post of Lord High Treasurer. During the course of conflict against Parliament, he temporarily entered into agreement with that body and also with the Scots against his wife's fulminations. It is probably safe to conclude, therefore, that even without Henrietta's admonitions, Charles's political course would not have been very different from what it in fact was and he would have ended his days with his head upon the block.

Such was my conclusion when I first undertook this study as a doctoral dissertation some years ago, and after subsequent review I find no reason to change the thesis. On offering it for publication, I realize with regret how belatedly my thanks to those who have assisted me is appearing in print. I remember with gratitude the help of the library administration at the University of Illinois in acquiring many of the documents on microfilm, and am especially indebted to the librarians in the pamphlet and manuscripts rooms of the British Museum for their generous assistance. Above all, I am grateful to the late Raymond Phineas Stearns, emeritus professor of history at the University of Illinois, who in the course of a conversation only a few months before his death encouraged me to attempt the publication of Henrietta's biography. All faults or inadequacies that might appear here, however, must be attributed to me.

CONTENTS

I   BIRTH TO BETROTHAL *page 3*

II   EARLY DISCORDS OF MARRIAGE *page 39*

III HALCYON YEARS *page 73*

IV   BRINK OF CONFLICT *page 94*

V   THE QUEEN AND THE TRIBUNAL OF THE PEOPLE *page 115*

VI   NEW TRIALS, NEW DANGERS *page 142*

VII FLIGHT TO FRANCE *page 170*

VIII HOPE AND HEARTBREAK *page 203*

EPILOGUE · TROUBLED TWILIGHT *page 230*

BIBLIOGRAPHICAL ESSAY *page 253*

INDEX *page 273*

Note on Dates

Two calendars were in use during the era with which this work is concerned. The Old Style or Julian calendar employed in England was eleven days behind the New Style or Gregorian calendar used in most European countries. In England, furthermore, the year began on March 25 for most purposes rather than on January 1. In this book dates are given according to the Old calendar with the year beginning on January 1.

Note on Foreign Coins

Money raised by Henrietta Maria on the Continent in support of Royalist arms is stated in sterling equivalents. To give comparative values of monetary units in seventeenth-century Europe is a precarious undertaking and can be only approximate at best for a time when mintage was not exact, wars were endemic, and sovereigns toyed with devaluation. Perhaps the most explicit source on seventeenth-century monetary exchange rates was the law merchant or commercial arithmetic book published to instruct merchants engaged in foreign trade. Of such books, I have consulted the following: Gerard Malynes, *Lex Mercatoria* (London,

1629); Giovanni Giacomo Lando, *Aritmetica Mercantile* (Venice, 1640); C. Naulot, "Nouveau Traité des Changes Étranges Qui Se Sont dans les Principles Places de l'Europe," in M. Jacques du Puys, *L'Art des Lettres de Changes* (Brussels, 1673); François Bertrand De Barreme, *Le Grand Banquier ou le Livre des Monnoyes Étrangères Reduits en Monnoyes de France* (Paris, 1696); Lewis Roberts, *The Merchant's Map of Commerce* (4th ed., London, 1700); and Jacques Savary, *Universal Dictionary of Trade and Commerce* (2 vols. in 4 parts, tr. Malachy Postlethwayt, London, 1757).

Four continental monetary units are mentioned in estimating the sums collected by Henrietta: the Dutch guilder and the French livre, crown, and pistole. For the purpose of this work, the guilder and livre each exchanged for two shillings sterling, the crown for six shillings, and the pistole for eighteen shillings, though these ratios did not hold through the remainder of the seventeenth century.

Henrietta Maria

QUEEN OF THE CAVALIERS

Abbreviations Used in Notes

MANUSCRIPT COLLECTION	LOCATION	ABBREVIATION
Additional Manuscripts	British Museum, London	*Additional MSS*
Manuscrits, Archives Nationale	Bibliothèque Nationale, Paris	*MSS Archives Nationale*
Carte Manuscripts	Bodleian Library, Oxford	*Carte MSS*
Clarendon State Papers	Bodleian Library, Oxford	*MSS Clar. S. P.*
Egerton Manuscripts	British Museum, London	*Egerton MSS*
Manuscrits Français	Bibliothèque Nationale, Paris	*MSS Français*
Harleian Manuscripts	British Museum, London	*Harl. MSS*
Manuscripts, Lambeth Palace Library	Lambeth Palace, London	*MSS Lambeth Palace Library*
Lansdowne Manuscripts	British Museum, London	*Lansdowne MSS*
Manuscrits, Bibliothèque Mazarine	Bibliothèque Mazarine, Paris	*MSS Mazarine*
Manuscrits, Bibliothèque St. Geneviève	Bibliothèque St. Geneviève, Paris	*MSS St. Geneviève*
Stowe Manuscripts	British Museum, London	*Stowe MSS*

CHAPTER I

BIRTH TO BETROTHAL

1609-25   "THIS day the queen was delivered of a daughter at the Louvre around ten o'clock in the evening; for which the court showed no gladness or rejoicing, and did not fire a single shot of the cannon to mark the event."[1] Thus did Pierre de L'Étoile record the birth of Henrietta Maria in his journal entry for November 26, 1609.[2] The queen to whom he referred was Marie de Medici, daughter of the Duke of Florence and descendant of the famous Florentine banking family. She already had provided three sons to assure the succession to the throne of France, and this newborn child, her sixth, was by the Salic law excluded from ever wearing the crown. Accordingly,

1. Pierre de L'Étoile, *Mémoires-Journaux* (12 vols., ed. G. Burnet, A. Champollion, E. Halphen, Paul Lacroix, Charles Read, and Tamisey de Larrogue, Paris, 1875–96), X, 83. Pierre de L'Étoile (1540?–1611) was descended from a family distinguished for serving the crown in civil capacity. Both his father and grandfather had served honorably in the Parlement. Pierre himself was first usher in the chancery, but he usually is remembered for his journals.

2. The date usually given for Henrietta's birth is November 25, 1609. See *La Grande Encyclopédie* (31 vols., Paris, n.d.), IX, 1116; also *Dictionary of National Biography* (63 vols., ed. Leslie Stephens and Sidney Lee, London, 1895–97), XXV, 429 (referred to throughout as *D.N.B.*). François de Bassompierre, a contemporary of Henry IV, agrees with the date L'Étoile gives; see Bassompierre, *Journal de Ma Vie: Mémoires* (4 vols., ed. Marie J. A. LaCropte, Paris, 1870–77), I, 255. By the Julian or Old Style calendar then used in England, Henrietta's birth date was November 14, 1609.

the birth of Henrietta, someday to be Queen of England and one of the most tragic of royal personages, was generally received with as little acclaim as L'Étoile indicated in his diary.

Henrietta's father, Henry IV, first of the Bourbon rulers of France, hardly turned his attention from the gaming table on hearing of his daughter's birth. She was, after all, the sixth child his queen had presented to him, a marginal child whose importance was further diminished by her sex. Besides, other interests weighed on his mind. Both love and war embroiled him. The greybeard of fifty-seven years was engaged in the pursuit of a new mistress, the sixteen-year-old wife of the Prince of Condé, while his military pursuits were directed toward the expulsion of Hapsburg power from the duchy of Cleves.

A few days following the birth of Henrietta, the Prince of Condé and his wife fled across the French border into the Spanish Netherlands to spare the princess the attentions of the king. Receiving this intelligence while playing at cards, Henry IV leaned toward his close companion, Marshal de Bassompierre, and whispered, "I am ruined."[3] He immediately withdrew from the playing table and called for members of his council to meet him in the nearby room where his wife was spending her accouchement. Even the Duke of Sully, the chief minister and treasurer, was summoned. The Duke of Sully gave his master some good advice. Asked what was to be done, he replied, "Nothing." Feigned indifference to the flight of Condé would convince the archduke in Brussels that the whole matter was not worth his attention, and without support in Brussels the prince and his wife would have to return to France within three months. But Henry's passion was too ardent to exercise patience. He followed other advice in dispatching guards with all haste to apprehend the fleeing couple if they had not yet made good their escape, and sent a special envoy to beg the archduke for their return if they had already reached Flanders.[4]

3. Bassompierre, *Mémoires*, I, 251, 255–260; L'Étoile, *Mémoires-Journaux*, X, 86–87.
4. Bassompierre, *Mémoires*, I, 261.

The flight of the Princess of Condé to Spanish territory, if not the cause impelling Henry to military action, probably heightened his zeal for the campaign he was planning against the Austrian Hapsburgs, who were dynastically related and politically allied to the ruling family of Spain. Contention and war between the Hapsburg rulers and the French kings had been intermittent during the previous century, when the Hapsburgs' threat to acquire preponderant power over the European continent had been countered by French resistance. During the first two decades of his reign, Henry IV had been preoccupied in restoring political order and economic vitality within France after the country had been burdened by thirty years of internecine religious and political wars. Having completed the task of internal restoration, Henry was able to turn his attention to foreign relations. The particular issue in dispute was the question of the succession to the duchy of Cleves, whose direct ruling line had died out. The Hapsburg ruler in Austria claimed that since he was Holy Roman Emperor, the fiefdom of Cleves had reverted to him, and he proposed to grant the duchy to his brother Leopold despite the protests of other contenders. The disputed territory lay in the Rhine valley, immediately south of the Dutch Netherlands. Henry was determined to thwart the extension of Hapsburg power in northern Germany. Throughout the winter of 1609–10 the noise of military preparation was heard in France. In late spring Henry's forces were on the march toward Germany, and daily the king was expected to depart from Paris and join his forces.[5]

Before setting off for wars, Henry was obliged to attend the belated coronation of his queen, who had not shared in her husband's ceremonial enthronement five years before their marriage. Marie de Medici insisted on the performance of this formality, for without it certain peccant factions might attempt to usurp her

5. Maximilien de Bethune, Duke of Sully, *Mémoires* (5 vols., Edinburgh, 1819), IV, 475–484, 505–506, 508; V, 170–172, 186; Hardouin de Beaumont de Péréfixe, *The History of Henry IV* (London, 1663), p. 341; *Recueil des Lettres Missives de Henry IV* (7 vols., ed. M. Gerger de Xivrey [*Collection de Documents Inédits*], Paris, 1853–76), VII, 859–861.

children's rights were their father to die while away on campaign.[6] Henry had fathered a generous number of illegitimate offspring, whose paternity he acknowledged and whose claims would be put forward were Marie's position as queen not incontrovertibly established. In accordance with the queen's wish, the coronation was solemnized at the church of St. Denis, situated about four miles north of Paris, on May 13, 1610.[7]

On the day following the ceremony, Henry returned to Paris. His usual jollity and ebullience were overcome by moroseness and pessimistic foreboding. Perhaps not too much should be made of the shifting moods of a middle-aged man, but Henry's mind was not impervious to predictions of his impending death, however much he outwardly scoffed at such prognostications. He had been warned that his wife's coronation would be closely followed by his own demise. In the afternoon he called for his carriage and asked to be taken to the Arsenal, where the Duke of Sully had offices. As he rode through the narrow, tortuous streets of the city, he saw that they were festooned in preparation for the celebration of the queen's coronation. On turning into the Rue de la Ferronerie, or the blacksmith's street, his carriage was stopped by congested traffic. At that instant an obscure friar, François Ravaillac, stepped onto a spoke of one of the carriage wheels, hoisted himself to the window beside which Henry was sitting, and struck the king three blows with a dagger. Henry was mortally wounded, the aorta leading from his heart having been severed. By the time his carriage returned to the royal residence, the king was dead.[8]

Henry's body was taken to its final resting place at the abbey church of St. Denis, burial ground for the kings of France. The infant Henrietta—she was about six months old—was carried to the funeral rites to cast holy water upon the bier of her father, as did the other legitimate children of the king. The performance

6. Bassompierre, *Mémoires*, I, 271.

7. *Ibid.*, pp. 272–273; L'Étoile, *Mémoires-Journaux*, X, 217–218, 224–225; Sully, *Mémoires*, IV, 522–524; *The Life and Death of Henrietta Maria de Bourbon* (London, 1685, reprint 1820), p. 3.

8. Bassompierre, *Mémoires*, I, 273; L'Étoile, *Mémoires-Journaux*, X, 218–231.

of this reverent duty marked the second visit of Henrietta to St. Denis, the earlier occasion having been the coronation of her mother only a few weeks before.[9]

Although Henrietta was too young to understand the gravity of these observances or the meaning of events during the first six months of her life, they reveal something of the character of the age in which she was born. One of the more obvious facts of those times was the development of the nation-state form of political organization. With some concession to quasi-feudal elements, Henry IV had suppressed internal strife and centralized political authority in the control of the monarch. He was primarily a national instead of a feudal ruler. The military campaign he was planning to secure Cleves from Hapsburg control was undertaken for national rather than for personal or dynastic reasons. In fact, Henry IV disclaimed any intention of retaining the territory as his own possession.[10] As well as the emergence of nationalism there was the persistence of religious conflict, since this problem deriving from the Reformation awaited the terrible experience of the Thirty Years' War before it subsided. In evidence of unsettled religious conditions, Henry IV was assassinated by a fanatic who protested against toleration of the Huguenots.[11] And the scientific method of inquiry into natural phenomena, then in process of development, had not dispelled prevailing superstitions concerning the spirit world and the physical environment. Dreams, for example, were widely taken to be omens of ill or good fortune, for both Henry and his wife were said to have had portentous dreams on the eve of his assassination.[12]

Much as these political, religious, and intellectual developments were to bear upon Henrietta's life in an impersonal way, she was more intimately influenced by her immediate circum-

9. *Life and Death of Henrietta Maria*, p. 4. The interval between the king's death and his burial was no unusual delay for the seventeenth century.

10. Sully, *Mémoires*, V, 187.

11. "The Trial of Ravaillac," *Bibliotheca Curiosa* (40 vols. in 9, ed. Edmund Goldsmid, Edinburgh, 1885), XII, 5–21.

12. Sully, *Mémoires*, IV, 522–524; L'Étoile, *Mémoires*, X, 224–225.

stances. Her association with other members of her family and with her nurses and teachers impinged on her awareness more acutely than did the historical forces of the age, at least during her early years.

The first of Henry IV's children, Louis the Dauphin, was eight years old when Henrietta was born. A year younger than Louis was Elizabeth. Four years after the birth of Elizabeth came Christine, and in the succeeding years the Duke of Orleans, who died before he was given a name, then Gaston, and last of all Henrietta.[13] It was only natural that Henrietta had closer association with Gaston, who was nearest her in age, than with any of the other children. Louis, being next in line to the succession, was taken from the royal nursery where his brother and sisters lived at about the time of Henrietta's birth and was placed under male governors and teachers. Elizabeth and Christine, married at early ages, left the royal household before they could appreciate Henrietta as other than a younger sister whose personality traits had made no strong impress on their memories.

These children of the king lived during most of their early years at the château of Saint-Germain-en-Laye, a palatial country seat about two hours' journey from Paris as the coach then traveled. A hunting lodge that had served French kings from the time of St. Louis, Saint-Germain-en-Laye was under Henry IV nothing other than a royal nursery. It was beautifully situated on a wooded crest sloping down to a bend of the river Seine. There were, to be sure, excursions for the children to other of the royal residences, principally to Fontainebleau, to St. Cloud, to the Luxembourg, and even to the Louvre, although Marie de Medici kept her children away from Paris as much as possible to avoid the danger of contagion. All of these palaces had been successively rebuilt or enlarged. Like Francis I of a century before, Henry IV was a great builder, keeping architects and workers busy fulfilling plans to enhance the royal residences. As Henrietta saw these palaces, they were splendid examples of French Renaissance archi-

13. Péréfixe, *History of Henry IV*, pp. 382–383.

tecture, since most of the construction did not antedate the time of Francis I.[14]

One can only wonder at the memories the children of Henry IV must have had of their childhood days at Saint-Germain-en-Laye. With its terraced gardens, its two broad stone stairways leading down to a quay along the river's edge, its famous grotto, and its many fountains, the old château must have furnished a pleasant setting. Pleasant as the setting might have been, descriptions of life at Saint-Germain-en-Laye indicate that there were bustle and confusion at times. Each child had his own retinue of servants to swell the staff of domestics that performed more general services around the palace. And in addition to Henry's legal offspring there were his eight natural children. Henry IV had an oriental concept of the family; he loved all of his children, whether legitimate or illegitimate, and thought they should be reared together.[15]

Presiding as governess over "the flock," as court wits jocularly referred to Henry's children, was Madame de Montglat.[16] The king and queen were so certain of Madame de Montglat's care in bringing up their brood that except for occasional supervisory orders the children were left almost wholly in her charge. Madame de Montglat was treated more as a close friend of the family than as a servant. Henry established an almost confidential friendship with her, often exchanging information on prevention of infectious diseases or recipes for concoctions to ease the gout, an affliction that handicapped him in his later years. The children were devoted to this large, thin, ugly woman, who was almost a mother to them, and yet their love for her was more an expression of respect and duty than of warm affection. Madame de Montglat kept the

14. Jean Héroard, *Journal* (2 vols., ed. Eudoxie Soulié and Edouard de Barthélemy, Paris, 1868), I, 223, 423; Lucy Crump, *Nursery Life 300 Years Ago* (London, 1929), pp. 32, 40; Louis Batiffol, *La Vie Intime d'une Reine de France* (Paris, 1911), p. 259 (referred to hereafter as Batiffol, *Vie Intime*); MSS *Français 3818*, fol. 13; Rodolphe Pfnor, *Monographie du Palais de Fontainebleau* (3 vols., Paris, 1863), I, 11–20.

15. Batiffol, *Vie Intime*, p. 264; Péréfixe, *History of Henry IV*, pp. 384–385.

16. Batiffol, *Vie Intime*, pp. 260–261, 263.

busy nursery in order and dispensed discipline whenever the children were disobedient. She had been instructed not to pamper them, and perhaps she was too busy to coddle her charges anyway. Incidents are not wanting to illustrate that wills sometimes clashed when the children proved recalcitrant, as is seen in one of the earliest letters Henrietta Maria ever wrote:

MAMANGAT

I pray you excuse me if you saw my little sulky fit which held me this morning. I cannot be right all of a sudden; but I will do all I can to content you; meantime, I beg you will no longer be angry with me, who am and will be all my life, Mamangat,
    Your affectionate friend,

HENRIETTA[17]

Here is an apology of a little girl who had been naughty—an early trace of petulance and self-will later to be shown in adult life. While the circumstances occasioning this note are no longer known, it can easily be imagined that Henrietta, after showing bad behavior toward the governess, was taken to her room by her undergoverness, Madame Saint-Georges, and was made to write the note of apology.

To the royal children, Madame de Montglat must have seemed closer than their own mother. Marie de Medici was not demonstrative in her affection for her children; she probably loved them, but at a distance. For weeks or even months at a time she remained away from them, and although she received reports from and answered with instructions to Madame de Montglat, even this show of interest was almost clinical in its detachment. Whenever she visited them at Saint-Germain-en-Laye, she was not an inti-

17. Mary Anne Everett Green, *Letters of Queen Henrietta Maria* (London, 1857), p. 4. The manner in which Henrietta addressed her governess in the note is interesting. The name Madame de Montglat was difficult for the younger children to pronounce, so in their infantile way they called her "Mamangat." In letters written years later after the children had become kings, dukes, and queens, they still affectionately addressed their former governess as Mamangat. See Armand J. du Plessis, Duke of Richelieu, Cardinal, *Lettres, Instructions Diplomatiques et Papiers d'État* (8 vols., ed. Denis M. L. Avenel [*Collection de Documents Inédits*], Paris, 1853–77), I, 150n (referred to hereafter as Richelieu, *Lettres*).

mately affectionate mother, but a parent who was to be respected and obeyed. In contrast to her husband, who romped gleefully with his children and insisted they call him "Pappa," Marie de Medici insisted upon the maintenance of a formal decorum in relations between parent and child. She received her children into her presence, but not in a familiar way, and recommended punishment or reward in accordance with the deserts of their behavior.[18]

Marie de Medici, herself a person without any claim to learning, gave scant attention to the education of her children. Years later Henrietta, then an exiled queen living in France, was to express her regret that she had received so little education, and especially that her ignorance of history had made it impossible for her to understand political conditions in England.[19] One biographer has written that Henrietta and her brother Gaston had François Savary de Breves as their tutor.[20] For many years the French ambassador at the court of the Ottoman sultan, de Breves was the foremost scholar of oriental literature in his day, but since he was dismissed from the court when Henrietta was not yet nine years old, his influence upon the development of her mind was not very marked. There is no certain knowledge of the books Henrietta studied, although there is evidence that she read verses or at least stories from the Bible, and it is probable that she learned verses emphasizing moral precepts from Pibrac's *Quatrains*.[21] Inasmuch as Henrietta was said to have had a lovely voice, she probably received some training in music, which was at that time receiving its modern form of notation. Her fondness for dancing and penchant for theatricals probably derived from childhood instruction

18. *MSS Français 3818*, fols. 26, 32, 34, 35, 38, 39; Héroard, *Journal*, I, 116; Batiffol, *Vie Intime*, pp. 255, 257.

19. Jacques Bossuet, "Oraison Funèbre de Henrietta Maria de France," *Oraisons Funèbres* (ed. P. Jacquinet, Paris, n.d.), p. 1.

20. Agnes Strickland, "Henrietta Maria," *Lives of the Queens of England* (8 vols., Boston, 1860), VIII, 9; "François Savary de Breves," *Biographie Universelle* (45 vols., 2nd ed. by Mme C. Desplaces, Paris, 1843–65), V, 502–503.

21. Guy du Faur, Seigneur de Pibrac (1529–84), a distinguished student of law, was sent on a number of foreign embassies in service of the king and was a member of the royal council under Henry III. He is best remembered for his *Quatrains*. "Seigneur de Pibrac," *Biographie Universelle*, XXXIII, 171–173.

or participation in those accomplishments. Performances of ballets, plays, and pageants by the royal children were frequently mentioned in commentaries on Henry IV's court. Often the adult members of the court, including the most grave persons on the king's council, were obliged to attend these juvenile presentations, for which they pretended an avid interest although inwardly they suffered agonies over the childish speech and awkward movements of the performers.[22]

Religious instruction and training in court etiquette took a leading part in Henrietta's education. Marie de Medici insisted that her children be given an awareness of their importance and dignity, and permitted only persons of noble rank to have audience with her son Louis. The mores of the time, however, permitted even in the company of the children a coarse language and ribaldry which would be considered shocking in a later age.[23]

The play of the children was so similar to childhood pastimes of today as hardly to need comment.[24] In short, they mimicked their elders. Girls played with dolls, doll houses, and doll dishes. They played games closely resembling blindman's buff and puss in the corner or amused themselves by pretending to plant a garden—very much as children might occupy themselves in almost any age.

Amid the concerns and pastimes of childhood, Henrietta remained an obscure younger daughter of the royal family. Court chroniclers hardly mentioned the daughters of Henry IV, or if they did they often confused the names of the three girls. Little as was written about Elizabeth and Christine, the two older daughters, Henrietta's personality was even less definite and less often mentioned in the records of those years.[25] She was usually present

22. Héroard, *Journal*, I, 117, 118, 120, 243, 260, 262, 285, 287, 376–377; Crump, *Nursery Life 300 Years Ago*, pp. 147, 151, 163, 170; Batiffol, *Vie Intime*, p. 260.

23. Héroard, *Journal*, I, 128; Green, *Letters of Henrietta Maria*, p. 2.

24. Crump, *Nursery Life 300 Years Ago*, pp. 74, 98, 99, 100–104; Héroard, *Journal*, I, 113, 114, 116, 248, 250.

25. K. A. Patmore, *The Court of Louis XIII* (London, 1909), p. 173; Batiffol, *Vie Intime*, p. 285.

on important state occasions, as at the coronation of her brother Louis in September, 1610, when she was carried by the Princess of Condé. On a few other occasions in later years Henrietta also appeared before public view. She attended the reception of Louis's Spanish bride at Bordeaux in 1615 and the marriage of Christine to the Duke of Savoy in 1619.[26] Apart from the incidental mention of her presence at such public affairs, Henrietta seems to have been overlooked by the recorders of court life during the first decade of her existence.

During most of Henrietta's preadolescent years, France was under the regency of her mother.[27] A large, fleshy, indolent woman, Marie de Medici wanted peace, peace at almost any price, so that she might enjoy the amenities of her position. She almost completely reversed the policies which had been promoted by her husband. Rather than take energetic measures to quell the rebellious nobility, she chose the easier course of bribing them. The millions of livres which the Duke of Sully had accumulated in the treasury flowed out to purchase an unstable order in domestic politics. The dowager queen trusted her Italian favorites, Concino Concini and his wife, for counsel, and ultimately dismissed her husband's advisers. As for foreign relations, Henry's policy of resisting the aggrandizement of Hapsburg power was forgotten. Understandable, perhaps, was the abandonment of his campaign to save Cleves from the grasp of the Austrian emperor, but more inexcusable was the alliance of France with Spain through a double marriage with the ruling family of that country: Princess Elizabeth was betrothed to Philip IV, and Louis was married to the Infanta Anne. Rarely had a ruler of France displayed greater ineptness or neglect in serving the security of the state.

Louis XIII, although coming into his majority in 1614, showed little propensity for government, and to prevent him from becom-

26. *Life and Death of Henrietta Maria*, p. 4.
27. James B. Perkins, *France under Mazarin* (2 vols., New York, 1902), I, 18–19, 63–68, 76; Henri Hauser, *La Prépondérance Espagnole* (vol. IX in the Peuples et Civilizations series, ed. Louis Halphen and Philippe Sagnac, Paris, 1933), pp. 286–294; *Egerton MSS 2884*, fol. 17.

ing interested in political affairs, his mother kept him occupied with trivial pastimes and worthless friends. Meanwhile, Louis nurtured his resentment against courtiers who looked on him with contempt. The insolence of Concini, the hated foreigner, especially grated on his pride. Finally his smoldering vengeance broke through. With the connivance of his falconer, Louis d'Albert, later to be made Duke of Luynes, Louis XIII overthrew the regency; Concini was murdered by a guard of officers sent to arrest him, and Marie de Medici was banished to Blois.[28]

Henrietta Maria did not accompany her mother into exile. One source states that she feared to show sympathy toward her mother because of the displeasure such an attitude might incite in her brother Louis.[29] Then only eight years of age, Henrietta probably was not apprehensive over any danger to her person. We can only conjecture what effect this disruption in the family might have had upon her. Because the queen mother had not been generous in her outward expression of affection for her children, and since she had lived apart from them much of the time, it might be supposed that Henrietta was insensitive to her mother's absence. The evidence of later years, however, indicates that Henrietta was much devoted to her mother.[30] It is not unlikely that during the years of her mother's exile Henrietta established a strong attachment for Madame Saint-Georges, who had always been closer to her than the head governess, Madame de Montglat. Discord in the family and separation from her mother must have created an emotional vacuum that had to be filled by someone, and Madame

28. Armand J. du Plessis, Duke of Richelieu, Cardinal, *Mémoires* (10 vols., ed. P. M. Charles, François Bruel, and Robert Lavallée [Société de l'Histoire de France], Paris, 1907–31), II, 207–208 (referred to hereafter as Richelieu, *Mémoires*); Hauser, *La Prépondérance Espagnole*, pp. 292–293; C. V. Wedgwood, *Richelieu and the French Monarchy* (London, 1949), pp. 45–46; Héroard, *Journal*, I, 159–160.

29. Richelieu, *Mémoires*, II, 210; *Life and Death of Henrietta Maria*, p. 4.

30. In 1638, Henrietta was to show tender solicitude and love for her mother when Marie de Medici, again exiled from the French court, sought refuge in England. See p. 108.

Saint-Georges[31] would appear to have been the person to supply this deficiency in the life of Princess Henrietta.

When in June of 1620 Marie de Medici was reconciled with her son and again admitted to the court, Henrietta began to receive more public attention, because it was time to consider a suitable marriage for her.[32] Only ten years of age, she was still too young to wed, but some political advantage might be gained by negotiating a contract which postponed the consummation of the marriage. To be sure, there had been many suggestions of matching her with one or another prince.[33] While she was still in the cradle, it was said, her father had mentioned an English marriage as a future possibility. Throughout the ensuing years there had been tentative suggestions, coming from either London or Paris, of a dynastic relationship between the two courts, but all earlier proposals concerned the two older sisters of Henrietta rather than Henrietta herself. No serious efforts were made in Henrietta's behalf until Louis's confidant, the Duke of Luynes, sought closer relations with England to offset the rivalry of Spain. In 1621 he sent an obscure person named du Buisson to England on the pretext of buying horses for the royal stable, but with secret instructions to sound out the attitude of the English court concerning a French match for Prince Charles. The next year Luynes sent his brother, Marshal de Cadenet, for the avowed purpose of initiating a marriage contract. By that time, however, James I had gone so far in contracting a marriage between his son and the Spanish Infanta Dona Maria that Cadenet's embassy appeared to be superfluous.[34]

31. Madame Saint-Georges, born Jeanne de Harlay, was the daughter of Madame de Montglat. During her earlier years she served under her mother in caring for the royal children. Later she became lady of honor to Henrietta Maria. See Richelieu, *Lettres*, I, 150n.

32. *Life and Death of Henrietta Maria*, p. 4; Richelieu, *Lettres*, II, 18.

33. *Stowe MSS 173*, fols. 142, 174, 205; John Rushworth, *Historical Collections* (8 vols., London, 1721–22), I, 1.

34. Leveneur de Tillières, *Mémoires* (ed. M. C. Hippeau, Paris, 1862), pp. 26–27; Richelieu, *Mémoires*, III, 116–117.

The negotiations involved in James's attempt to conclude a match with Spain were to have important results for Henrietta. Apart from the fact that James I had ended the Elizabethan conflict with Spain and considered peaceful relations with that country peculiarly his own policy, by 1622 he had added reasons for desiring a Spanish alliance. In 1619 James's son-in-law, Frederick, Elector of the Palatinate, had accepted the crown of Bohemia offered to him by the nobility of that kingdom after they had overthrown their reigning sovereign, Ferdinand of Austria. The incident was in large measure an outcome of religious division and political problems arising from the Reformation, and it touched off the terrible conflict of the Thirty Years' War. Frederick was leader of the Protestant princes in Germany, while Ferdinand, who had been educated by Jesuits, supported the Catholic Counter-Reformation. The Czech nobility of Bohemia had revolted against their Hapsburg king because they feared his encroachment against their Protestant religion. Ferdinand, who was the Holy Roman Emperor as well as Archduke of Austria, could look to his Hapsburg relatives in Spain for assistance against the Protestant states. After occupying the throne of Bohemia for only a few months, Frederick was driven out of the country by imperialist forces, and when a Spanish army occupied the Palatinate, he became a prince without a country. It was the plight of Frederick that made James all the more eager to acquire a marriage alliance with Spain. He hoped that a dynastic relationship with the Spanish Hapsburgs would induce them to evacuate the Palatinate and restore Frederick to his patrimony.[35] Improbable though it was that the Spanish king would act against Hapsburg interests by handing over the Rhenish lands he had so recently acquired, the particular difficulty on which negotiations had stuck was the Spanish demand that the Catholic religion be tolerated in England. Besides insisting

35. Francesco de Jesus, *Narrative of the Spanish Marriage Treaty* (tr. and ed. Samuel Rawson Gardiner [The Camden Society], Westminster, 1869), p. 105; Rushworth, *Historical Collections*, I, 1; *Cabala, Mysteries of State* (London, 1654), pp. 112, 113.

that the infanta enjoy full security in exercising her faith, including her own chapels and train of priests, and that the children of the marriage be reared as Catholics up to their twelfth year without prejudice to their hereditary claims if they persisted in that religion, the Spanish government set down the further condition that the English king prevail on Parliament to abrogate all laws which had been enacted against Catholic recusants.[36] James was unable to grant this last condition, because he knew the militantly Protestant parliament would react vehemently against such a proposal. James I had gone so far in his concessions to the Spanish, however, as to promise secretly that he would not enforce anti-Catholic laws which had been passed by Parliament. It was on the basis of this promise that a Spanish request for a dispensation to allow the marriage of the Infanta Dona Maria and the Prince of Wales was sent to the pope early in 1623.[37]

At this point in the negotiations, James's favorite, the Marquis of Buckingham, hit upon a madcap scheme intended to hasten the royal marriage and to enhance his own fame. Buckingham proposed that he and Charles travel incognito to Spain, where the prince, under the tutelage of his companion and with the benefit of the latter's worldly wisdom, could woo the infanta personally and bring matters to a speedy conclusion. An arrogant, reckless young man on whom James showered every favor, Buckingham quite overpowered the judgment of the still younger Charles. The aging king saw the folly in Buckingham's proposal. If Charles and "Steenie," as James affectionately called Buckingham, went to Spain, they would place themselves in an unfavorable position for bargaining; they would appear to come as suppliants begging for the hand of the infanta. Nevertheless, after much wheedling and coaxing, the old king consented to let them undertake the venture.[38]

36. Jesus, *Spanish Marriage Treaty*, pp. 107, 130.

37. *Cabala*, pp. 258–259; Thomas Frankland, *The Annals of King James and King Charles the First* (London, 1681), pp. 37, 44; Rushworth, *Historical Collections*, I, 4, 14, 34; Jesus, *Spanish Marriage Treaty*, pp. 179, 197.

38. Edward Hyde, Earl of Clarendon, *The History of the Rebellion and Civil*

Charles and Buckingham, accompanied by only two servants, started out in the manner of knights-errant on February 17, 1623. They quickly reached the Channel and crossed over to France. Thinly disguised by false beards and announcing themselves by no great stretch of the imagination as Tom and John Smith, they lingered at the court in Paris for several days. There, witnessing the rehearsal of a ballet which the ladies of the court were to present, Charles saw Henrietta Maria for the first time, but he scarcely noticed her, for his eyes were fixed on Queen Anne, who, being the older sister of Dona Maria, might give some portent of the one for whom he made his distant journey.[39]

Spurring their horses in a hard ride through southern France and across the Pyrenees, James's "Dear Sweet boys, worthy to be put into a new Romanso," arrived at the house of the British ambassador in Madrid on March 2, 1623.[40] Here they were to remain for the next six months. The Spanish ministers refused to concede any more generous terms for a marriage treaty than had been granted to James through more distant dealings. Although the Spanish people were cordial in receiving their unexpected visitors, it was not long until disappointment was expressed on both sides. Charles failed to obtain a single private interview with the infanta, who was thoroughly frightened by the rashness of the two English gentlemen, and the Spanish court was offended by Buckingham's presumptuous behavior.[41] At length it appeared to Charles and Buckingham that they were being put off and played for fools. It was obvious the Spanish would not trade the Palatinate for a marriage, as the Count of Olivares, first minister to Philip IV,

---

Wars in England (7 vols., Oxford, 1849), I, 16–19 (referred to hereafter as Clarendon, *History of the Rebellion*); *D.N.B.*, LVIII, 330; Isaac Disraeli, *Commentaries on the Life and Reign of Charles I* (2 vols., ed. and rev. B. Disraeli, London, 1851), I, 29.

39. Henry Ellis, *Original Letters* (12 vols. in 3 series, London, 1824–46), ser. 3, III, 121–122; Rushworth, *Historical Collections*, I, 76; Philip Yorke, Earl of Hardwicke, *Miscellaneous State Papers* (2 vols., London, 1778), I, 399 (referred to hereafter as Hardwicke, *State Papers*).

40. *Cabala*, pp. 14–15; Rushworth, *Historical Collections*, I, 98–100.

41. Jesus, *Spanish Marriage Treaty*, pp. 230, 232; *Cabala*, p. 221.

made clear to Charles. Before sailing from Spain for the homeward journey, Charles did sign a marriage contract, but its fulfillment was contingent on a dispensation from the pope and on the infanta's residence in Spain until toleration for English Catholics had been sincerely demonstrated.[42] Charles's signature was deceptive, for he really had little intention of honoring the agreement.[43]

Arriving back in England on October 5, the two venturers were hailed by a people overjoyed to discover that the infanta had been left behind in Spain.[44] The prince and the duke[45] felt themselves fully in harmony with the attitude of the populace. Buckingham, smarting from injured pride, blamed the Spanish for the failure of his mission, and Charles was no less chagrined, because it was apparent Spain would never return the Palatinate to its rightful owner unless forced to do so. On the insistence of his two "dear boys," James I reluctantly agreed to convene his last parliament for the purpose of procuring sufficient tax revenues to launch military operations against Spain.[46]

In his speech opening the meeting of Parliament, James explained that the members had been assembled to advise him whether the marriage contract with Spain should be carried into effect. The limited time did not permit him, he said, to give a detailed account of the treaty, but he assured his hearers that he had never agreed to anything contrary to the laws regarding religion. "It is true," he continued, "that at times for reasons best known to myself, I did not so fully put those laws into execution, but did wink and connive in some things, which might have hin-

42. *Ibid.*, p. 15; Jesus, *Spanish Marriage Treaty*, pp. 214–215; Rushworth, *Historical Collections*, I, 89; Hardwicke, *State Papers*, I, 417, 419, 428; *Calendar of State Papers, Venice* (38 vols., ed. Allen B. Hinds and others, London, 1864–1940), XVIII, 75–76 (referred to hereafter as *Cal. S. P. Ven.*).

43. Rushworth, *Historical Collections*, I, 103, 104.

44. *Cabala*, p. 13; Ellis, *Original Letters*, ser. 1, III, 160, 164; Rushworth, *Historical Collections*, I, 104.

45. James I raised Buckingham to the rank of duke during the latter's sojourn in Madrid.

46. Samuel Rawson Gardiner, *History of England from the Accession of James I to the Outbreak of the Civil War, 1603–1642* (10 vols., London, 1896–99), V, 177; *Cabala*, p. 197.

dered more weighty matters. . . ." The first response of Parliament was to present a petition insisting that enactments against recusancy be stringently enforced; furthermore, that in any future marriage treaty with the prince of another state, the king must refuse to relax the execution of laws against "Popish Recusants." In reply to the request, James promised that he would "be careful that no such conditions be foisted in upon any other Treaty whatsoever. . . ."[47]

Subsequently, after hearing Buckingham's speech in report on his journey to Spain, a speech delivered with almost regal pomp and deleted of facts which would have alarmed the Protestant sensibilities of the audience, Parliament advised the king to revoke the treaty and exonerated Buckingham from any suspicion of devious dealings in forming the marriage agreement.[48] This vindication of the duke for past actions did not mean Parliament was ready to trust his leadership in the future. Parliament was hardly less bellicose toward Spain than was Buckingham, but its members would support a war only on their own terms and under leaders who had the confidence of the nation. For the defense of the realm, Parliament did vote a sum of £300,000, a modest amount to serve the purpose for which it was designated, but did not make an open declaration of war against Spain.[49]

Between crown and Parliament there was decided difference of opinion concerning the type of war that should be waged against Spain.[50] The members of Parliament thought of war in the Elizabethan sense, as a sea war involving attacks on Spanish shipping and colonies. Such a war was comparatively cheap and brought in

47. Rushworth, *Historical Collections*, I, 115–116, 142–144.

48. *Journals of the House of Commons*, I, 720–724; *Stowe MSS 183*, fol. 29; Clarendon, *History of the Rebellion*, I, 26–27.

49. Godfrey Davies, *England under the Early Stuarts* (Oxford, 1938), p. 57.

50. *Debates in the House of Commons in 1625* (ed. Samuel Rawson Gardiner [The Camden Society], Westminster, 1873), intro. p. iii; *Calendar of State Papers, Domestic Series, of the Reign of James I, 1603–1625* (5 vols., ed. Mary Anne Everett Green, London, 1857–59), 1623–25, p. 185 (referred to hereafter as *Cal. S. P. Dom.*); Rushworth, *Historical Collections*, I, 36, 190; *Cabala*, pp. 244–247; Ellis, *Original Letters*, ser. 3, III, 118; *MSS St. Geneviève 820*, fol. 95; *D.N.B.*, LVIII, 331, 332.

profits to private raiders. If the economic underpinnings of Spain were destroyed by attacks on her overseas commerce and colonies, Parliament reasoned, then the Palatinate would fall back into the hands of Frederick. More presciently, James saw that a land war involving a huge outlay of money would be necessary to bring about the return of the Palatinate. Buckingham's plans encompassed both views. He conceived a war of maximum effort on both land and sea—a formidable undertaking for a country such as England, which had never been accustomed to heavy war taxes.

Buckingham was perceptive enough to understand the necessity of acquiring a powerful continental ally if he intended to carry out his plans.[51] For this reason his thoughts turned to France, where he had already made overtures. On embarking at Santander for the journey from Spain, he secretly had sent to Paris a reformed English friar named Gray. Through acquaintance with one of the ladies in the entourage of Marie de Medici, this envoy was able to obtain an audience with the queen mother herself. He explained to her that while a marriage contract had been signed at Madrid, the prince and the Duke of Buckingham were so displeased by the ill treatment they had received there and by the duplicity of the Spanish ministers that the agreement probably would be rescinded. Accordingly, he continued, any hope of a marriage between the Prince of Wales and the only remaining daughter of France would be well received in England. Marie listened with sympathy and replied that though such matters would have to be considered through official channels, she felt obligated to express her gratitude for the harmonious relations that had existed between England and France during King James's reign and to mention her personal indebtedness to that monarch for the kindness he had shown her when she ruled as regent.[52]

To follow up this initial inquiry, Lord Kensington was dispatched to Paris late in February, 1624.[53] Upon arriving at the

51. *Debates in the House of Commons in 1625*, intro. pp. iv–vi.
52. *MSS St. Geneviève 820*, fols. 2–8; Jesus, *Spanish Marriage Treaty*, pp. 274–275; Richelieu, *Lettres*, VII, 535.
53. *MSS St. Geneviève 820*, fol. 135; Richelieu, *Mémoires*, IV, 37. Henry Rich,

Louvre, he went to the apartment of his old friends, the Count and Countess of Chevreuse. Kensington was, in fact, one of the many lovers whom Madame de Chevreuse could list during the course of her venturesome life. The court was busy preparing for a masque that evening, but shortly after his arrival Kensington was given a brief informal audience with the queen mother and was even permitted to meet Henrietta. On the basis of this first meeting with Henrietta, Kensington wrote the prince that she was "the sweetest creature in France." He continued to extol the merits of Madame, as Henrietta was called, in his letter to the prince: "Her growth is very little short of her age; and her wisdom is infinitely beyond it. I heard her discourse with her mother, and the Ladies about her, with extraordinary discretion, and quicknesse."[54] Kensington was playing cupid to fire the young man's interest in the princess, a role for which he was better suited than for serious political dealings.

The prince was not without interest. Nor was Henrietta. Kensington carried on his person a locket containing a miniature portrait of Charles, which he readily showed to people around the French court who inquired of the prince's appearance. This liberality evoked the customary courteous remarks of what a fine, handsome young man the prince appeared to be, which comments Madame did not fail to overhear. Curious though she was, her girlish modesty prevented her from asking the English ambassador to see the portrait. Let Kensington tell the rest of the story as he related it in a letter to Charles:

> But at last (rather than want that sight the which she was so impatient of) she desired the Gentlewoman of the house where I am

---

Viscount Kensington and later Earl of Holland (1590–1649), continued under Charles I to enjoy the favor he had first received under James I. He was a handsome courtier, more able in the drawing room than on the battlefield or in the political arena. During the English Civil War he at first supported the Parliamentary cause but later joined the Royalist forces. Captured by Parliamentary armies, he was tried before the high court of justice, condemned, and beheaded. See C. H. Firth's article on him in *D.N.B.*, XLVIII, 111–114.

54. Ellis, *Original Letters*, ser. 1, III, 178.

lodged, that had been her servant, to borrow of me the picture in all the secresie that may be, and to bring it unto her, saying, she could not want that Curiositie as well as others towards a person of his infinite reputation. As soon as she saw the party that brought it, she retired into her Cabinet, called onely her in; where she opened the picture in such haste, as showed a true picture of her passion, blushing in the instant at her own guiltinesse. She kept it an hour in her hands, and when she returned it, she gave with it many praises of your person.[55]

So well did Kensington's business prosper at the French court that he asked permission of Marie de Medici to convey expression of the prince's esteem in a private interview with Madame. The mother wished to know what he proposed to say to the girl. Playing on what trace of romance still slumbered in the old queen's soul, Kensington at first caviled, but then confided that in representing the feelings of the prince he would tell Madame that he no longer spoke out of courtesy, "but out of passion, and affection, which both her [Henrietta's] outward and inward beauties (the virtues of her mind) so kindled in him." "Allez, allez," answered the mother with a smile. "Il n'y a point de danger en tout cela. Je me fie en vous, je me fie en vous." Kensington claimed to have been worthy of the trust the mother placed in him, although he did cheat a little in sweetening his words: "Neither did I abuse her trust, for I varied not much from it in delivering it to Madame, save that I amplified it to her a little more, who drank it down with joy, and with a low Curtesie acknowledged it to the Prince; adding, that she was extremely obliged to his Highnesse, and would think herself happy in the occasion, that should be presented of meriting the place shee had in his good graces."[56]

Adept as Kensington was in making sallies of love, he proved less astute in dealing with the political aspects of the marriage proposal. From Buckingham's standpoint the diplomatic purposes in opening conversations with France were quite as important as

55. *Harl. MSS 1581*, fol. 24; *Cabala*, p. 280.
56. *Ibid.*, p. 290; *Harl. MSS 1581*, fol. 24.

the need to find Prince Charles a wife; the marriage itself was to serve as a corollary to an alliance which would be directed against Spain. Only a few weeks after reaching Paris, however, Kensington wrote King James that a French marriage should not be made dependent upon an agreement providing French assistance for the recovery of the Palatinate, because such a demand would offend Louis XIII, who did not wish to make his sister a pawn in international agreements.[57]

The real import of Kensington's letter was France's refusal to be tied to England by a diplomatic alliance, written or oral. The two countries had political interests that were similar to some degree but not identical in all respects. To be sure, Louis and his ministers wished to stem the extension of Hapsburg power in the German states and to prevent English alignment with Spain, but they did not wish to support Protestantism in Germany by restoring Frederick to the Palatinate, and they wanted to deal with their own internal problems—the submission of the nobility and the quasi-independent Huguenots to royal control—before embroiling themselves in major foreign undertakings. Besides, there was a better place to shut off Spanish inroads to Germany than in the Palatinate.

In an eastern canton of Switzerland was a valley called the Valtelline, which offered a route from Milan, over which the Spanish governed, to the Tyrol, a territory belonging to the Austrian Hapsburgs. From the Tyrol, Spanish armies could be marched through the Rhine valley up to the Low Countries, where a revolt had broken out against Spanish rule during the reign of Philip II in the previous century and where the seven northern, or Dutch, provinces still struggled for their independence. Not uncommonly in that age of religious intolerance, a conflict flared up in the Valtelline between the Catholics and Protestants, whereupon the former called in Spanish assistance, which resulted in Spanish occupation. Some time previously France had concluded a treaty assuring protection to the Valtelline from foreign intervention. If France

57. *Cabala*, p. 275.

24

acted out of respect for that treaty, forcing the Spanish out of the Valtelline and closing that region to the overland march of Spanish armies into the Rhineland, she could thwart the concerted efforts of the Austrian and Spanish Hapsburg rulers to extend their hegemony over Germany. This end could be attained without an English alliance, without restoring a Protestant ruler in the Palatinate, and without involvement in a major war, since clearing the Spanish forces from the Valtelline would be only a minor military undertaking.[58]

Although the national interests of England and France were not close enough to form the basis of a diplomatic alliance, Buckingham persisted in his efforts to obtain one. By May, 1624, Kensington's shortcomings were so obvious that the Earl of Carlisle was sent to Paris to deal with the more serious topics under consideration.[59] Much to his disappointment, Carlisle learned that France would not conclude a marriage agreement without a provision requiring protection for Catholics in England. The treaty previously signed with Spain was to form the pattern for a marriage agreement with France.[60] James I, mindful of the promise he had made to Parliament regarding the inviolability of the recusancy laws, thought it impossible to meet the French demands. Fearful that the English would break off negotiations, Louis's first minister, the Marquis La Vieuville, assured Carlisle that the demands made in behalf of English Catholics were not to be taken seriously, but were intended only to facilitate the procurement of a dispensation from the pope. He said it would be satisfaction enough if James merely sent a signed letter declaring his intention of allow-

58. Richelieu, *Mémoires*, IV, 219, 223–225.

59. *Ibid.*, p. 38n; *MSS St. Geneviève 820*, fol. 115; Jesus, *Spanish Marriage Treaty*, p. 276; *Cal. S. P. Ven.*, XVIII, 345; Richelieu, *Lettres*, VII, 534. James Hay, first Earl of Carlisle (d. 1636), was one of James's Scottish favorites, but he did not enter the king's service until the succession to the English throne. Carlisle was noted for his spendthrift habits, which his master indulged by generous grant of office and income. See S. R. Gardiner's article on him in *D.N.B.*, XXV, 265–267.

60. Hardwicke, *State Papers*, I, 460, 465, 551–553; *Additional MSS 32092*, fol. 136; *Harl. MSS 1581*, fol. 28; Richelieu, *Mémoires*, IV, 51.

ing Catholics liberty to practice their religion privately. La Vieuville's pliant attitude was to cause his downfall. He had not consulted his king, who was determined to accept nothing less than a solemn contract signed by both James and Charles. On learning of La Vieuville's misrepresentations, Louis XIII dismissed him from office and appointed Cardinal Richelieu to head his council.[61]

Richelieu insisted that stipulations suspending execution of laws against English Catholics be made a part of the main body of the treaty, which would be a public agreement. Carlisle, pointing out the promise James had made regarding the religious laws to his last parliament, said a public statement was impossible. The English ambassador could concede no more than a secret verbal promise that the condition of Catholics in England would be alleviated. Richelieu would never agree to this, but he did agree that the religious articles of the treaty be made a separate secret agreement in writing signed by both James and Charles.[62]

At this stage it appeared the talks would be terminated, as they probably would have been had Buckingham not intervened. On August 12 the king sent a letter to the Earl of Carlisle instructing him to end negotiations if the French were unwilling to confirm La Vieuville's explanation of the religious articles. The courier carrying this dispatch was called back by Buckingham, who opened the letter and, after consultation with James, so altered its wording that conversations would be continued.[63]

As finally drawn up, the marriage treaty[64] granted Henrietta full freedom of religion in England and gave her charge of the religious education of any children that might be born to her up to their thirteenth year. At all places where she resided she was to have her own chapel, which would be open to attendance for English Catholics. To perform religious functions in the chapels, she

61. *Ibid.*, pp. 62–63; *MSS St. Geneviève 820*, fol. 50; Richelieu, *Lettres*, VII, 535.

62. Richelieu, *Mémoires*, IV, 64–66; *MSS Français 21006*, fols. 59, 60, 63.

63. Hardwicke, *State Papers*, I, 524–525; *Cal. S. P. Dom.*, 1623–25, p. 328.

64. *MSS Français 3692*, fols. 43–48; *Additional MSS 34217*, fols. 46–47; *Harl. MSS 295*, fol. 257.

was to have in her house twenty-eight priests, almoners, and chaplains, who were to be permitted to wear their religious habits at any
time and in all places. Her domestic establishment was to consist
of French Catholics chosen by the King of France. The secret part
of the treaty[65] pertaining to the alleviation of the condition of
Catholics in England was contained in a separate paper signed by
James and Prince Charles. By terms of this portion of the treaty, all
Catholics who had been imprisoned because of their religion were
to be set at liberty, English Catholics were to be searched after no
more or otherwise molested on account of their religion, and,
finally, Catholics deprived of property seized since an amnesty
granted in July of 1623, when England was negotiating the Spanish
treaty, were to be restored what had been taken from them.

Superficially, it might have appeared in the fall of 1624, when
the terms of the marriage treaty were concluded, that France had
secured the better part of the bargain. She had gained an ally to
offset the Hapsburgs, acquired full guarantee for the king's sister
to remain in her religion, and extended protection to English
Catholics. All of these advantages were enjoyed without a written
or definite commitment to assist England's foreign enterprises and
left the French government free to act in any contingency as her
own particular interests might dictate. But if Richelieu had dealt
shrewdly with the English, he failed to appreciate the intensity of
Protestant sentiment in that country.[66] Like the Spanish, Richelieu
assumed that the king in England could force his people to change
their religious opinions and attitudes. Moreover, he did not understand the power of Parliament in religious matters. The recusancy
laws passed by Parliament could not be treated with impunity, and
how Charles and his father were to fulfill their promises for any
extended length of time can only be questioned. James I had also
to remember the pledge he had made to Parliament in the previous
spring, when he promised that in any marriage treaty he would

65. *Le Mercure François* (25 vols. in 27, ed. J. and E. Richter, Paris, 1611–44),
XIII, 193–194, 195; Hardwicke, *State Papers*, I, 574; *MSS Français 3692*, fol. 22.
66. *MSS St. Geneviève 820*, fol. 213; Richelieu, *Mémoires*, IV, 58; Jesus, *Spanish
Marriage Treaty*, p. 143.

accept no terms contrary to the laws of England. Since the statement of Catholic liberties was embodied in a separate engagement rather than in the marriage treaty itself, James could argue that he had not broken the letter of his promise, but it is difficult to avoid the conclusion that he had violated its meaning. However much the French ministers might have congratulated themselves, the treaty was based on hope and ambition rather than on conditions that really existed, and could hardly prove permanent or lasting.

The French marriage treaty had important results on English domestic politics in the fall and winter of 1624–25. James twice postponed the meeting of Parliament, first in October, 1624, and again in February of the following year, although he was desperately in need of parliamentary grants to support a hireling army under the freebooter Ernst von Mansfeld, whom he had engaged to march against the Palatinate.[67] The reason for these postponements was not difficult to discern. James knew that if he called Parliament before the marriage of Prince Charles and Henrietta Maria had been performed, there would be embarrassing questions from that body concerning the terms of the treaty, and Parliament might ask him to abrogate the agreement, as indeed it had done with respect to the Spanish treaty. This request would be inadmissible, for an alliance with France was a cornerstone of Buckingham's foreign policy.[68] What James wished to do, therefore, was confront Parliament with a fait accompli. Once the marriage had been consummated, it would be too late for Parliament to destroy the treaty. The members of Parliament were not in the dark concerning the real reasons for these postponements, whatever other excuses James offered. After the first prorogation, Thomas Wentworth expressed the opinion of many another member of Parliament in a letter to Sir George Calvert, the king's secretary:

67. Ellis, *Original Letters*, ser. 1, III, 180; Hardwicke, *State Papers*, I, 533, 537–541. Graf Ernst von Mansfeld (1580–1626), an enemy of the Hapsburgs, who he believed had wrongfully excluded him from his paternal estates, fought as a mercenary in the employment of a number of kings and princes.
68. *D.N.B.*, LVIII, 332.

Now that you have given us a put off till February, we are at good
Ease and Leisure to pry (the true Effects of the want of Imploy-
ment), saucily out of our own Calling into the Mysteries of the State;
to cast about for a Reason of this sudden Change. In a Word, we
conclude, that the French Treaty must first be consummate before
such unruly Fellows meet in Parliament, lest they might appear as
agile against this, as that other Spanish Match. For my Part I like it
well, and conceive the Bargain wholesome on our Side, that we save
three other Subsidies and Fifteenths.[69]

If the meeting of Parliament was delayed by Charles's impending marriage, the marriage in turn was delayed by haggling between the French court and the pope over a dispensation. At last
the difficulties were settled, so that by the latter part of March, 1625,
the papal authorization for Henrietta's marriage to a Protestant
prince was completed.[70] Along with the dispensation, the pope sent
a letter to Henrietta Maria, saying that were it not for the hope
afforded by her character that she as a queen in a heretical country
would be the guardian of her oppressed fellow religionists, he
would not have granted permission for her marriage to a Protestant
prince. He admonished her to be an Esther to her oppressed people,
or a Bertha, whose marriage to the Kentish King Ethelbert brought
religion into Britain. In concluding his letter, the Holy Father
wrote that the eyes of the world were turned upon her in expectation that she would fulfill the hope placed in her. Henrietta, in

69. Thomas Wentworth, Earl of Strafford, *The Earl of Strafford's Letters* (2
vols., ed. William Knowler, London, 1734), I, 24. Sir George Calvert, first Lord
Baltimore (1580?-1632), was educated at Oxford. Apparently a bright young
bureaucrat, he was appointed secretary to Robert Cecil and in 1619 was made
first secretary to James I. In 1625 he became a convert to the Catholic faith and
resigned his office. It was he who made application for a charter establishing the
colony of Maryland. See the article by G. T. Bettany in *D.N.B.*, VIII, 269-272.
Thomas Wentworth, first Earl of Strafford (1593-1641), of whom there will be
more to say in later chapters, was educated at Cambridge and was a member of
most of the parliaments between 1614 and 1629. He opposed Buckingham's war
policy against Spain, but his opposition to the crown stopped short of infringement
on the king's executive powers. See S. R. Gardiner's article in *D.N.B.*, LX, 268-283.
70. Richelieu, *Lettres*, II, 18-19; Richelieu, *Mémoires*, IV, 68-70; V, 8-10, 15.

response to this expression of trust, wrote that nothing was so dear to her as the safety of her conscience and the good of religion, and promised to bring up her children in the Catholic faith.[71]

The royal wedding was imminent, but James I did not live long enough to witness the event; he died rather unexpectedly on March 26 after an illness of three weeks. Charles did not wish his father's death to hold up the wedding any longer than a decent respect demanded.[72] It was necessary that his wedding precede the meeting of Parliament, and a meeting of Parliament was imperative if Charles was to acquire sufficient revenue to fight the Spanish. In these circumstances the obsequies for James I were observed with what some people considered unseemly haste.

At the time of James's death, Catholics were already enjoying relief from persecution, as had been promised in the secret articles. In late December of 1624 James had instructed his judges to cease enforcement of the recusancy laws and to release Catholics held in prison because of their religion. Proceedings against Catholics in church courts were dropped, and fines imposed on them since the revocation of the Spanish alliance were returned. As king in his own right, Charles continued his father's amnesty toward Catholics. A directive to Lord Keeper Williams on May 1, 1625, ordered that warrants be issued to judges and other officials "to forbear all manner of proceeding against His Majesties Catholic subjects."[73]

On the same day that Charles ordered cessation of penalties against Catholics, he was married by proxy to Henrietta Maria. The wedding took place before the west door of the Cathedral of Notre Dame in Paris, since in those times a marriage ceremony including a Protestant as one of the principals was not permitted within the walls of a Catholic church. All of the regal pomp belong-

71. MSS Français 3692, fol. 34; Green, Letters of Henrietta Maria, p. 7.

72. Mercure François, XI, 336–337; Hardwicke, State Papers, I, 568–569; Salvetti Correspondence (MSS of Henry Duncan Skrine, Historical Manuscripts Commission, Eleventh Report, Appendix, part I, London, 1887), pp. 5, 7, 10; Rushworth, Historical Collections, I, 167.

73. Calendar of State Papers, Domestic Series, of the Reign of Charles I, 1625–1649 (23 vols., ed. John Bruce and others, London, 1858–97), 1625–26, p. 16.

ing to the age was employed to celebrate the wedding.[74] From the archbishop's palace, where the members of the wedding procession were to gather, a gallery leading to the nearby cathedral was especially constructed for the occasion. Although the marriage rites were not to be performed until four o'clock in the afternoon, Henrietta arrived at the episcopal residence by nine in the morning to begin the long process of dressing in her bridal attire. Charles's intended proxy, Buckingham, detained in England by the funeral of the king, was replaced by the Duke of Chevreuse, who was a distant relative of the groom and Louis's choice for the honor.

The wedding procession, as it moved along under the gallery decorated with violet-colored silk, must have presented a revelry of colors. Yards of black and purple velvet, cloth-of-gold-and-silver, and scarlet silk and satin had gone into the making of the gowns and uniforms. Henrietta, walking between her brothers, Louis and Gaston, wore a bridal gown of cloth-of-gold-and-silver sprinkled with golden fleurs-de-lys and garnished with diamonds. A small crown graced the top of her head, and three princesses of the blood held her train. The Duke of Chevreuse was attired in a black velvet suit with slits to reveal its cloth-of-gold lining, a scarf covered with diamonds in rose pattern glittered across his chest, and a hooded coat embroidered with cloth-of-gold and diamonds completed his sparkling array.

The procession was arranged according to a precise order: first came the captain of the guard and his company, followed by a hundred of the king's Swiss guards with drums beating and standards unfurled, and then by six royal trumpeters; following in succession were the master of ceremonies and his assistants, the Knights of the Order of the Holy Ghost, seven heralds-at-arms, the marshals of France, and the dukes and princes; the bride and her two brothers were placed toward the end of the line, ahead of the queen mother

74. *Mercure François*, XI, 355–365; *Lansdowne MSS*, the *Burghley Papers*, XCIII, part 1, fol. 37; "The Glorious Triumph and Order of the Ceremonies Observed in the Marriage of the High and Mightie Charles King of Great Britain with Lady Henrietta Maria" (London, 1625), unpaged pamphlet.

and Queen Anne. In all, the wedding procession must have comprised not many fewer than three hundred persons.

On reaching the canopied platform before the church door, Louis surrendered his place at the side of his sister to the Duke of Chevreuse, and Cardinal Rouchefaucault pronounced the nuptial benediction. The assemblage then filed into the cathedral to hear a nuptial mass. Within the great church, tapestries from the valuable royal collection relieved the bare stone of the walls, and the gallery leading from the archbishop's palace continued through the nave as far as the choir. At the entry to the choir, Lords Kensington and Carlisle, being Protestants representing a Protestant country, took their leave of the rest of the company and retired to the nearby palace. The royal family and their immediate attendants observed the mass from a richly covered dais which had been built in the center of the choir.

In the evening a wedding banquet was celebrated in the great hall of the episcopal residence, where merriment reigned as dukes and counts served platters of food to the royal diners. From the outside the noise of a jubilant populace now and then penetrated the thickness of the walls. The guilds of the city paraded before the banquet tables in the uniforms of their organizations, and the Swiss guards demonstrated a marching drill. Intermittently the thunder of cannon resounded in the distance, while the reflection of festive bonfires in the streets danced on the darkening windows of Paris. This was Henrietta's day. Madame the little princess, so long the obscure youngest child of Henry IV, had become an important person, for now she was Queen of England.

Two weeks after the wedding Buckingham arrived in Paris for the ostensible purpose of conducting the new queen to her realm. His presence soon evoked strong comment, either favorable or unfavorable, on every side.[75] The men around the court hated him, whereas the women found him handsome and fascinating. His visit gave him an opportunity to show off some of the finery he had intended to wear as Charles's proxy for the wedding. One of the

75. *Salvetti Correspondence*, p. 19.

twenty-seven suits of clothing that he had had tailored especially for the occasion was described as a "rich white satin uncut velvet suit, set all over, both suit and cloak, with diamonds, the value whereof is thought to be worth fourscore thousand pounds, besides a feather made with great diamonds; with sword, girdle, hatband and spurs with diamonds. . . ."[76]

Insufferable as Buckingham's ostentation and vanity might have been, what most offended the French was his effrontery in making romantic approaches to their queen, with whom, it was said, he consorted on familiar terms even from the first meeting, as though they had been intimate for years. Unloved and neglected by her husband, the queen was not indifferent to Buckingham's attentions, although she little understood the true character of her would-be lover. Even before Buckingham went to France, the friendship between him and Queen Anne had been fostered by Madame de Chevreuse, who was well experienced in affairs of the heart, and Lord Kensington, recently made Earl of Holland, also had a part in recommending the handsome duke.[77]

Buckingham had a more serious purpose in coming to France than to escort Henrietta to England or to court Queen Anne, for now that England and France had been linked by a royal marriage, he sought to complement that association by concluding a military pact against Spain.[78] Richelieu was no more ready to sign such an alliance after the marriage than he had been before the event, but he had reasons for treating the English courtier with consideration. He wished to keep England at war with Spain and to prevent the English from assisting the French Protestants in their opposition to royal authority. Nevertheless, there was no reason to join French interests and the English attempt to recover the Palatinate, because France's fight in the Valtelline was already half won, and the cardinal wanted no agreement that would prevent his country from establishing peaceful relations with Spain should the opportunity

76. Hardwicke, *State Papers*, I, 571.

77. Françoise Bertaut, Madame de Motteville, *Mémoires sur Anne d'Autriche et Sa Cour* (4 vols., ed. M. F. Riaux, Paris, n.d.), I, 15.

78. Richelieu, *Mémoires*, V, 89.

offer itself. In reply to Buckingham's importunity Richelieu said that France fought in the Valtelline merely to honor a treaty with the inhabitants of that area, that France hoped to live in harmony with England, and that if the English government assisted the Huguenots, France would be less able to give England support in her war against Spain. As for French support against Spain, Richelieu conceded no more than a verbal promise to continue subsidy for the feckless mercenaries which King James had employed to drive Spanish forces out of the Palatinate.[79]

Realizing how ephemeral Richelieu's verbal promise might prove and having failed to achieve the anticipated sequel to the marriage treaty, Buckingham was furious. His failure to secure a firm political alliance with France caused his plan for fighting Spain to fall asunder. Without the French alliance it would be almost impossible to get Parliament to follow his leadership, and without parliamentary support it was difficult to perceive where funds for fighting the war against Spain could be obtained. A less foolhardy man might have revised his ambitions to suit the circumstances, but Buckingham was only stirred to greater anger.[80]

By the end of the first week of Buckingham's stay, during which the nightly revelries around the court became the talk on the streets the next day,[81] it was time for Henrietta to start on the journey to the country marriage had destined for her. With all of her company and attendants she was to go by way of Amiens to Boulogne, where English ships waited to transport her and her followers to Dover. The king, the queen, the queen mother, and Gaston were to accompany her to the coast. From there her household of two hundred servants and twenty-eight priests and the official escorts—Buckingham, Holland, Carlisle, and the Duke and Duchess of Chevreuse—would continue with her to England. Included in her household was Madame Saint-Georges, her trusted friend since nursery days, who was to be Henrietta's lady of honor.

79. *Ibid.*, pp. 87, 88, 90, 93, 94.
80. *D.N.B.*, LVIII, 333.
81. *Mercure François*, XI, 366.

Among her clergymen were the young and aggressive Bishop of Mende, acting as governor over the other priests, Father Sancy, her confessor, and the venerable and benign Father Berulle, serving as the principal of her Oratorians.[82]

The bridal journey began on May 23. Henrietta's leave-taking of the city was marked by ceremonies considered appropriate to indicate the importance of the event, and a parade of the city archers, the militia, the guilds, the trumpeters, and other groups representing Paris did her the honor of escort as far as St. Denis. The Queen of England rode out of Paris in a red velvet litter carried by two mules draped in crimson cloth and adorned with aigrettes.[83]

Reaching Amiens four days later, the bridal party was detained by the festivities the city had prepared to commemorate the royal marriage. After the heightened activity of the last three weeks and several days' journey by coach, Henrietta probably would have welcomed a release from the pageants, ballets, fireworks, military drills, parades, dances, and plays presented before her. But since the fathers of the city had outdone themselves, it seems, in giving welcome to the youngest sister of their sovereign, Henrietta had to sit through the performance of these tiring displays. A further wait was made necessary in Amiens by the illness of the queen mother, for whom the journey had been somewhat trying. Already the king had been left behind in Compiègne because of another of his recurrent illnesses.[84]

While the queen mother lingered in bed, others of the bridal party, in keeping with the lighthearted ways of the court, lingered along moonlit paths. Seconded by the good offices of Madame de Chevreuse, Buckingham continued to make entreaties of love to the French queen. One evening the queen obtained from her captain of the guard a key giving admittance into a walled garden next to the house where she was lodged. Her husband's order prohibiting the use of this garden might have made her risk more

82. Bassompierre, *Mémoires*, p. 204.
83. *Mercure François*, XI, 367–368.
84. *Ibid.*, pp. 370–373.

tempting. As the queen and Buckingham strolled along one of the lanes of the garden, they became separated from the rest of their company. The queen's page, probably perceiving Buckingham's displeasure at his presence and not unwilling to do his small part in the intrigue, lagged far behind. The duke and the queen turned a corner where they were screened by a high hedge. Moments of silence followed. Suddenly the queen let forth a scream which pierced the night air, whereupon her page and other romantic couples in the garden rushed to the place from which the distress had sounded, there to find the frightened queen and, standing a short distance away, the disconcerted duke.[85]

While the bridal party sojourned at Amiens, Charles in England insisted that his queen depart as soon as possible, for Parliament was shortly to convene, and unless Henrietta were to arrive soon he could not be at the English coast to meet her.[86] It was decided that the queen mother, although improved, would not go on to Boulogne and that Queen Anne would remain in Amiens with her. Henrietta was to leave forthwith, having of her immediate family only Gaston to accompany her to the French coast.[87]

The queen mother was able to escort Henrietta a short distance out of Amiens, where the leave-taking between mother and daughter took place. Here Marie de Medici gave Henrietta a letter, purportedly her own but actually written by Father Berulle, as a final admonition to her daughter.[88] This letter Henrietta was always to keep with her to be reread at intervals in order that her mother might in a sense ever be near to give counsel and assistance. Henrietta was reminded in the letter that as God had blessed her, so was she to do her duty toward Him while here on earth. "Do not forget," the letter continued, "that you are a daughter of the Church and that this is the highest position you possibly can hold." She was sent to England as protector of the Catholics there; her efforts were

85. Motteville, *Mémoires*, I, 16.
86. *Cal. S. P. Ven.*, XIX, 83.
87. *Cabala*, p. 254.
88. This letter will be found in full in Richelieu's *Mémoires*, appendix of vol. V, 275–281; *Mercure François*, XI, 39.

to be used upon her husband the king that he might mitigate their sufferings. "Be to them an Esther, who had the grace of God to be the defender and deliverer of His people from her husband, Ahasueres. . . . Do not forget them, my daughter; God has sent you into that country for their sake; for it is His people who have suffered for so many years." She was not to forget in her charity those people of another religion, who because of their heresy were afflicted by God. Through her influence and kindness she might get them to leave their error and become converts to the true faith. "After God and religion . . . your first duty is to the king to whom God has joined you by the sacrament of marriage. Love him as your husband and honor him as your king. . . . Be sweet, humble, and patient to his will." Besides marital love, she owed to her husband love of another sort, the "love of a Christian, loving his soul and his salvation." She was to pray for her husband's conversion each day, that he might return to that religion for which his grandmother, Mary of Scots, had died.

Thus was Henrietta sent to England, as though she were a missionary of the Propaganda going forth to fight the battle for God and the Church. This was a precarious attitude for a queen going into a country where the people had often manifested their hatred toward the Catholic Church, where Parliament had enacted laws against Catholicism, and where the same body had repeatedly petitioned the king for more exact and stringent enforcement of those laws.

A few days after taking leave of her mother, Henrietta stood upon the sandy beach at Boulogne[89] and, while waves lapped at her feet, looked over the billows of the Channel toward England. This was her first sight of the ocean. In the swelling waters was a power not of her own making. So was it also in the determination of matters more immediate and personal to her. She went to England as queen upon the arrangement of others and for the convenience of the state. How could the future be other than ominous for her? She was to be a Catholic queen in a Protestant country at

89. *Cal. S. P. Dom.*, 1625–26, p. 41.

a time when religious controversy was still violent and religious differences were still deeply felt. The diplomatic foundations on which her marriage had been established were already beginning to crumble. Richelieu had no better reason to expect mitigation of religious penalties in England than Buckingham had to hope for a military alliance with France. Henrietta, looking over the waters, probably had little thought of these hazards, but there must have been a tug at her heart when the fifteen-year-old girl thought of the friends and the country she was to leave behind.

CHAPTER II

EARLY DISCORDS OF MARRIAGE

1625-29 ❦ IT WAS a sad little queen who arrived in Dover at about seven o'clock on the evening of Sunday, June 12, 1625. A girl for the first time among a strange people with a strange language and a strange religion, Henrietta could hardly hold back her tears. Even before she had sailed from Boulogne, her melancholy had been apparent, for from there Sir Tobie Matthew, who acted as her interpreter, had written to the Duchess of Buckingham: "Methought I discerned in her countenance a little remnant of sadnesse, which the fresh wound of parting from the Queen Mother might have made. . . ."[1] To Charles, who had been waiting in Canterbury for her arrival on the English coast, she sent a message from Dover saying that she would be unable to see anyone until the following morning.

Henrietta's state of mind being what it was, the best that England might have offered could hardly have consoled her. But as if

1. *Salvetti Correspondence* (*MSS of Henry Duncan Skrine, Historical Manuscripts Commission, Eleventh Report,* Appendix, part I, London, 1887), p. 21; Armand J. du Plessis, Duke of Richelieu, Cardinal, *Mémoires* (10 vols., ed. P. M. Charles, François Bruel, and Robert Lavallée [Société de l'Histoire de France], Paris, 1907-31), V, 142; Arnold Harris Mathew and Anette Calthorp, *The Life of Sir Tobie Matthew* (London, 1907), p. 263; *Cabala, Mysteries of State* (London, 1654), p. 253; *Le Mercure François* (25 vols. in 27, ed. J. and E. Richter, Paris, 1611-44), XI, 394.

her own sadness were not affliction enough, the English seemed to add injury through the poor accommodations they prepared for her.[2] On her first night in England she was given quarters in a dank, old, run-down castle near the port where she disembarked. The furnishings were antiquated and worn. Such a bed as she slept in during her first night would long have been discarded in France. Only one table was provided for her officers and servants, making it necessary for some of them to walk into the town of Dover to buy their supper on the evening of their landing.

The next morning at about ten o'clock, while Henrietta was having breakfast, news reached her that the king had come from Canterbury and awaited her presence in the hall below. Without remaining at table a moment longer, she went to meet the person to whom her own life was thenceforth bound. On seeing Charles, she kneeled before him, and uttering a short speech she had prepared, declared that she came to his country to be used and commanded as he might wish. Charles pulled her to her feet, embraced her, and covered her face with kisses. The royal couple then retired to a private room for about half an hour, after which time they again appeared before the whole company, and Henrietta introduced her principal officers and servants to the king.

Noticing Charles looking down at her feet, Henrietta perceived that he had been told of her short stature, and finding her a little taller than he had expected, was asking himself whether her height might be increased by high-heeled shoes. Thereupon Henrietta raised her skirt to show her feet and purportedly said, "Sir, I stand upon mine own feet. I have no helps by art. Thus high I am, and am neither higher than lower."[3]

To further understanding with her new husband, she explained that, being young and inexperienced among a people whose ways were strange to her, she likely would make mistakes, but that if she did, she wished Charles himself to tell her of them so that she

2. Richelieu, *Mémoires*, V, 141; *Mercure François*, XII, 230.
3. Henry Ellis, *Original Letters* (12 vols. in 3 series, London, 1824–46), ser. 3, III, 197–198.

could avoid repeating her errors. Henrietta had honest intentions of adopting the customs of her husband's people insofar as it was possible for her to do so.[4] At dinner that day she ate venison and other roast meats, while her confessor, standing in back of her, angrily reminded her that it was the eve of St. John the Baptist and that she should fast.

Charles, like most of the English, was probably much pleased by the appearance of his vivacious, black-eyed wife.[5] Just what impression he made upon her during this first meeting is unrecorded, although later comments made by members of her French household would cause us to believe that it was not a favorable one. What most impressed the French, and probably Henrietta as well, was the poverty of Charles's court.[6] Having entered the queen's service in anticipation of a good living, and little understanding Charles's financial dependence on a parsimonious parliament, the queen's followers soon complained of the simplicity of life in England as contrasted to the splendor of the French court. When the king presented himself at Dover, they immediately pointed to the roughness of his attire and the paucity of his attendants—not at all as the King of France would have appeared for such an occasion. The English court was simple and without ceremony as compared to the court in France. The appearance of Charles belied the portraits they had seen of him, and his morose and indifferent behavior seemed to accentuate the austerity of his surroundings.

A clash between Charles and the queen's household occurred almost at the outset, and was indicative of the trouble that would almost inevitably ensue so long as the queen's French retinue remained in England. When in the afternoon following the king's arrival the court started out for Canterbury, Henrietta's lady of

---

4. John Rushworth, *Historical Collections* (8 vols., London, 1721–22), I, 170; Ellis, *Original Letters*, ser. 3, III, 198.

5. *Ibid.*, p. 206; *Cabala*, p. 253.

6. Rushworth, *Historical Collections*, I, 424; Isaac Disraeli, *Commentaries on the Life and Reign of Charles I* (2 vols., ed. and rev. B. Disraeli, London, 1851), I, 200 (referred to hereafter as Disraeli, *Commentaries*); Leveneur de Tillières, *Mémoires* (ed. M. C. Hippeau, Paris, 1862), p. 90.

honor, Madame Saint-Georges, took a place in the coach in which Charles and Henrietta were to ride, since it was the custom in France for one in her position always to accompany her mistress. Charles, not understanding the assumption on which Madame Saint-Georges had acted and unwilling to tolerate it if he had, ordered her to get out of the carriage. An unhappy scene followed. Charles imperiously expected to be obeyed, while Henrietta tempestuously insisted that Madame Saint-Georges accompany her. Leveneur de Tillières, Henrietta's chamberlain, thought the young queen should have shown more consideration for her husband's wish. Upon persuasion of some of the queen's officers, Charles finally gave in to his wife's demand, but he did not forget what he considered an affront on the part of Madame Saint-Georges.[7]

That night the king and queen slept at Canterbury.[8] As on the queen's first evening in England, so again on her second night the bed provided for her outraged her French followers. It began to appear there was not a bed in England suitable for royal occupancy. If anything, the bed at Canterbury, one usually assigned to ambassadors extraordinary traveling on mission to or from London, was worse than the one Henrietta had slept in at Dover. Charles, native to all the hardships of England and blissfully indifferent to the French complaints, permitted only two of his servants into the bedroom to help him undress. Hastily dismissing them, he then bolted all seven doors giving access to the bridal chamber.

The following morning the queen's melancholy had deepened, whereas Charles was unusually jocund and loquacious. The day's progress brought them to the home of the Countess of Lennox near Gravesend, where they rested for a day before making their entry into London on the sixteenth.[9]

At that time London was beset by another of the city's recurrent plagues—just punishment, as the Catholics explained it, for Eng-

7. *Ibid.*

8. *Mercure François*, XII, 395; Tillières, *Mémoires*, p. 91; Ellis, *Original Letters*, ser. 3, III, 198.

9. Tillières, *Mémoires,* p. 91; *Salvetti Correspondence*, p. 21.

land's heresy. During the week of the queen's arrival a hundred citizens had died of the contagion, and the toll was mounting daily. To spare Their Majesties the danger of infection in the narrow, teeming streets, arrangements were made for Henrietta and Charles to travel by barge on the Thames.

Oblivious to the dangers of a London plague, the queen's French followers complained that entering the city by way of the Thames withdrew the new queen from the plaudits of her subjects and made it impractical to provide the ceremonies and honors that should have been accorded to her.[10] From the viewpoint of the English, on the other hand, the queen received a rousing and spontaneous welcome. Despite a downpour, Londoners lined the river bank or shouted their greetings from boats and houses along the river's edge as Their Majesties, both clothed in green, waved in response from the opened window of their barge. Fifty ships of the Royal Navy discharged salvos in salute to England's new queen. That was something she had never witnessed before, the English proudly assured themselves. Perhaps a few companies of colorfully uniformed Swiss guards would have done more to stir the queen's pride in her new country, since the French as yet had little appreciation of sea power.[11]

The royal barge finally docked at Somerset House, a palace with grounds reaching down to the bank of the river Thames. Formerly the home of Charles's mother, it was now assigned to his wife. Here also the queen found the furnishings inadequate, for the bed of state, an heirloom that had belonged to Queen Elizabeth, was of such antique design that Henrietta had never seen one like it.[12]

Two days after the queen's arrival in London, Charles went before his first parliament to deliver the opening address.[13] His speech was a simple appeal for funds without explanation of his plans for waging the undeclared war against Spain. The men sitting

10. Richelieu, *Mémoires*, V, 142; Ellis, *Original Letters*, ser. 1, III, 196–197.
11. *Ibid.*, pp. 196, 200.
12. Richelieu, *Mémoires*, V, 142–143; Ellis, *Original Letters*, ser. 3, III, 206.
13. Rushworth, *Historical Collections*, I, 171, 172, 189; *D.N.B.*, LVIII, 333.

in Parliament were in no mood to give docile assent to the king's request for money, because they had no confidence in Buckingham, in whose hands Charles had placed the conduct of foreign policy. They were aware of Buckingham's failure to fulfill the expected results of the French marriage treaty, as was apparent from Richelieu's negligence in supplying materials for Count Mansfeld's army, which had been employed by the late King James to drive Spanish forces out of the Palatinate.

Parliament was especially incensed by the religious results of the marriage treaty, for it was clear that the laws against Catholics were not being enforced. In slanted disapproval of the French marriage the members warned the king against the danger of "papists" foisted upon him by foreign rulers. The presence of the queen's priests at the court in their clerical robes rankled the Puritan soul. Not so rash as to reprimand their king for permitting English Catholics to attend the queen's chapel, they nevertheless petitioned him not to permit attendance of his subjects at the chapels of Catholic ambassadors resident in London.[14]

Unless given some part in determining how appropriations were to be expended, Parliament would not vote a supply to further Buckingham's foreign ambitions.[15] At one point in the debate on supply Buckingham was asked, "But where is the enemy?" He replied that Parliament had only to put the sword in his hand by voting a sufficient amount of money for war, and he would prove worthy of his country's confidence. Parliament did make an initial grant of two subsidies, but this sum was only one-seventh of the £1,000,000 Charles needed for foreign affairs.

Tardy as the members of Parliament were in voting much-needed money for carrying on the war against Spain, Charles could no longer keep them in London, because of the danger of the plague, which was spreading daily. Parliament was recessed on July 11 and ordered to reconvene in Oxford on August 1. Already

14. Rushworth, *Historical Collections*, I, 181.
15. *Ibid.*, pp. 179, 189; Godfrey Davies, *England under the Early Stuarts* (Oxford, 1938), p. 58.

the king and queen had sought safety from the plague by removing to Hampton Court.[16]

After but a few weeks of married life it was apparent that so long as the French household remained in England, Charles could not live on satisfactory terms with his wife. Buckingham was the first to whom Charles told his dissatisfaction. As if his own shoulders were broad enough to bear all of the world's ills, Buckingham took it upon himself to set matters aright.[17] At Hampton Court he spoke menacingly to Henrietta, saying that the king her husband would not long endure her indifferent attitude, and that if she did not show more affection toward him, she would make herself the most unhappy woman in the world.

Since the details of Henrietta's domestic life during the early period of her marriage were reported mostly by the French, the story was almost inevitably one-sided. And yet the narrative as it stands gives these events as seen from Henrietta's position. In relating the story of Henrietta's early marital difficulties, the French made Buckingham the bête noire who deliberately poisoned relations between husband and wife to prevent her from displacing him in the king's favor. To what extent Buckingham was aware of the queen's power to influence her husband might be questioned, although it seems certain, as the queen explained years later to Madame de Motteville,[18] that Buckingham was in part the cause of early misunderstanding between the royal couple.

On the other hand, Charles was not without genuine grievances against the young and high-spirited queen. In the company of her French attendants she was gay and frolicsome, but when her husband appeared she became sullen and distant. Seeking only the companionship and company of the French ladies she had brought with her, she was not becoming acquainted with her husband's people and was not learning the English language. Charles was

16. Ellis, *Original Letters*, ser. 3, III, 208, 209; Rushworth, *Historical Collections*, I, 177; *Salvetti Correspondence*, p. 24.

17. Tillières, *Mémoires*, pp. 92–93.

18. Françoise Bertaut, Madame de Motteville, *Mémoires sur Anne d'Autriche et Sa Cour* (4 vols., ed. M. F. Riaux, Paris, n.d.), I, 19–20.

faithful to his wife, but in turn he expected to be obeyed. On the point of obedience he was very sensitive. Like many people of weak personality, he could be almost cruel at times in his attempt to command respect. From the first he seemed to be strongly attracted to his quick-witted and fun-loving wife, and though he wanted to love her, she always evaded him.

In an attempt to draw the queen away from the exclusive company of her French attendants and bring her into better relations with English persons at the court, it was suggested that certain English women of high rank be made ladies of the queen's bedchamber. When Buckingham asked the queen to grant this honor to three of his womenfolk—his wife, sister, and niece—Henrietta replied that since King James's wife had had only two ladies for her bedchamber, precedent did not demand more than the three French women presently serving in that capacity. Having been refused his request, Buckingham then went to see the French ambassadors on the matter.[19] The ambassadors were not unfavorable to his suggestion, but when the Bishop of Mende, who was at the head of the queen's clergy, heard of the proposal, he placed an absolute veto upon it, saying that to place "Huguenot" women around the queen as Buckingham proposed to do would seriously hazard her religion. Much as the French feared the English would attempt to impinge upon the religious faith of the queen, there was nothing to indicate the English had any intention of effecting her conversion by cajolery or threats.

While bickering over the queen's household preoccupied the court, there were more serious public matters calling for the king's attention. As arranged on the recess of Parliament in mid-July, that body was to reconvene in Oxford at the beginning of August. Henrietta did not accompany Charles all the way to Oxford, but resided at Woodstock, an estate nearby the town. Parliament did not last out half the month.[20] In response to the king's repeated demands for money, the members finally suggested that a board be estab-

19. Tillières, *Mémoires*, pp. 93, 94.
20. *Ibid.*, p. 95; Rushworth, *Historical Collections*, I, 194.

lished to guide the conduct of the war, rather than leave its direction in the hands of Buckingham alone. Refusing to share his power over foreign policy with Parliament, the king dissolved his first parliament on August 12, 1625.

Although Charles had denied Parliament any control over foreign relations, he did surrender to continuing protests against clemency for English Catholics.[21] He saw that it was impossible to honor the provisions on religion in the marriage treaty and at the same time live in harmony with his own subjects. Since the treaty with the French had failed to elicit French support for the war against Spain, Charles decided to placate Parliament by enforcing the religious laws. By removing this contention between himself and Parliament, Charles hoped for more success in obtaining money from that body. In the latter part of August, the laws against Catholics were again put into execution. All religious orders, excepting those priests of the queen's household, were banished from England, and English parents were ordered to bring back any children sent abroad to be educated in Catholic schools or seminaries.

To save his policy toward England from failure, Richelieu determined to send Sieur de Blainville to that country on a special mission. In the original set of instructions,[22] evidently written in late July or early August, Blainville was informed that his mission to England had three purposes: to maintain the alliance with England, to foster the comfort and happiness of the queen, and to bring about more exact compliance with the promises the king had made concerning the suspension of religious laws. While these purposes were related and interdependent, all considerations were to be made subsidiary to the national interests of France in retaining the cooperation of England against Spain. On matters pertaining to the queen's household, Richelieu tended to be flexible, even to the

21. *Ibid.*, pp. 180, 198; *Harl. MSS 161*, fol. 236; *Additional MSS 34324*, fol. 242; *Salvetti Correspondence*, p. 31.

22. Tillières, *Mémoires*, p. 101; Armand J. du Plessis, Duke of Richelieu, Cardinal, *Lettres, Instructions Diplomatiques et Papiers d'État* (8 vols., ed. Denis M. L. Avenel [*Collection de Documents Inédits*], Paris, 1853–77), II, 125–126, 126–127n, 128, 129 (referred to hereafter as Richelieu, *Lettres*).

point of allowing consideration of Buckingham's proposal to place three of his women relatives in the queen's bedchamber, and although Blainville was to make no agreement on the removal of Madame Saint-Georges from the queen's entourage, Richelieu conceded that ultimately such a step might be necessary.

The English were not deceived by Blainville's mission. Thomas Lorkin, an English agent then in Paris, wrote to Buckingham that Blainville came to England as nothing other than a spy. Lorkin's information was not ill founded.[23] In his instructions Blainville was told to inform certain persons on the French pension list that their salaries would be forthcoming and that they were to continue their secret work of informing on the English government. He was to foment discord between the "Puritans" in Parliament and the Duke of Buckingham, and to renew France's historic friendship with the Scots by soliciting the good offices of Scottish members of the court. He was also to cultivate the friendship of certain important persons, including the Lord Keeper of the Seal, the Chancellor of the Exchequer, and Buckingham's mother—all of whom were believed to be friendly toward French interests and cryptically Catholic.

Not long after the writing of the first set of instructions for Blainville, the French ambassadors Ville-aux-Clercs, the Marquis d'Effiat, and the Duke of Chevreuse returned to France, and Father Berulle was recalled from England to report on matters affecting the queen.[24] The reports received from these emissaries shocked the French court and called forth a second set of instructions, which were given to Blainville before his departure.

In the second directive to Blainville, Richelieu was adamant in his demands.[25] There was no longer any talk of replacing Madame Saint-Georges or of admitting English women to the queen's bedchamber; both proposals were forbidden. The French minister

---

23. *Cabala*, pp. 300, 302; Richelieu, *Lettres*, II, 130, 133, 134, 135.
24. *Salvetti Correspondence*, p. 27; Richelieu, *Mémoires*, V, 149.
25. Richelieu, *Lettres*, II, 137–140.

was almost peremptory in his demand that the renewed enforcement of the laws against Catholics be suspended. If the English in response pointed to the French policy toward the Huguenots, they were to be told that that referred to an entirely different matter, for the French king had never made any agreement allowing England to intercede in behalf of his Protestant subjects, and the English could be sure that nothing would stop His Christian Majesty in his determination to subdue the Huguenots.

Back in England, following the dissolution of Parliament, the king left for New Forest, a royal hunting preserve, while the queen with her court went to Titchfield, the estate of the Earl of Southampton. During her stay at Titchfield the queen committed a mistake which did her no good in the opinion of the English public, whose favorable attitude she had every reason to cultivate.[26] The Countess of Denbigh, sister to Buckingham, arranged a Protestant service to be held in the great hall of the house in which the queen was residing. Courtesy and usage demanded that the countess obtain the queen's consent before taking such a step, but she had in no way consulted the queen. Henrietta, zealous for her own religion, felt the affront keenly. With an exceeding lack of that graciousness which becomes a queen, Henrietta and a group of her French friends several times walked through the hall where Protestant services were being held, laughing and talking loudly all the while and leading little dogs that added to the din with their barking.

Henrietta was in no better standing at the court when early in November, 1625, Blainville arrived in England. At the time of Blainville's arrival, Buckingham was away from the court supervising the preparation of a fleet at Portsmouth to be sent against Spain. The king and queen, still evading the threat of the plague in London, were living near Southampton. In the first audience granted to the French ambassador, Charles was anything but friendly. He informed Blainville that he would brook no inter-

26. Tillières, *Mémoires*, V, 100–101.

ference from the French in the management of the queen's household, and that as for treatment of the Catholics, his policy was in the interest of his state and was none of France's concern. In contrast to Charles's hostility, the duke on returning from Portsmouth, where he had assembled the fleet, was very cordial toward Blainville.[27]

Having dispatched the fleet against Cadiz, Buckingham left shortly afterward for Holland to cement an alliance among England, the United Provinces of the Netherlands, and Denmark for upholding the Protestant cause in Germany.[28] From Holland, Buckingham intended to go to France in hope that he could prevail upon Richelieu to join a northern alliance. Whether Buckingham expected to resume his love affair with the French queen where he had left off during June is questionable. In going to France for either purpose, political or personal, he showed great temerity, for there were courtiers in Paris sworn to kill him if he ever set foot in the country. Richelieu realized that to admit Buckingham to the court would be an insult against Louis XIII, and that a mission on the part of Buckingham would not result in a lessening of political and religious tension between England and France. Accordingly, the French ambassador in Holland told Buckingham that his presence was not welcomed in France.[29]

Close upon Buckingham's return to England, the fleet returned from Cadiz. Again Buckingham's plans had failed. In fact, the expedition against Cadiz, ill provided and poorly led, proved a fiasco of almost comic proportions. On the return trip, however,

27. Richelieu, *Mémoires*, V, 150, 172.
28. *Salvetti Correspondence*, p. 34; *Harl. MSS 6988*, fols. 43, 71; Richelieu, *Mémoires*, V, 162.
29. *Ibid.*, p. 163. It is not improbable that at about this time Buckingham received from Madame de Chevreuse the letter treating of his wish to visit the French court. She wrote that while the queen was still favorably inclined toward him, there was so much enmity against his person that his coming would be dangerous. "Do what you will, I dare not advise you; to come is dangerous, not to come is unfortunate." Madame de Chevreuse employed awkward and transparent symbols in her letter. A heart referred to the Queen of France, a fleur-de-lys to the king, and an anchor to Buckingham himself, who held among other offices that of the Admiralty. See *Cabala*, pp. 298–299.

four French ships charged with transporting contraband of war to Spanish ports were seized and taken to England, where the proceeds from the sale of their cargoes were retained by the government.[30] The seizure of the French ships was to have more important results than the attempt against Cadiz.

French relations with England had reached such a state that Richelieu perceived the distinct possibility of war between the two countries at a time when war with England did not fit into his plans. He thought the French ambassador in Holland had been much too abrupt in his manner of denying Buckingham's wish to go to France. In appeasement of ill feeling that might have been engendered by the refusal made to Buckingham, Richelieu sent a special envoy, Nicholas de Bautre, for the purpose of inviting English emissaries to France, Buckingham again excepted, to further the settlement of differences existing between the two crowns.[31]

Henrietta continued to have altercations with Charles. One evening early in December, just after she had retired with her husband to their bedchamber, she presented to him a list of those persons she wished appointed to administer her dower lands. When her husband dismissed the matter by remarking that he would consider it the following morning, she replied that several of her French followers were included in the list. She had, in fact, placed the Bishop of Mende at the head of the list as general manager of all her estates. It probably gave her a feeling of importance to reward her friends, and she was likely guided in her selections by members of her French household who were hungry for remunerative offices. The king told her she could rest assured he would not permit the appointment of any Frenchmen, whereupon the queen became irate, and after a few insults had been passed back and forth, she told her husband he could keep the estates and give her a pension in lieu thereof. Thinking it scandalous for a woman to argue with her husband in such a manner, Charles reminded his

30. Rushworth, *Historical Collections*, I, 196–197; Richelieu, *Mémoires*, V, 169–170.

31. *Ibid.*, pp. 171–172.

wife to consider to whom she was talking with so little respect and said he wished to hear no more on the subject.[32]

Henrietta seems to have been resilient. Between quarrels with her husband she could still manage to enjoy herself. During Christmas week she witnessed a play at Hampton Court presented by the common players and was busy preparing a pastoral in which she herself would act when the court returned to London.[33]

London was not considered safe for the court's return until the last week of January in the following year.[34] From the time of Henrietta's marriage in the preceding May, about sixty thousand persons were said to have died of plague in the city.

Their Majesties' absence from London had delayed the coronation, which finally took place on February 2, 1626. The ceremonies were on a modest scale, since Charles's straitened financial circumstances did not allow much expenditure for the purpose. Fearing that her own religious beliefs would be violated by the Protestant observances, the queen refused to be enthroned along with her husband.[35] She even refused to attend the rites in Westminster Abbey, although a screened place from which she could look upon the ceremony had been provided for her. Instead, she watched the procession from Westminster Hall to the abbey church from a window of the gatehouse at Whitehall Palace.

When a few days after the coronation Charles's second parliament convened, there occurred an incident, petty in many respects, of the kind that not uncommonly exacerbates relations between husband and wife. Henrietta's chaplain had arranged a place at Whitehall Palace from which she could watch the ceremonious procession marking the opening of Parliament, but Buckingham suggested that the queen witness the event from the home of his

32. "The King's Cabinet Opened," *The Harleian Miscellany* (12 vols., London, 1808–11), V, 540–541.

33. *Calendar of State Papers, Domestic Series, of the Reign of Charles I, 1625–1649* (23 vols., ed. John Bruce and others, London, 1858–97), 1625–26, pp. 179, 193 (referred to hereafter as *Cal. S. P. Dom.*).

34. *Salvetti Correspondence*, pp. 41, 44.

35. Ellis, *Original Letters*, ser. 3, III, 216–217, 220; *Harl. MSS 390*, fol. 8.

mother. Exactly why Buckingham wished such an arrangement is not very clear, unless the presence of the queen among his own womenfolk would impress upon members of Parliament his continued favor with the king. Shortly before the procession was to begin, Charles came to escort his wife to the place designated in accordance with Buckingham's wish, but on reaching the exit of Whitehall Palace the queen begged to be allowed to comply with the plan her chaplain had made for her, because she feared the unexpected drizzle outdoors might ruin her hairdress. Charles readily granted her request. Buckingham, however, was much agitated by Charles's concession, and reminded him that a king who could not command his wife would make a poor impression on an obdurate parliament. Before Buckingham could reach the queen with a message rescinding the king's permission, Sieur de Blainville, having somehow learned what was in the air, had conducted her to the home of the Countess of Buckingham. This act of compliance only deepened Buckingham's feeling of outrage, because the queen appeared more obedient to her French attendants than to her lord. Buckingham then appeared before the queen and the other ladies she had so recently joined to convey the king's order that she forthwith return to Whitehall Palace. At first the queen, probably with embarrassment, tried to demur, saying that she was well enough satisfied where she was, but she finally yielded to her husband's command. For some days after this event Charles refused to see his wife unless she wished to ask his forgiveness. Since their separation lasted for several days, Henrietta evidently was not as pliant to her husband's will as members of her French retinue, to whom we are chiefly indebted for information on this event, seem to indicate. When she did go to him, she said that though she could perceive no fault in herself, she asked him to forget his hurt if she had given offense.[36]

In a dispatch to the King of France describing the incident that occurred on the opening day of Parliament, Blainville made no reference to his having advised the queen in the matter; he merely

36. Tillières, *Mémoires*, pp. 120–122.

said that the queen sent for him to escort her to the home of the countess. In English opinion his role in the misunderstanding that arose between the king and queen was not so passive. Dispatched by a foreign government under conditions of which the English were not unaware and instructed to support the French party at the English court, he appeared to be creating a dangerous opposition within the government. To Buckingham's request that Blainville not be received in the queen's presence, Henrietta rejoined that since he was commissioned to the English court by her brother, she was forced by diplomatic protocol to refuse the duke's suggestion. Charles circumvented his wife's refusal by sending Blainville a note informing him he was forbidden to come to the court. The French emissary protested that because he was sent as a representative of his sovereign, his own personality was not an issue in the dispute and that therefore he could not receive the king's command. Shortly thereafter, Blainville sought to alleviate his difficult situation by moving to a house several miles from London to wait out his time.[37]

In pursuing a strong and aggressive policy in his dealings with English officials, Blainville was out of touch with the government in France, where foreign policy had changed after the ambassador went to England. Richelieu had decided not to push at that time the demands assigned to Blainville. In response to Richelieu's invitation to send ambassadors extraordinary to France—Buckingham excluded—the Earl of Holland and Sir Dudley Carleton were dispatched to the French court.[38] On the day before Holland and Carleton left, Blainville sent the Bishop of Mende to France to counteract complaints the English ambassadors would almost certainly make against the French party in England. Blainville was now carrying out his own program in relations with the English. His poor intelligence with his home government resulted in part

37. L'Abbé M. Houssaye, "L'Ambassade de M. de Blainville," *Revue des Questions Historiques*, XXIII (1878), 194, 201; Richelieu, *Mémoires*, VI, 221; Ellis, *Original Letters*, ser. 3, III, 223.
38. Houssaye, "L'Ambassade de M. de Blainville," pp. 185, 187; Tillières, *Mémoires*, p. 114.

from the interception by English agents of the dispatches he sent to France.[39]

The main task of Holland and Carleton, besides requesting the recall of Blainville, was to try again to bring the French marriage treaty to fruition by obtaining a definite written alliance against Spain. That the French might be free from internal difficulties to concentrate their strength against Spain, the English ambassadors prevailed upon the Huguenot leaders to sign a disadvantageous treaty with Louis XIII.[40] Still, Richelieu refused an alliance. Having left Henrietta to her fate for a time at least, the French court reacted mildly to stories of her domestic difficulties, although certain groups felt strongly about the treatment given to Blainville.[41] Early in March, just before Holland and Carleton returned to England, the blow fell. It was suddenly announced that Richelieu had reached accord with Spain over differences concerning the Valtelline.[42] Richelieu had hoodwinked the English all along. France was now at peace, uneasy as it was, both at home and abroad, and her leaders could use all the nation's energy for the subjugation of the Huguenots.

Because of the cordial reception that had been given Holland and Carleton in France and in hope that a conciliatory attitude might further the success of their mission, Charles had meanwhile readmitted Blainville to his court. In March, Blainville received from the King of France a note of reprimand for the trouble he was reported to have caused in England, and early in April he received his recall.[43]

During the period of renewed friendliness toward France, Charles and Buckingham apparently tried to alleviate the unhap-

---

39. Houssaye, "L'Ambassade de M. de Blainville," pp. 189, 193.

40. *Salvetti Correspondence*, p. 43; Richelieu, *Mémoires*, V, 220, 225–226; Tillières, *Mémoires*, p. 122.

41. *Cabala*, pp. 296–297; *Salvetti Correspondence*, p. 54; *Harl. MSS 1581*, fol. 48.

42. Tillières, *Mémoires*, p. 129; Richelieu, *Mémoires*, V, 260; *Salvetti Correspondence*, p. 54.

43. Richelieu, *Mémoires*, VI, 228; *Salvetti Correspondence*, p. 60; Houssaye, "L'Ambassade de M. de Blainville," pp. 201–202.

piness of the queen. A Florentine correspondent resident in London wrote in March, 1626, of the sincere affection which existed between the royal couple.[44] But if we can believe Henrietta's chamberlain, Buckingham's friendship could be sinister. In a conversation with the queen he talked of love, possibly with intent of instructing her on the subject. When the queen, feeling her womanly modesty offended by the liberties he was taking in the conversation, chilled on the subject, the duke turned to religion. However astute the duke might have been on the topic of love, his remarks on the Catholic religion revealed an abysmal ignorance. Before the talk was over the conversation took a worse turn, for the duke attempted to convince the queen that she should dismiss her French household.[45]

Somewhat later he went to Madame Saint-Georges and told her that with her influence over the mind of the queen, she could do much to better relations between Henrietta and Charles. Madame Saint-Georges replied that she thought the king and queen got along satisfactorily. Buckingham said it was true that they lived amicably enough during the day, but that the queen did not respond as she should to her husband's embraces at night. Very likely with embarrassment, Madame Saint-Georges rejoined that she did not meddle into those affairs. Buckingham then told Charles of the conversation with Madame Saint-Georges, who he said had promised to speak to the queen. To Charles it seemed that his wife did become more affectionate toward him, but when Buckingham reminded him that he had Madame Saint-Georges to thank for the favor of his wife, the king was deeply disturbed.[46]

For some time past Charles had thought of getting rid of the queen's household. Already three English ladies—the Countess of Denbigh, the Duchess of Buckingham, and the Countess of Carlisle—had been placed in the queen's bedchamber.[47] Finally, in June, 1626, the king found a pretext for sending the queen's French

44. *Salvetti Correspondence*, p. 49.
45. Tillières, *Mémoires*, p. 126.
46. *Ibid.*, p. 127; *Cabala*, p. 296.
47. Ellis, *Original Letters*, ser. 1, III, 210–211; Richelieu, *Lettres*, II, 244.

attendants back to France. According to the story told to him, the queen and a group of her friends, while strolling through the parks surrounding St. James's Palace, had stopped at Tyburn gallows and uttered a prayer in behalf of Catholics who out of loyalty to their religion had been executed there.[48] In English eyes, of course, these martyrs had been guilty of treason. How much truth there was in this story, which the queen hotly denied, is questionable. By the time it reached the king, it had probably been embellished with added detail. Nevertheless, Charles had a good excuse for "cashiering the Monsieurs," and in anticipation of the act Sir Walter Montagu was sent to the French court on a minor pretext to determine whether the French were in a position to retaliate with force against the intended breach of the marriage treaty. Montagu returned with good news: because the French king was occupied with suppressing a court conspiracy against Richelieu, the time for expulsion of the French could not be more propitious.[49]

A few days later Carleton left for Paris to explain why the French household was being sent home.[50] After giving Carleton time to reach the French court, where he would be in a position to offer explanation, the decisive step was taken.

On the morning of August 9 the council was convened, and Charles's resolve was made known to the members. Charles's purpose, as he informed the councilors, was to expel the French from

---

48. *Additional MSS 39228*, fol. 6; *Mercure François*, XIII, 155–156; Hugh Williams, *A Gallant of Lorraine* (2 vols., London, 1921), II, 464.

49. Tillières, *Mémoires*, p. 139; Richelieu, *Mémoires*, VI, 231. After attending Cambridge University, Walter Montagu (1603–77) had traveled extensively on the Continent, where he acquired a knowledge of modern languages. He carried out a number of foreign missions for the Duke of Buckingham. While on an assignment to France during the early stages of the marriage negotiations, he formed with Henrietta a friendship that lasted until her death. Montagu later became a convert to Catholicism and ultimately abbot of the Benedictine monastery at Pointoise in France. As Abbot of Pointoise, he was to figure prominently in an attempt to force the conversion of Henrietta's youngest son, the Duke of Gloucester (see Epilogue). *D.N.B.*, XXXVIII, 270–271.

50. *Salvetti Correspondence*, p. 82; Richelieu, *Mémoires*, VI, 232; Rushworth, *Historical Collections*, I, 424. Sir Dudley Carleton, employed in the foreign service of England ever since he was given his first assignment by James I in 1610, was considered one of the most astute diplomats of his day. *D.N.B.*, III, 996–999.

court so that he could possess Henrietta as his wife. At one o'clock, shortly after the king and queen had dined, Charles went to the queen's apartment, where he found her enjoying herself in the company of two of her women friends, and told her that he had something he wished to say to her in his own room. Answering that she could just as well hear him where she was, the queen asked what he wished to say. On the excuse that he wanted to speak about a private matter, Charles ushered her ladies out of the room, bolted the doors, and informed his wife he was sending her French followers back to their home country. Exactly what followed in the talk between husband and wife was largely conjecture, despite what was reported. Be that as it may, the queen's ladies who had been barred from her room very definitely heard the cries and wails of their mistress, and in their curiosity went out to a court beneath the queen's apartments to look up at the windows from which the cries of despair issued. On hearing her friends in the court, the queen rushed to a window, broke out several panes of glass, and grasping onto the grating, lifted herself up to appeal to the women gathered below. At that moment the king tore his wife away from the window against her wails of protest.[51]

Charles intended to take his wife to the country after expelling her French servants, so that in a changed setting she might more easily forget her loss, but Henrietta reacted in such a way that he was unable to take this means of easing her grief. She refused to go

---

51. Tillières, *Mémoires*, pp. 143, 144; Richelieu, *Mémoires*, VI, 233; Ellis, *Original Letters*, ser. 1, III, 239. Following the expulsion of her French servants, Henrietta sent letters to her mother, Louis XIII, and Richelieu in appeal for help. Let one such letter to her mother serve as an example:

MADAME,
    Have pity on my misery, as you would demand succor in your afflictions. I have no hope but in God and you. Remember that I am your daughter, and the most afflicted person in the world; if you do not take pity on me, I am beyond despair. You have pitied the poor people who asked you for alms; I ask your assistance and will be to my death, Madame, your very humble and very obedient daughter and servant.

Charles, Comte de Baillon, *Lettres de Henriette-Marie, Reine d'Angleterre* (Paris, 1877), p. 350.

to bed or to eat until she had been promised she could retain a few of her servants. She asked to see her confessor. The two priests Charles had designated for her, neither of whom was French, she rejected because they had taken the religious oaths and hence were considered renegade Catholics. Moved to pity, Charles permitted Father Philip, whom she trusted, to remain in her service, and also allowed her to keep a French nurse and Madame Vantelet as well as a few other French servants of lesser importance.[52]

All of the other French officers, clergymen, and servants were taken to Somerset House to await shipment to France.[53] They were recompensed for expenditures they had made while in the queen's service, and in mitigation of their feeling of outrage, were given presents of considerable value.[54] Charles was eager to see them gone. When after several days they still lingered within the confines of Somerset House, Charles wrote to Buckingham: "I have receaved your Letter by Dic Greame, this is my Answer. I command you to send all of the French away tomorrow out of Toune. If you can, by faire meanes (but strike not long in disputing) otherwise force them away, driving them away lyke so manie wyld beastes until you have shipped them, and so the Devill goe with them. Let me heare no answer bot of the performance of my command."[55]

Meanwhile, in France, Carleton was performing the onerous task of explaining the reason for the ejection of Henrietta's household. Louis XIII shortly afterward ordered Carleton to leave the country, in empty retaliation against Charles's act of expulsion. Incensed though the French were, they reacted more mildly than might have been expected.[56] Henrietta's mother wrote a letter telling her daughter to obey her husband in all things except religion,

52. *MSS Français 3692*, fols. 4, 5; Ellis, *Original Letters*, ser. 1, III, 238; Tillières, *Mémoires*, pp. 145–146.
53. Ellis, *Original Letters*, ser. 1, III, 237, 243; Tillières, *Mémoires*, p. 146; Richelieu, *Mémoires*, VI, 235–237.
54. Ellis, *Original Letters*, ser. 1, III, 246; Tillières, *Mémoires*, pp. 147–148.
55. *Harl. MSS 6988*, fol. 11.
56. Richelieu, *Mémoires*, VI, 238; *MSS Français 3692*, fol. 53; *Cabala*, p. 301.

and in a conversation with the English ambassador in Paris the queen dowager denied any feeling of anger toward the Duke of Buckingham.

By the time the outcasts from England reached France, François de Bassompierre, a nobleman of an old Lorraine family, was preparing to go to England on embassy. In addition to effecting the restoration of the queen's household, Bassompierre was to encourage England's war against Spain, to seek easement of punishment for English Catholics, and to ask for restoration of the goods and ships which the English had continued to seize since the fall of the previous year.[57] His mission, except for the added complications of the queen's household, was about the same as that assigned to Blainville twelve months earlier.

On reaching England late in September, 1626, he was given a most unfriendly reception. He was told that he would be given no allowance from the treasury for his maintenance in England, a rebuff which implied that he was not even recognized as an ambassador. Until he had sent Father Sancy, whom he brought as his confessor, out of the country, he was further told, he would not be granted an audience at court. At first he could not understand the English objections to Father Sancy, and although the English repeatedly insisted on this matter, Bassompierre stood fast upon his rights as an emissary accredited by the French government.[58]

Finally permitted to present his credentials and letters from the French king at a formal meeting of the court, he was told to make no speech on that occasion, since the king feared this provocation would cause his wife to break out crying before the whole assembly. This limitation placed upon Bassompierre showed the emotional state of the queen a month after she had been deprived of her French associates. After being recognized by the court, the

57. Richelieu, *Mémoires*, VI, 243–244; Richelieu, *Lettres*, II, 243–253; *MSS Français 3692*, fols. 8, 85.

58. François de Bassompierre, *Journal de Ma Vie: Mémoires* (4 vols., ed. Marie J. A. LaCropte, Paris, 1870–77), III, 255–256, 258; Richelieu, *Mémoires*, VI, 328–329; *MSS Français 3692*, fols. 60, 66.

envoy was free to visit the queen at Somerset House any time he wished. This liberty enabled a person as fair-minded as Bassompierre to see both sides of the story. Witnessing several quarrels between the king and queen, he began to see that Charles had a spirited, self-willed wife, and probably taking a man's viewpoint, found himself sympathizing with the king. In fact, Bassompierre himself became involved in quarrels with the queen, and on one occasion told her that if she did not change her attitude, he would forthwith return to France and tell Louis XIII who really was at fault.[59]

Bassompierre's amiability soon won him many friends around the English court. With Buckingham he appeared to form a most cordial and informal relationship, although the sincerity behind the duke's show of friendship, as will later be seen, might be questioned. In December, when Bassompierre's stay in England was drawing to a close, Buckingham entertained Their Majesties and Bassompierre as guests of honor in his palatial London residence, known as York House.[60] Bassompierre described this home as the most sumptuous and most richly furnished house he had ever seen. Among the displays presented at dinner was a pageant showing the sea that divided England from France, and above it the French queen mother sitting on a throne among the gods and beckoning with her hands to the King and Queen of England and of France, the Duke and Duchess of Savoy, and the Elector and Electress Palatine to come and join her among the gods, thereby to put an end to the discords of Christendom. This display was "a fanciful mystical conceit," as one writer described it, expressing Buckingham's wish for an alliance against Spain. Most of the night was spent in dancing and other amusements, and the festivities ended with the serving of a splendid refection of sweetmeats at four o'clock in the morning. Their Majesties remained to sleep at

59. Bassompierre, *Mémoires*, III, 259–269, 265–278 *passim; MSS Français 21007*, fols. 66, 67.

60. *Salvetti Correspondence*, pp. 94–95, 97, 101, 102; Bassompierre, *Mémoires*, III, 274.

the duke's house, where the entertainments were renewed later in the day.

Having gone to England without great expectation for the success of his mission, Bassompierre was well pleased with the concessions he was able to obtain. The council agreed to allow the queen twelve priests appointed by Louis XIII, and also a bishop to serve as the queen's grand almoner and governor to her clergymen. In addition, the French were to send two ladies for the queen's bedchamber and a few servants. No agreement was reached concerning cessation of raids on French commerce or relief for Catholics in England.[61]

When Bassompierre informed the queen of what he had been able to obtain in her behalf, she was indignant and castigated him severely. He had not done enough for her. On returning to his lodgings, Bassompierre was approached by Father Sancy, who began to intercede on Henrietta's behalf, asking that Bassompierre negotiate further with the council to satisfy her wishes. For the first time Bassompierre realized why the English had so strongly objected to the presence of Sancy in England. The English knew him from the days when he was a member of the queen's household. He was nothing short of a spy. All along, while Bassompierre had been debating with the council, Sancy had been exchanging notes with Henrietta, no doubt telling her to insist on certain minimum demands, and probably had been in communication with other Catholics in England as well. The old soldier Bassompierre was at the end of his patience, and Father Sancy caught the brunt of his ire.[62]

Bassompierre returned to France at the end of the year. As he waited for passage at Dover, he saw armed English ships bringing in French merchantmen as prizes. Another matter that disturbed him during his wait in Dover was Buckingham's wish to accom-

61. *MSS Français 3692*, fols. 84, 148, 150, 183–184, 191–192, 199, 200. These folios relate to topics discussed in negotiation of the agreement with Bassompierre. A copy of the treaty is found in fols. 183–184.

62. *MSS Français 3692*, fol. 175; Williams, *A Gallant of Lorraine*, II, 492.

pany him back to France as England's return for his embassy.[63]
Buckingham even sent horses and carriages to Dover in anticipation of travel from Calais to Paris. Knowing that Buckingham
would do well to come out with a whole skin if he appeared in
France, Bassompierre had to exercise all of his diplomatic skill in
dissuading his impetuous friend from making the journey. Finally
it was agreed that Bassompierre would cross the Channel and prepare the way for Buckingham's reception at the French court.[64]

If Richelieu had accepted the result of Bassompierre's mission
as sufficient basis for harmonious relations between England and
France, it would have been awkward to deny Buckingham's proposal to go to France. But Richelieu had adequate reasons for scorn-
ing Bassompierre's achievement. For one thing, Bassompierre's
mission treated only one part of his assignment, and that perhaps
the least important part in Richelieu's opinion. Even on this point
Bassompierre had not exacted as much as was expected; and of
course nothing was said on religion or raids against French commerce. Since France now had no external wars or internal disturbances as she had had during Blainville's mission, there was no
reason for the French king to demand less from England than he
had a year earlier. Bassompierre's achievement in England was not
enough to justify Buckingham's presence at the French court. The
French had not forgotten the English favorite's insult to their
queen when he was last in France, and Richelieu, knowing that he
could not satisfy the demand for an alliance as Buckingham
wished, had no desire to see the duke.[65]

Late in the year the Duke of Epernon seized the English wine
fleet of about two hundred ships at Bordeaux. At a meeting of the
privy council in December, 1626, the English ministers retaliated
by ordering the seizure of all French shipping, and English raiders
were soon scurrying along French coasts and making runs into
smaller French harbors to ferret out their prey. By the end of the

63. *MSS Français 3692*, fols. 193, 209; Richelieu, *Mémoires*, VI, 338.
64. *Salvetti Correspondence*, p. 102; Richelieu, *Mémoires*, VI, 339.
65. *Ibid.*, VII, 42–43, 45–47.

year the two countries were practically at war.[66] Richelieu had little reason to want a war with England, for he did not have sufficient sea power with which to strike back at English fleets. On the other hand, any military threat Buckingham might make against France was considerably reduced in its potential by the antipathy felt toward him in Parliament, which in the previous spring had brought impeachment proceedings against the duke. Inasmuch, however, as Louis XIII was preparing to subjugate the port city of La Rochelle, the English navy could make the reduction of the Huguenot bastion doubly difficult for the King of France.

Early in May, 1627, Buckingham, dressed in a hat with magnificent plumes and a coat with a long collar, the best of military fashion in that day, was seen at Plymouth officiously directing the preparation of the fleet with which he personally was to scour the seas and storm the coasts of France. In June he invited Their Majesties to a fête at York House. The duke himself took part in a ballet depicting the preparation of the navy and its departure from England.[67] During the same month Henrietta wrote her mother of Charles's desire for peace between the two countries: ". . . I can say with truth," she avowed, "that I have always recognized in him this desire to an extreme. . . ." Expressing her own wish, she added, "As for me, madam, it would be the greatest satisfaction that could ever happen to me. . . ."[68]

About a month later, shortly after Buckingham had left with the fleet, Charles departed from London to hunt in various locations where game was plentiful, while the queen went to drink the waters at Wellingborough, a place that was to become a favorite vacation resort for her. From here the queen wrote the Lord Trea-

66. *Calendar of State Papers, Venice* (38 vols., ed. Allen B. Hinds and others, London, 1864–1940), XX, 54–55, 68 (referred to hereafter as *Cal. S. P. Ven.*); *Cal. S. P. Dom.*, 1625–26, p. 486; Tillières, *Mémoires*, p. 160.

67. Edward Hyde, Earl of Clarendon, *The History of the Rebellion and Civil Wars in England* (7 vols., Oxford, 1849), I, 52, 55; *Harl. MSS 6988*, fols. 50, 87; *Salvetti Correspondence*, pp. 116, 118.

68. Mary Anne Everett Green, *Letters of Queen Henrietta Maria* (London, 1857), p. 11.

surer, Richard Weston, asking that she be given £2,000 as soon as she returned to London and also requesting that she be paid other money due her.[69]

On All Saints' Eve, Henrietta consulted a prophetess, Eleanor Davies, whose fame as a prognosticator was already widespread in London. The questions Henrietta asked this woman revealed the main concerns on the queen's mind during the third year of her marriage.[70] The first question she asked was when she would be with child. To this the seer vaguely answered, "Oporet habere tempus," which was translated for the queen by the Earl of Carlisle. Next, the queen wished to know what success would accrue to the Duke of Buckingham, who was away on his expedition against the French. As for his honor, the prophetess replied, he should not bring home much, but his person would soon return. Then the queen wanted to know whether she was to be happy, and if so, for how long. She was told that she would be happy for sixteen years. At this point in the interview Charles entered the queen's apartment, and on learning what was taking place expressed his displeasure by immediately ending the interview. A few days later he sent an officer to forbid Eleanor Davies from again seeing the queen and above all from making predictions about affairs concerning the king.

On November 8, 1627, Buckingham returned with the fleet from his expedition, which as it finally developed was an attempt to take the French island of Rhé, off the channel leading to the port of La Rochelle. This military venture ended in a rout with terrible losses for the English, as many families who counted sons among the missing could attest. When Buckingham rode up to London from Plymouth, the king met him with open arms and many apologies that he had not been able to reinforce the venturer as had been planned.[71] In the following month Richelieu returned

69. *Salvetti Correspondence*, p. 122.

70. George Ballard, *Memoirs of Several Ladies of Britain* (Oxford, 1752), pp. 275–276.

71. *D.N.B.*, XX, 335. "On October 20 the English army on Rhé consisted of 6,884 men. On November 8 no more than 2989 landed at Plymouth." See also

to Henrietta the prisoners the French had seized on Rhé.[72] This special concession to the queen, as if to indicate that her influence was greater than Buckingham's, must have been a bitter pill for the duke to swallow.

During the months after Buckingham's return from Rhé, public feeling against the king's favorite was expressed with increasing intensity. In the parliament of 1628, Sir Edward Coke named Buckingham as the cause of England's troubles. "What shall we do," he asked. And then, in reply to his own question, he continued, "Let us palliate no longer, if we do, God will not prosper us. I think the Duke of Buckingham is the cause of all our Miseries; and until the King be informed thereof, we shall never go out with Honour, or sit with Honour here; that Man is the Grievance of Grievances. . . ."[73] In June a London mob attacked and killed a certain Dr. Lambe, a necromancer whom Buckingham was supposed to have consulted.[74] Actually this was a vicarious attack against Buckingham himself, since Dr. Lambe probably would never have come into public notice had it not been for his purported association with the duke.

Buckingham was at Portsmouth preparing to set out with a fleet for the relief of La Rochelle, which was besieged by forces of the French king, when the hand of an assassin ended his plans to aid the Huguenots. John Felton, Buckingham's murderer, thought he was performing a public service in dispatching the duke, and many an Englishman placed no less value on his act. "God bless thee, little David," shouted a woman to him as he was being taken by barge to the Tower.[75]

A servant sent by Henrietta was the first to bring news of Buck-

Sir Simonds D'Ewes, *Autobiography and Correspondence* (2 vols., ed. James Orchard Halliwell, London, 1845), I, 366; *Harl. MSS 6988*, fols. 30, 43, 53; *Salvetti Correspondence*, p. 136.

72. Richelieu, *Lettres*, II, 740.

73. Rushworth, *Historical Collections*, I, 607.

74. *Ibid.*, p. 618; *Harl. MSS 390*, fol. 415; *Salvetti Correspondence*, p. 161.

75. *Harl. MSS 390*, fol. 437; Ellis, *Original Letters*, ser, 1, III, 258; Sir Philip Warwick, *Memoirs of the Reign of Charles I* (London, 1702), p. 32.

ingham's death to France.[76] Whether he was sent for this particular purpose is not certain, but he probably was not. At least Henrietta gave no indication of triumph over the death of the person who had caused her much unhappiness. She tenderly comforted the king in his grief over the loss of one who had been so near to him. Even more ingratiating in the eyes of the king, she went to Buckingham's wife and mother to offer her condolences.[77]

It was in the days following Buckingham's death that the deep affection between Henrietta and Charles, one of the most endearing of royal romances, began to flourish. By her outpouring of sympathy, the queen begot love. Charles always needed someone on whom to lean, and in supporting him during his season of sorrow, Henrietta awakened an affection in her own heart for the one who needed her care.

Through many trials the queen at last achieved her victory. With the French household and Buckingham now out of the way —the two factors which had kept the king and queen apart all along—the natural affinity the royal couple must always have felt for one another could grow unhindered. Only a month after Buckingham's death, persons around the court were remarking of the new relationship that had arisen between the king and queen, and of the consequent influence Henrietta was almost certain to have upon her husband. Writing in a report to his home government in September, 1628, the Venetian ambassador in London declared, "I must add that every day she concentrates in herself the favor and love that were previously divided between herself and the duke. . . ."[78]

In August, 1628, the king had left London to hunt as usual, while the queen had gone to Wellingborough, where she delighted in the country dances presented before her. At the end of the month they were together again. The queen, who because of the impoverished condition of the court never had enough money to

76. *Cal. S. P. Ven.*, XXI, 297.
77. *Salvetti Correspondence*, p. 165.
78. *Cal. S. P. Ven.*, XXI, 311.

spend, asked her husband for two pounds sterling to give in alms to a poor Frenchwoman. When the king asked who this person was, she replied, "I, Sire, am the penniless pauper." [79]

With the removal of Buckingham, there began to be talk of peace between England and France. The Venetian ambassadors in either country, eager to have France free of the English war so that she could concentrate against Spanish forces in northern Italy, were untiring in their efforts to bring about a cessation of the pointless hostilities. Alvise Contarini, the Venetian ambassador in London, had the Earl of Holland ask the queen whether she would use her good offices with the king in urging him to accept negotiations for a peace. Henrietta accepted his suggestion with alacrity. She told Charles that while she did not pretend to meddle into his political affairs or to influence his judgment, she would be happy if peace were established between those most dear in her heart—that is, between her husband and her brother. As for the effect of the queen's plea, Contarini wrote, "I know that her entreaties have made an impression, in addition to my own." [80] Earlier he had informed the doge in Venice that if peace were concluded between England and France, the queen might be instrumental in bringing it about.

Although there was some contention about the settlement of the queen's household, Contarini did not think Henrietta would make much trouble on this point. She was learning to live with her English friends. Concerning the sending of another French household to England, Contarini declared, "I do not think the queen is very anxious to have them, foreseeing disagreements, which might impede her growing influence, while the king is obviously disinclined to have Frenchmen in his household." [81] Contarini was certainly right in the last part of his statement. Charles had no intention of again accepting a large body of French servants to

79. *Ibid.*, pp. 213, 242; *Salvetti Correspondence*, p. 158.
80. *Cal. S. P. Ven.*, XXI, 293, 310, 362–363.
81. *Ibid.*, pp. 287, 315.

surround his wife. In reference to a comment of Charles on this matter, Contarini wrote, "He repeated that if the French came here, the peace would not last, as their heat does not agree with the phlegm here." On the same subject, Contarini later said, "The King has more regard for his domestic peace, which he pretends the French have always disturbed, than for anything else."[82]

The agreement made with Bassompierre about the queen's household was, Charles maintained, a dead letter. Richelieu suggested the question be settled by personal negotiation between Henrietta and her mother. Knowing the superior attitude that Marie de Medici would take, Charles would hear nothing of this suggestion. For all of her growing influence over her husband, Henrietta was reluctant to endorse Richelieu's proposal. In a letter to the Venetian ambassador in France, Contarini added this postscript: "At this moment the queen, instead of the promised letter to the queen mother, sends me word very confidentially that she does not want to displease the king by interesting herself too far in this matter, and asking me to supply her place by attesting that she is perfectly satisfied with the services and with the court in its present state, and she is very anxious that this shall not disturb the principal matter."[83] It was in no small measure due to the queen's conciliatory attitude that negotiations had led to the exchange of unofficial emissaries by the end of the year.

Added to the conciliatory attitude of the queen were other developments, which by the spring of the next year made peace between England and France almost inevitable.[84] By that time the Rochellese, for whose cause the English were supposed to be fighting, had surrendered their city to the besieging army of Louis XIII. Furthermore, Charles dismissed his fifth parliament in March of 1629, and resolved to rule England without a representative body. Since he was no longer to have monetary support from Parliament,

82. *Ibid.*, pp. 340, 375.
83. *Ibid.*, p. 380.
84. Warwick, *Memoirs*, p. 36; *Cal. S. P. Ven.*, XXI, 503, 600.

Charles would have to withdraw from foreign ventures simply because he would not have financial resources to engage in wars. And then, on March 25, came the announcement that the queen was pregnant. From Holland the Venetian ambassador sent a dispatch to his government stating, "They speak openly here of peace between England and France. . . . The French ambassador has no news from his court on the subject. . . . He remarked to me that the pregnancy of the queen of England had given a great impulse to this reconciliation." [85]

A treaty ending hostilities between England and France was signed on April 4 and was to be publicized in both countries in May. It was a status quo ante bellum agreement, with the added provision that all differences existing between the two states would be settled by later negotiation.[86]

The king and queen were at Greenwich when the peace was declared on Sunday, May 10, 1629. The next day the queen went to London to have a *Te Deum* sung at her chapel in Somerset House. On the following Tuesday night, she was prematurely delivered of a male child, who lived only two hours. During her ordeal her life was in great danger; it was a question of saving the queen or the child. When consulted on the matter, the king, who was constantly at his wife's bedside, said he "would rather save the mold than the cast." The letter Charles wrote to the queen mother telling her of the misfortune was the first he had addressed to her in three years.[87]

The Marquis of Chateauneuf came from Paris in June, 1629, to discuss those questions which, according to the recent treaty terms, were to be settled through negotiation. Chateauneuf found Charles sensitive and fussy over small points pertaining to diplomatic niceties. Charles's pride was hurt; it galled him to think he and Buckingham had been defeated by the French. To Henrietta he admitted the injury he felt when Louis XIII had the English standards captured at Rhé set up in the Cathedral of Notre Dame, and

85. *Ibid.*, XXII, 58.

86. Richelieu, *Mémoires*, X, 219; Thomas Frankland, *The Annals of King James and King Charles the First* (London, 1681), pp. 363–364.

87. D'Ewes, *Autobiography*, I, 411–412; *Cal. S. P. Ven.*, XXII, 68–69, 70.

further stated that only Christian forbearance enabled him to listen to overtures of peace.[88]

For all of the Christian sentiment of forgiveness that Charles could muster, he still was not willing to concede much.[89] After tedious dealings, he finally agreed to let the French send six priests in addition to the two Henrietta already had, but refused to accept a bishop as her chief almoner. At first he absolutely refused to discuss appointment of other servants for the queen's household, saying that he would arrange those matters for his wife as he desired. With reluctance he finally granted the queen mother of France the privilege of appointing one lady of the bedchamber for Henrietta's service, although the appointment was to be deferred until some indefinite time in the future.

In the end Chateauneuf's mission proved no more successful than had that of Bassompierre. The talks in fulfillment of the treaty finally ended with nothing agreed to on the treatment of Catholics in England or compensation to France for incursions against French commerce.

At the same time conversations were held with Chateauneuf, dealings were also under way for a peace with Spain. In effect the war against Spain had proved abortive. Even before Buckingham started on his expedition to Rhé, he had sent agents to consult with the Spanish concerning a treaty, which was not concluded until eighteen months after accord was reached with France.[90]

Thus, neither England nor France had been able to achieve the diplomatic and political purposes they had hoped to gain from the marriage of Henrietta and Charles. Instead of regaining the Palatinate for his brother-in-law Frederick, Charles was forced to withdraw from foreign wars after determining to rule without Parliament, the only organ of English government possessing adequate power of taxation to support extensive military endeavors. In withdrawing English military power from the Continent,

88. *Ibid.*, p. 127; Richelieu, *Mémoires*, X, 220–223, 226–227, 238.
89. *Ibid.*, pp. 245, 246, 272.
90. *Ibid.*, pp. 265, 268, 269, 270; *Salvetti Correspondence*, pp. 105, 157, 158.

Charles's disappointment was no greater than Richelieu's. Richelieu had hoped to engage the English against Spanish and Austrian forces in Germany, thereby relieving France of military involvement in that region so that she might strengthen herself through internal reforms.

Nor had Richelieu been any more successful in building up a Catholic party in England to foster opinion favorable toward France. Every one of Charles's parliaments had presented petitions urging the king to more vigorous measures against Catholics, and it was largely because of the avidly Protestant attitude of the House of Commons that Charles dismissed Parliament with finality in 1629.[91] Of course, it was Parliament that became the unforeseen factor in disappointing the diplomatic aims of France and England,[92] and the political ambitions interwoven with the marriage of Charles and Henrietta in turn precipitated the dispute between Charles and his parliaments.

Until the diplomatic purposes of the marriage treaty had been frustrated, Charles and Henrietta could not have been happy as husband and wife. Political considerations introduced too many complexities, such as the queen's household and Buckingham's attempts to pursue an aggressive foreign policy. Now, however, the happy years began for Henrietta, the years of childbearing and the years during which she possessed her husband's heart completely. And yet hers was but a tentative happiness. Difficulties and unsolved problems remained in the background. The constitutional position of the king and of Parliament was still unsettled, and the prejudices against Catholicism remained unabated. Of the seriousness of these lurking dangers, Henrietta was largely unaware. She had entered the halcyon period of her life, the time when she was to know the joy of being a woman.

91. Rushworth, *Historical Collections*, I, 660.
92. Davies, *The Early Stuarts*, pp. 64–65.

CHAPTER III

HALCYON YEARS

1630-35   ON A May night in 1630, the inhabitants of a small Gloucestershire town reveled around flickering bonfires. England had cause to rejoice. The queen had given birth to a prince,[1] thereby establishing the succession. "When the news came of the Prince's birth," wrote a contemporary, "there was great Joy shown by all the rest of the Parish, in causing Bonfires to be made, and Bells to be rung, and sending Victuals into those of the younger sort, who were most busily employed in the Publicke Joy." But not all of the townsmen were happy over the event behind the celebration, for "from the rest of the Houses, being of Presbyterian or Puritan Party, there came neither Man, nor Child, nor Wood, nor Victuals; their doors being shut close all the evening, as in a time of general mourning and disconsolation."[2]

Among the more extreme Protestant groups, the Puritans and Presbyterians especially, were those who were not pleased that their Catholic queen had given them a future ruler, but preferred instead to think of one of the sons of the Protestant Frederick of the Palatinate, brother-in-law to Charles I, as assurance for the

1. The exact date of the prince's birth was May 29, 1630. *Harl. MSS 6988*, fol. 133.

2. Peter Heylin, *Cyprianus Anglicus: The History of the Life and Death of William Laud* (London, 1671), p. 198.

73

succession in England.[3] To them Protestantism appeared to be fighting a losing battle against the sweep of the Catholic Counter-Reformation on the Continent. They had only to remember the fall of La Rochelle in France and the recent successes of the emperor in Germany to arouse their fears of the papacy. A prince under the religious influence of a strongly Catholic mother was for the Puritans an inadmissible danger to Protestantism in England.[4]

Many Protestants believed Henrietta to be aggressive in the interest of her own faith. During the preceding month of March, the new French ambassador, the Marquis of Fontenay-Mareuil, had brought with him twelve Capuchin monks, eight of whom were to serve in the queen's chapel in accordance with the marriage treaty as modified in 1629.[5] The Puritan soul rankled at the sight of Capuchins in their cassocks moving about the court or on some private mission into the city. They took the presence of the hated monks to be added evidence of the queen's power over her husband.

Catholics around London, assuming the admission of Capuchins to indicate a more lenient attitude toward their religion on the part of the king and his officers, repaired more openly and in ever larger numbers to attend mass in the queen's chapel or the chapels of foreign ambassadors resident in the city.[6] The Puritans were immediately aroused. In part to placate their protests,[7] the council ordered that none of His Majesty's subjects were to attend

3. *Ibid.*

4. Frances Verney, *Memoirs of the Verney Family* (4 vols., New York, 1892–99), I, 93–95.

5. *Calendar of State Papers, Venice* (38 vols., ed. Allen B. Hinds and others, London, 1864–1940), XXII, 301 (referred to hereafter as *Cal. S. P. Ven.*); *Le Mercure François* (25 vols. in 27, ed. J. and E. Richter, Paris, 1611–44), XVI, 443–444; Cyprien de Gamache, *Memoirs of the Mission in England of the Capuchin Friars of the Province of Paris, from the Year 1630 to 1669* (in vol. II, 293–501, of Thomas Birch, *The Court and Times of Charles I* [2 vols., London, 1848]), p. 298. The French king intended the two Oratorians who had remained with Henrietta following the expulsion of the French household to be sent back to France, but she refused to comply with her brother's orders. Four of the Capuchins that Fontenay-Mareuil brought with him were to serve his own chapel.

6. Birch, *Court and Times of Charles I*, II, 66–71.

7. *Cal. S. P. Ven.*, XXII, 304–305.

religious services in the homes of ambassadors.[8] On Sundays pursuivants were placed within twenty paces or so of the doors of embassies to apprehend those English subjects who were leaving after attending mass.[9] As a result, incidents involving violence were not wanting. Claiming their rights under diplomatic immunity, ambassadors remonstrated against the ruling of the council, saying that the declarations of that body could not apply to the embassies, which in effect were territories of foreign princes.[10] On an April Sunday a party of communicants leaving the chapel of the French ambassador was set upon by pursuivants. A part of the group was caught and carried off to jail, while the remainder ran back to find sanctuary within the walls of the embassy. A short time afterward some of the French officers issued forth with swords in hand to chase away the pursuivants who continued to hover outside the door of the building, but they also were forced to retreat from the English police.[11]

English subjects who attended the queen's chapel were, in deference to Her Majesty, treated with more consideration. Agents were posted outside the chapel to warn them against violating the law, and those who persisted in entering were not arrested until the day following. Nevertheless, there were exceptions to the general practice. Marie Aubert, wife of the queen's chief surgeon, was seized by a pursuivant on coming from Somerset House. Although she showed him a warrant from the king excusing her from the decree of the council, the officer dragged her through the street with such violence that she, then being great with child and weak from fasting, was prematurely delivered of a dead infant.[12]

The queen was outraged by the council's action against Catholics. For days she refused to speak to any of its members, but above

8. *Calendar of State Papers, Domestic Series, of the Reign of Charles I, 1625–1649* (23 vols., ed. John Bruce and others, London, 1858–97), 1629–31, p. 209 (referred to hereafter as *Cal. S. P. Dom.*).

9. *Cal. S. P. Ven.*, XXII, 308.

10. *Ibid.*, p. 304.

11. Birch, *Court and Times of Charles I*, II, 76–77.

12. *Cal. S. P. Dom.*, 1631–33, p. 142.

all the rest she blamed the Lord Treasurer,[13] Richard Weston, who since Buckingham's death had increasingly assumed the place of leadership among the king's advisers. Placed between the mounting anger of the Puritans, who suspected him of Catholic proclivities despite his denial of any such inclination, and the tart asperity of the queen, who could not appreciate the attitude or importance of the Puritans, Weston suffered the censure of both sides.

One of the best assurances the Puritans had against Catholicism or a Catholic successor to the throne was the king himself. No less than the Puritans did he oppose the education of his successor in the rites of the Catholic Church. He ordered that no Catholic servants attend the queen during her confinement, and even refused to permit a doctor sent from France to see the queen.[14] Soon after the prince's birth, Charles sent word notifying the two Capuchins whom the queen had brought to St. James's Palace to remain with her during her lying-in that they must take no measures regarding the baptism of the infant, but that the king personally would look after the christening of his son.[15] Although by the marriage treaty all children born of Charles and Henrietta were to be trained in their mother's religion during their childhood, the king ordered that the ceremonies for baptism conform with those prescribed by the Anglican Church.[16]

Following the christening of Prince Charles, the king started his annual progress to royal residences outside London, and the queen joined him not long afterward. The affection between husband and wife continued to flourish. During the previous spring the queen's mother had sent a present of linen for Henrietta's accouchement. In a note sent along with his wife's letter of thanks, the king declared, "The only dispute that now exists between us

13. *Cal. S. P. Ven.*, XXII, 309.

14. Birch, *Court and Times of Charles I*, II, 63; *Cal. S. P. Ven.*, XXII, 345; Armand J. du Plessis, Duke of Richelieu, Cardinal, *Lettres, Instructions Diplomatiques et Papiers d'État* (8 vols., ed. Denis M. L. Avenel [*Collection de Documents Inédits*], Paris, 1853–77), III, 520–521 (referred to hereafter as Richelieu, *Lettres*).

15. Gamache, *Memoirs*, p. 306.

16. *Lansdowne MSS 1054*, fol. 89.

is that of conquering each other by affection, both of us esteeming ourselves victorious in following the will of each other."[17]

Early in August Their Majesties returned to London temporarily to see the baby prince.[18] Of the infant, Henrietta wrote to Madame Saint-Georges a month later: ". . . he is so fat and so tall, that he is taken for a year old, and he is only four months. . . . I will send you his portrait as soon as he is a little fairer, for at present he is so dark I am ashamed of him."[19]

After the birth of the prince the severity of measures taken against Catholics abated, so that by the end of 1630 "the state of religion was quiet and the Catholics enjoyed a sweet and agreeable peace."[20] This change in policy even the Catholics attributed to the increased appeal the queen could exercise over the heart and mind of her husband, since she was now mother of his child. And by October there were rumors that the queen was again pregnant, although her trip to Cambridge the following February to witness three plays offered by students there gave lie to that report.[21]

Much as the king loved his wife, the extent of her influence over him, despite what her enemies might have thought,[22] was as yet uncertain and ill defined. Nor did the queen have any definite policy of her own to support. Her actions were based upon personal considerations, upon her like or dislike of some person, rather than upon policy. To be sure, there were those around the court whom the queen did not like, Weston being the principal one among them.

If opposed to Weston because he concurred with the council's measures against Catholics, her dislike of him arose in the first instance from his close-fisted policy in handling the finances

17. Mary Anne Everett Green, *Letters of Queen Henrietta Maria* (London, 1857), pp. 14–15.

18. *Cal. S. P. Ven.*, XXII, 379, 388.

19. Green, *Letters of Henrietta Maria*, p. 17.

20. Gamache, *Memoirs*, p. 303.

21. *Cal. S. P. Ven.*, XXII, 431, 456; Henry Ellis, *Original Letters* (12 vols. in 3 series, London, 1824–46), ser. 2, III, 267.

22. *The Memoirs of Edmund Ludlow* (2 vols., ed. C. H. Firth, Oxford, 1894), I, 10.

of the royal household.[23] At a time when Parliament could not be looked to for supply, the discharge of funds from the treasury had to be closely supervised even against the demands of a queen who wished to spend money freely. Weston, hard pressed to find extra-parliamentary sources of public revenue, tried to make ends meet by limiting expenditures, and consequently the king's household operated under limited means.

It was said that during the period of her lying-in the queen was, because of the mean furnishing of her palace, much embarrassed by the visit of the old Duchesse de Tremouille, who had come to England to see her daughter. Her request to visit the queen was at first denied. When finally she was admitted to the room in which the queen was lying, the window curtains were drawn so that the visitor could not so easily perceive the poverty of the furnishings in the room and the shoddiness of the queen's personal effects.[24]

Also, Weston's personality contributed little to win the queen's friendship. In the presence of Her Majesty he could be more curt than was his wont in refusing her wishes, and then in private would torture himself wondering why the queen did not look upon him with more favor. Driven by this despair to soliciting friends for information, he finally would go to the queen and try to make apology, often giving the names of his informers and in so doing making personal relations around the court more strained than ever.[25]

As might be assumed, Weston had opponents among the officials and servants of the king, and these opponents sought to employ the influence of the queen to overthrow the chief minister. The leader of Weston's opposition was Lord Holland,[26] who had

23. *Cal. S. P. Ven.*, XXII, 142; "Richard Weston," *D.N.B.*, LX, 366.
24. *Cal. S. P. Ven.*, XXII, 359.
25. Edward Hyde, Earl of Clarendon, *The History of the Rebellion and Civil Wars in England* (7 vols., Oxford, 1849), I, 72.
26. François de Val, Marquis of Fontenay-Mareuil, *Mémoires* (2 vols., ed. M. Petitot [vols. 40 and 41 of *Collection Complète des Mémoires Relatifs à l'Histoire de France*], Paris, 1826), II, 360 (referred to hereafter as Fontenay-Mareuil, *Mémoires*).

ridden to office on the train of Buckingham. Holland was ambitious for position and aspired to fill his benefactor's place after the duke's assassination. In 1631 the cabal around the queen made a timid effort to lessen Weston's power by appointing Francis Cottington, lately returned from embassy to Spain, First Secretary of State, and in so doing to win him from the following of Weston, since he would owe his position to the good offices of the queen. Cottington, however, fearing that he might totally ruin himself in the confidence of the king if the venture failed, refused to accept the office unless Weston approved.[27] If Weston by no means enjoyed the measure of influence over the king that Buckingham had exercised, the faction opposed to him was not yet strong enough to bring about his reduction.

As a sister to the King of France, Henrietta understandably was interested in affairs beyond the English Channel, although in French politics as in English concerns her intrigues usually arose from the desire to assist one or another of her friends rather than to promote long-range policies. So it was that she became involved in her mother's attempt to overthrow the leading French minister, Cardinal Richelieu, who formerly had been the dowager's secretary. Louis XIII stuck by his minister, and the queen mother, too long an annoyance to the peaceful order of the state, was confined in a castle at Compiègne. Somewhat later she made her escape to Flanders, from where she continued her intrigue against Richelieu.[28] Henrietta sympathized with her mother. To Fontenay-Mareuil, whom she despised as the creature of Richelieu, she protested vehemently because of what she considered ill treatment of the queen dowager. The dismissal of Richelieu was little enough, she told the ambassador, for the King of France to grant his mother.[29]

With Fontenay's predecessor, the Marquis of Chateauneuf, the queen's relations had been close and amiable, largely due to his

27. *Cal. S. P. Ven.*, XXII, 510.

28. Françoise Bertaut, Madame de Motteville, *Mémoires sur Anne d'Autriche et Sa Cour* (4 vols., ed. M. F. Riaux, Paris, n.d.), I, 48–49.

29. *Cal. S. P. Ven.*, XXII, 538, 544.

deliberate attempt to cultivate her friendship. Led on by the feminine wiles of Madame de Chevreuse, Chateauneuf had joined the camp of Richelieu's enemies and was fast assuming leadership in the party.[30] Believing that Henrietta's support might later be valuable, he took a sympathetic interest in the queen's household problems, indeed far too great an interest to please Charles, and understood her animosity toward Weston.[31]

Even after Chateauneuf's return to France, the liaison which had been established between him and the queen's party at the court did not end. As his chief agent in England, Chateauneuf employed the Chevalier de Jars, who had been chased out of France as a result of involvement in a plot against Richelieu in 1626. Schooled in the manners of the gallant, de Jars was another parasitic courtier who worked his way into the queen's good graces by his witty and entertaining conversation, and who pleased Charles as a boon companion and an opponent in tennis matches.[32]

Fontenay-Mareuil was not unaware of de Jars's role as Chateauneuf's henchman in England. In order to acquire evidence against the schemers who were planning the overthrow of Richelieu, Fontenay in the summer of 1631 hired housebreakers to steal the cabinet in which de Jars kept his correspondence. At once a hue and cry was sounded against this thievery of Fontenay, and was taken up by the queen herself. But despite her entreaties and demands, Charles refused to take any measures against the French ambassador or to protest his action to the French king.[33]

Meanwhile, from her place of refuge in Brussels, the French queen mother made repeated efforts to secure admission to England. In 1632 messengers were sent on two different occasions from Flanders for this purpose, and the Spanish ambassador in London also brought what influence he could to move Charles to grant

30. Leopold von Ranke, *A History of England in the Seventeenth Century* (4 vols., tr. C. W. Boase and others, Oxford, 1875), II, 144–146.

31. *Cal. S. P. Ven.*, XXII, 169, 331, 450.

32. *Ibid.*, pp. 527–528; Birch, *Court and Times of Charles I*, II, 123.

33. *Cal. S. P. Dom.*, 1631–33, p. 68.

the request of his exiled mother-in-law.[34] Henrietta's coterie, having Lord Holland as its chief spokesman, also supported the appeals of Marie de Medici. The council, in which Weston was the strongest member, took an opposite stand. Weston wanted no dealings with Marie de Medici; he was aware that the dissatisfied factions in both the English and French courts were linked together for the attainment of common interests, and that therefore Marie de Medici was his enemy as well as Richelieu's.[35] As a matter of fact, Chateauneuf wanted the queen mother in England, where he hoped she could strengthen the queen's party in bringing about the overthrow of Weston and his replacement by Holland. Were Holland to gain Weston's office, the queen mother would be in position to profit from Holland's promise that as director of English political affairs, he would bring strong pressure upon the King of France to permit her return. And the return of Marie de Medici to France could have but one outcome: the overthrow of Richelieu and his policies. It was known that Weston was much too cautious to venture upon a policy which, involving unfriendly relations with the government of France, might require the calling of a parliament to furnish military supplies.[36]

The related plots against Weston and Richelieu worked to a rapid climax. In November, 1632, the French court was at Bordeaux, where Richelieu fell ill with what was believed to be a fatal sickness. While Richelieu lingered on the edge of death, Chateauneuf danced merrily at royal entertainments. He even departed from Bordeaux abruptly to escort the French queen and her ladies on a trip to La Rochelle, leaving the earth, as he supposed, to gather its carrion.[37] Unfortunately for Chateauneuf, Richelieu survived. The issue was now clearly drawn. Besides the

34. *Cal. S. P. Ven.*, XXII, 585, 640.
35. *Ibid.*, p. 554.
36. Victor Cousin, *Madame de Chevreuse* (5th ed., Paris, 1869), p. 110; Louis Batiffol, *The Duchesse de Chevreuse* (New York, n.d.), pp. 151–152; Hugh Williams, *A Fair Conspirator* (New York, 1913), pp. 99–104.
37. Cousin, *Madame de Chevreuse*, p. 392.

incident at Bordeaux, the letters which Fontenay-Mareuil had seized in London definitely implicated Chateauneuf as well as de Jars in the scheming against Richelieu.[38] Among those papers were thirty-one letters written by Henrietta. She had had the temerity to assert in one of them that Chateauneuf was no instrument of Richelieu's, and that he would make a better minister in her brother's interest than did Richelieu.[39]

In February, 1633, Richelieu struck against his enemies. Chateauneuf was deprived of the office of Keeper of the Seal and cast into prison, where he was to remain until after the death of Richelieu almost ten years later.[40] The Chevalier de Jars, recently returned to France, was also arrested and sentenced to death, only to be reprieved at the last moment. He was, in fact, standing on the scaffold when the order commuting his sentence to imprisonment arrived.[41]

Thus was the party in opposition to Richelieu shattered. In this defeat the queen's cabal in England also suffered a severe setback. Henrietta had been defeated in her first attempt at serious political intrigue. Weston remained in power, and having survived the trial, was stronger than ever. As did Louis XIII, Charles I stood by his minister against the entreaties of the queen. In lesser matters Charles would listen to his wife and even give in to her supplications, but when important and fundamental policy was involved, he was adamant against her persuasion, following the policy which he believed to be for his own best interest and for the welfare of the state.

Divergence of views on political matters did not disturb the personal relations between Charles and Henrietta. They remained lovers. In December the king had a mild case of smallpox. Dreaded as the disease was in those days, the queen refused to remain apart

38. *Ibid.*, pp. 397–410. This reference consists of published papers that Richelieu prepared for his case against Chateauneuf.

39. *Ibid.*, p. 397; Richelieu, *Lettres*, IV, 433.

40. *Cal. S. P. Ven.*, XXIII, 83; *Mercure François*, XVIII, 923; Cousin, *Madame de Chevreuse*, p. 111.

41. Motteville, *Mémoires*, I, 56.

from her husband, sharing his bedroom at night and staying with him during his long hours of convalescence.[42]

Shortly after the king's recovery, the queen presented her pastoral, *The Shepheard's Paradise*, which she and the ladies of her court had been rehearsing since the preceding September.[43] The play, written by Sir Walter Montagu, one of the queen's group of close associates, was interminably long, requiring almost eight hours for its performance.[44] That the queen took the leading role and memorized her lines required no little industry on her part, since she was not proficient in English.

On January 11, 1633, the day after the play was offered, William Prynne issued his *Histrio-mastix*, a volume of about one thousand pages in which he condemned the witnessing and enactment of dramas and reviled women who appeared on the stage as actors.[45] By profession Prynne was a barrister of Lincoln's Inn. As a Puritan polemicist he was unsparing in his invective. In his book he declared women actors to be "notorious whores." Writing that St. Paul forbade women to speak in church, he concluded, "and dares then any Christian woman to be more than whoreshly impudent as to act, to speake publiquelie on a Stage (perchance in man's apparel and cut haire) in the presence of sundrie men and women?"[46] If offended by the bad taste of Prynne's diatribe, many an Englishman must have agreed with the substance of what Prynne said regarding women actors, since it was not the custom in England for women to act upon the stage until after the Restoration. But when Prynne condemned nearly all of the good old English pastimes, including hunting, public festivals, bonfires, Maypoles, and "dressing up of a House with Green-Ivy," he alienated what support he might have had to sustain him in the former charge.[47] Perhaps his most indiscreet charge was the assertion that the wit-

42. Ellis, *Original Letters*, ser. 2, III, 274; Birch, *Court and Times of Charles I*, II, 204–205.
43. Ellis, *Original Letters*, ser. 2, III, 271; *Cal. S. P. Ven.*, XXIII, 28.
44. *Ibid.*, p. 63.
45. Birch, *Court and Times of Charles I*, II, 222.
46. Ellis, *Original Letters*, ser. 2, III, 280–281.
47. John Rushworth, *Historical Collections* (8 vols., London, 1721–22), II, 220.

nessing of plays was the "cause of untimely ends in Princes," and the citation of Nero's fate as evidence.[48]

It was well known in England that the queen especially delighted in theatricals, so Prynne's attack, distributed just one day after the performance of her much-heralded pastoral, seemed directly pointed at her. Such was the conclusion of the court of Star Chamber.[49] Although Prynne in his defense said that the book had been written several years before the production of the queen's pastoral, the work was evidently added to from time to time, and those pages heaping damnation on actresses came toward the end of the volume, as if they had been appended during the preceding fall, when it was widely known the queen was preparing to act a part in her presentation.[50] Prynne ultimately suffered a heavy and humiliating punishment for his writings, not escaping the justice of the court until his ears had been clipped.[51]

If through the court of Star Chamber Henrietta had vengeance upon Prynne, she was not so victorious in her clashes with the Lord Treasurer, Weston. During the spring of 1633, in fact, two of her closest associates, the Earl of Holland and Henry Jermyn, suffered a rebuff as a result of a dispute with the king's minister. Jerome Weston, son of the Lord Treasurer, while returning through Flanders from a special diplomatic assignment, took from the pouch of one of the king's diplomatic couriers two letters, one written by the queen and the other by Holland.[52] In so doing, Jerome Weston, as the king later stated, was acting entirely within his powers and was justified in his suspicions, since it was not customary for private letters to be contained among official cor-

48. *Ibid.*, pp. 232, 235, 236.
49. *Ibid.*, pp. 221, 240.
50. Sir Bulstrode Whitelocke, *Memorials of English Affairs during the Reign of Charles I* (London, 1732), p. 18; Rushworth, *Historical Collections*, II, 224–225.
51. *Ibid.*, p. 233.
52. *Cal. S. P. Dom.*, 1633–34, p. 11. Henry Jermyn, Earl of St. Albans (d. 1684), held numerous offices in the queen's service, beginning in 1628 and continuing until her death except for the period when he was banished from court for refusing to marry Eleanor Villiers. After Charles's execution in 1649, Jermyn was Henrietta's closest male associate, serving as her chief adviser and factotum while she was exiled in Paris. *D.N.B.*, XXIX, 342.

respondence,[53] although this practice seems to have been employed
by the queen and Holland for some time. When the younger
Weston returned the letters to the king, their contents were found
to be harmless, being offers to mediate in behalf of de Jars, who
was then under sentence in France. Nevertheless, Holland was
angry over what Jerome Weston had done and sought satisfaction
through the gentlemanly expedient of a duel. The younger Weston accepted Holland's offer, but then permitted his father to inform the king of the challenge. Charles was determined that no
duels would be fought around his court, and was incensed that the
place of meeting was to have been in one of the royal gardens at a
place just below the windows of the apartment in which Jerome's
family lived. Both Holland and his second, Henry Jermyn, were
banished from the court, the former being put under house arrest
at his home in Kensington, the latter placed in the keeping of a
Sir Abraham Williams. The strength of Charles's determination
in carrying out this measure was matched against the effort of the
queen to defend her two followers from disgrace.[54]

Another scandal concerning Jermyn was shortly thereafter
brought to light. He had gotten with child one of the queen's ladies,
Eleanor Villiers, a niece of the once-favored Buckingham. On
being questioned, the disconsolate girl said she had loved Jermyn
so much that she had never exacted a promise of marriage from
him as a condition for their intimacy. For his part, Jermyn pointed
to his imprisonment and lack of means as excuse in refusing to
honor the girl by marriage.[55]

Ladies of Puritan families avoided the queen's court because
of such scandalous incidents. Immorality was thought to be rife
in the queen's circle, and the reputation of Her Majesty did not
escape the implications of gossip. While without blemish herself,
the queen was tolerant of the misdoings of others. She coaxed the
king for the return of her two friends, on whom she had been

53. Cal. S. P. Dom., 1631–33, pp. 14, 72.
54. Ibid., pp. 3, 12, 16; Cal. S. P. Ven., XXIII, 100.
55. Thomas Wentworth, Earl of Strafford, Letters and Dispatches (2 vols., ed.
William Knowler, London, 1739), I, 174; Cal. S. P. Dom., 1633–34, p. 50.

most dependent, and it was not long until she again enjoyed their company.[56]

During the summer of 1633, Charles and Henrietta were temporarily separated when the king went to Scotland for the coronation in his northern kingdom. The queen wrote him almost every day of his absence, and on returning, the king, as if by his haste to show the impatience of his love for her, rode from Berwick to London in four days.[57] Perhaps the knowledge that his wife was again pregnant increased his desire to be with her,[58] but those people of Puritan bent made jest of his uxoriousness. Sir Ralph Verney laughingly excused himself from a meeting with a friend, adding, "for according to the example of our gratious sovereign,

56. Verney, *Memoirs of the Verney Family*, I, 72; Bartholomew Warburton, *Memoirs of Prince Rupert and the Cavaliers* (3 vols., London, 1849), I, 74–75. Regarding Henrietta's moral innocence, Father Gamache wrote to Rome: "Father Philip asserts that she has no sin, except those of omission, of which he is a great enemy, and does not spare correction. As to faith, or sin of the flesh, she is never tempted. When she confesses and communicates, she is so earnest, that she surprises her confessor and all. No one is admitted in her bedrooms except ladies, with whom she sometimes retires, and employs herself on light, but innocent matters." Panzani's dispatch of August 25, 1636, as quoted in Green, *Letters of Henrietta Maria*, p. 32.

57. Verney, *Memoirs of the Verney Family*, I, 105. Sir Ralph Verney (1613–96) is remembered principally for the detailed notes he compiled on the meetings of the Long Parliament during its early years. Staunchly opposed to Laud's reforms in the Anglican Church, he took the side of Parliament in the Civil War. In 1643, however, he went into exile because he was unwilling to accept the Covenant approved by Parliament. He returned in 1653, was imprisoned by Cromwell two years later, but survived to live out his days. *D.N.B.*, LVIII, 264–265.

58. Thomas Rouse, *Diary* (ed. Mary Anne Everett Green [The Camden Society], Westminster, 1856), p. 75. The queen was to give birth to James, Duke of York, on the following November 14. James was actually Henrietta's third child to survive birth, Princess Mary having been born on November 4, 1631. Since the queen was frequently bearing children during these years, it would be monotonous to mention the birth of each child in the main body of this work. Accordingly, Henrietta's other children and their birth dates are listed here:

Princess Elizabeth	December 29, 1635
Princess Anne	March 17, 1637
Princess Catherine	January 29, 1639
Henry, Duke of Gloucester	July 8, 1640
Princess Henrietta Anne	June 16, 1644

Harl. MSS 6988, fol. 133.

A. Van Dyck. *Charles I of England and Henrietta of France.* Pitti Palace, Florence.

I must obey my wife and she commands my presence on the 26th." [59]

One person who more accurately estimated the queen's influence at the English court was Richelieu. Henrietta had been a disappointment to Richelieu, having failed completely to promote his interests at the court, for which purpose he had intended her as a bride of England. But the loss on Richelieu's part, as events subsequently worked out, was not so crucial as might have been expected, since Charles's inability to get along with Parliament meant that he lacked material resources to play much part in European politics.[60] Nevertheless, Richelieu wanted the queen's friendship rather than her enmity, and still hoped to draw her away from alignment with his enemies.

When the Marquis de Poigny was sent to replace Fontenay-Mareuil in 1634, Richelieu informed the new ambassador that he might find the queen distant and aloof in his first audience with her. The minister attributed her coolness to the government in France not so much to her own inclination as to misguidance by friends around her.[61] He singled out Madame Vantelet, a lady of the queen's bedchamber and the sole remaining servant whom the queen had originally brought with her from France, as one who had done much to cement the friendship between Henrietta and Chateauneuf. Madame Vantelet's French pension had been cut off because of her disloyalty to Richelieu. Yet he believed that were Poigny to hold out hope of its restoration, she might again serve the government of France.[62]

Richelieu was aware that it would be easier to bring about a change in Madame Vantelet's loyalties than to convince the queen to give up a friend, for one of Henrietta's strongest characteristics was unswerving devotion to anyone whom she liked.[63] Previous attempts of the French king to obtain the return of Father Philip after

59. Verney, *Memoirs of the Verney Family*, II, 12; Lucy Hutchinson, *Memoirs of the Life of Colonel Hutchinson* (London, 1848), p. 85.

60. Richelieu, *Lettres*, III, 520, 523.

61. *Ibid.*, IV, 561.

62. *Ibid.*, p. 562.

63. *Cal. S. P. Ven.*, XXIII, 284.

the Capuchins were sent to London met with obdurate resistance from Henrietta. So annoyed did she become with the French king's insistence in this matter that she dropped civilities and told her brother that, no longer wishing his protection, she demanded he not delve into affairs which she considered strictly her own concern.[64] She had spoken with finality, and Father Philip was to remain with the queen as her confessor until the end of his life.

A second purpose behind Henrietta's marriage to Charles—the protection of Catholics and the fostering of the faith in England—she had served much better than she had Richelieu's political designs. Her benefit to Catholicism resulted not so much from planned activity or program as from her personal influence. Her chapel was open at all times to other Catholics, her Capuchins also administered to her fellow religionists, and her supplications in behalf of recusants often moved the king to grant amnesty.[65]

While Catholics enjoyed the greatest peace they had known for many years, the condition of the Catholic Church in England was one of chaos and turmoil. Long a persecuted and outlawed body, the Catholics were without organization or discipline. The bishops appointed to govern them for intermittent periods since the latter part of Elizabeth's reign had had to carry on their work surreptitiously,[66] and the last bishop had left England with Cha-

---

64. *Ibid.*, p. 545; Richelieu, *Lettres*, III, 507–508.

65. *Calendar of Clarendon State Papers* (3 vols., ed. O. Ogle, W. Dunn Macray, and W. H. Bliss, Oxford, 1872–76), I, 51 (referred to hereafter as *Cal. Clar. S. P.*); Rushworth, *Historical Collections*, II, 284–285; *Cal. S. P. Dom.*, 1635–36, p. 53. Although there is abundant evidence of letters of grace and pardon given to recusants during these years, some of which resulted from application made to the queen by the petitioners, Charles's policy toward Catholics was not wholly due to the queen's influence. At a time when Laud's direction of the Church of England was bringing the forms of worship nearer the Roman practice, Charles was not likely to have a deep feeling of revulsion against the Catholic religion. So long as the Catholics quietly practiced their religion and were no threat to royal authority, the king had no desire to persecute them. See Arnold Oscar Meyer, "Charles I and Rome," *American Historical Review*, XIX (Oct., 1913), 13–26.

66. Gregorio Panzani, *Memoirs* (in *The History of the Decline and Fall of the Roman Catholic Religion in England* [tr. Joseph Berington, London, 1813]), p. 119.

teauneuf's return to France.[67] Without the restraining hand of a governor, some of the clergy had become lax and corrupt.[68] Disputes had arisen between the secular and regular clergy over conflicting jurisdictions. The Jesuits claimed special authority to hear confessions in any parish, whereas the regular clergy denied such powers. There was controversy as to whether a Catholic might subscribe to the Oath of Allegiance.[69] A disciplined order like the Jesuits, trained to exercise their offices in secrecy, opposed the sending of a bishop to England, while the regular priesthood clamored for a bishop who might put the aggressive Jesuits in their proper place.[70]

In an attempt to bring about order among the Catholics in England, the pope sent Gregorio Panzani as his mediator. Panzani, traveling incognito, reached England late in 1634. He immediately sought a meeting with the queen, for it was only by her protection and assistance that he could carry out his work. The queen's almoner, Jacques de Noel, Abbot of Peron, whom Panzani solicited for an introduction to Her Majesty, would have no part in the secret mission, but Henrietta's confessor did not hesitate in presenting the legate to the queen.[71] Henrietta took up the furtherance of Panzani's cause with alacrity and obtained the king's consent for the priest's presence in England so long as he carried out his work in secrecy.[72] Some time after the coming of Panzani, the king had to laugh when old Secretary Coke hushedly informed him of rumors that a priest who might be very dangerous to the kingdom had recently arrived from Rome.[73]

67. Richelieu, *Lettres*, III, 423.

68. *Cal. S. P. Ven.*, XXIII, 69.

69. *Cal. Clar. S. P.*, I, 62, 63, 64, 120; Panzani, *Memoirs*, pp. 141–142.

70. *Ibid.*, pp. 122–126, 140; *Cal. Clar. S. P.*, I, 62.

71. *Cal. S. P. Ven.*, XXII, 321.

72. *Ibid.*, XXIII, 68–69; Panzani, *Memoirs*, pp. 132–134.

73. *Ibid.*, p. 154. John Coke (1563–1644) had become one of the principal secretaries of state in 1625. Long employed in various administrative posts, he displayed every characteristic of a toady, though his behavior might have resulted from his purported commitment to the doctrine of divine right of kings. Upon dismissal from office in 1639, he retired to his estate in Derbyshire. *D.N.B.*, XI, 244–246.

According to his instructions, Panzani's assignment, difficult as it would have been in the achievement, was within imaginable limits. He was to settle disputes among the clergy, to try to obtain official permission for a Catholic bishop in England, and to obtain exemption of Catholics from all oaths imposed by the government.[74] Once he was in England, however, Panzani's ambitions soared. He took the ritualistic reforms being introduced into the Anglican Church by Archbishop Laud as a certain sign of England's inclination toward Rome.[75] He was misled by the silly palaver of Secretary Windebank, who avowed that he was himself a Catholic at heart.[76] Windebank and the emissary talked of an accommodation between England and Rome, and to initiate the religious union, tried to draw up an Oath of Allegiance which the pope would approve.[77] On hearing of Panzani's presumption, Cardinal Barberini, papal vice-chancellor, in effect told him to stop talking nonsense and to get on with his business in England.[78]

The king gave a flat refusal to Henrietta's entreaty for a Catholic bishop in England. But he was not to remain impervious to the campaign of Henrietta and Panzani. The queen inveigled her husband into a private meeting with the legate, at which the king respectfully removed his hat and the envoy in return kissed the king's hand. Charles was reported to have declared that he would have given his right hand rather than that England ever should have broken religious communion with Rome.[79]

Barberini placed strong emphasis upon personal relations with

74. Panzani, *Memoirs*, pp. 171–173.

75. *Ibid.*, pp. 136, 139.

76. *Ibid.*, p. 162. Sir Francis Windebank (1582–1646) held relatively minor administrative posts until his sudden elevation to the council in 1632, a promotion attributable to the fact that he seemed an agreeable person to leading members of that body. His hope of reuniting with Rome led to his cordial reception of the pope's representatives in England. In 1642 he fled to France on being asked by the Long Parliament to answer ten questions regarding his conduct in office. Shortly before his death in Paris he was received into the Catholic Church. *D.N.B.*, LXII, 162–166.

77. Panzani, *Memoirs*, p. 178; *Cal. Clar. S. P.*, I, 43.

78. Panzani, *Memoirs*, pp. 148, 155.

79. *Ibid.*, pp. 135, 161.

Charles in order to promote Panzani's mission. Knowing the king's fondness for Italian art, Barberini engaged to procure a certain statue of Adonis which Charles especially desired.[80] He also promised the queen to procure the services of the busy and much-sought-after sculptor Giovanni Bernini to make busts of Their Majesties.[81] Later in 1635, while the queen was in childbed,[82] she received a shipment of Italian paintings as a gift from Barberini. Charles was so impatient to see these treasures that they were unpacked in the room where Henrietta was lying. The king was overjoyed with the contents—paintings by Albani, Correggio, Veronese, and da Vinci—but the queen, less appreciative than her husband of artistic works, expressed disappointment that no devotional pictures were included in the shipment.[83]

On the surface at least, it appeared Panzani had more success in his dealings at the court than in his negotiations with the Catholic clergy. An instrument of concord was signed in November, 1635, by all of the clergy except the Jesuits, from whom Panzani could obtain no more than a grudging agreement not to oppose the sending of a bishop.[84] The king, on the other hand, agreed that in mitigation of the sufferings of Catholics, justices of the peace, pursuivants, and other lesser officials would henceforth act not upon their own initiative in prosecution of recusants but only upon direction from the council.[85] Of more importance, Charles gave permission for the exchange of personal representatives between the queen and the pope.[86]

Actually, Charles was not overwhelmed in his relations with Rome. His promise in easement of Catholics had meaning only to the extent it was enforced. His admission of the exchange of envoys between the queen and the pope was undertaken with the

80. *Ibid.*, p. 197.
81. *Ibid.*, p. 193.
82. Of Princess Elizabeth. See note 58.
83. Panzani, *Memoirs*, p. 251.
84. *Ibid.*, pp. 125, 178, 182–183, 217–218, 219, 220, 227.
85. *Ibid.*, p. 250.
86. *Ibid.*, pp. 187, 201.

belief that he could gain more than he gave in his relations with the papacy, as was indicated in the instructions he gave to Walter Brett, who was designated to be the queen's representative in Rome. Brett was to obtain the pope's support for the restoration of the Palatinate to Charles's nephew Louis, to move His Holiness to promote a marriage between the King of Poland and one of Louis's sisters, and to procure removal of the papal ban against the Oath of Allegiance. In return for these concessions, Charles agreed to permit the residence of a Catholic bishop in England.[87]

When Panzani left England early in 1636, the queen, whose career had begun so inauspiciously amid misunderstanding and calumny, seemed established on a new pinnacle of favor and fortune. She was later in retrospect to describe herself during these middle years as being the "happiest Queen in the world." To be sure, a queen who was loved by her husband and who so splendidly performed her duty of populating the royal nursery could hardly be insignificant in the nation's life.

But Henrietta counted for more than wife of the monarch and mother of his children. She now exchanged personal embassies with the pope and was beginning to be looked upon as protectress of Catholics in England, a role for which she had been designated at the outset of her marriage. While more was expected of her than she could perform, and while the extent of her services was at that time exaggerated in the estimation of many people, Richelieu thought her efforts in behalf of the persecuted Catholics achievement enough to merit his letter of commendation in 1634.[88]

Unpopular though Henrietta was among the Puritans,[89] she could not be attacked with impunity, as Prynne through sad experience had learned. Moreover, she had her supporters in England. About a year after the publication of the *Histrio-mastix,* the four Inns of Court, one of which had counted Prynne a member, pre-

87. *Ibid.,* pp. 154-155, 206-207; *Cal. S. P. Ven.,* XXII, 495-496; *Cal. Clar. S. P.,* I, 73-74. Walter Brett died while on his way to Rome. The next spring, in 1636, William Hamilton was sent as the queen's agent. *Cal. Clar. S. P.,* I, 97.
88. *MSS Français 15993,* fol. 22.
89. Hutchinson, *Memoirs of Colonel Hutchinson,* p. 87.

sented an elaborate masque as a countermand to Prynne's attack. The queen was so highly pleased with the first performance at Whitehall that it was produced a second time under the auspices of the Lord Mayor.[90]

Fast though her love held Charles, her influence over him was not unqualified. Writing in 1634, Fontenay-Mareuil declared that the queen could act only in accord with the king's humor.[91] In her rifts with Weston, the king had supported the Lord Treasurer rather than his wife, but Weston, or the Earl of Portland as he had since become, died in 1635. In a vicarious sense, the queen achieved a victory over Weston during his closing hours, for the Lord Treasurer, who had been a persecutor of Catholics in his life, became a convert on his deathbed.[92] With Weston out of the way and with no certain candidate for his position, it was rumored that the queen would name her own choice to fill his office.[93]

Little wonder, therefore, that those of strong Protestant persuasion looked upon her influence with misgivings. Already Charles had surrendered more than many of them had thought possible. Who could tell what future course the queen might give to the nation's development? "Lord," they prayed, "open her eyes that she may see her Savior, whom she hath pierced with her superstition and idolatry."[94]

90. Whitelocke, *Memorials*, pp. 19–22; *Cal. S. P. Ven.*, XXII, 32–36, 180.
91. *MSS Français 15993*, fol. 19.
92. Gamache, *Memoirs*, p. 332.
93. William Laud, Archbishop of Canterbury, *Works* (7 vols., ed. James Bliss, Oxford, 1854–60), VII, 232–233.
94. Birch, *Court and Times of Charles I*, II, 225.

CHAPTER IV

BRINK OF CONFLICT

1636-40 ✥ RICHELIEU pondered: the release of de Jars would be a small enough price to pay if the Queen of England convinced her husband to join France in an alliance against Austria.[1] True enough, de Jars had been a nuisance to Richelieu and had always connived with the pro-Spanish faction to work his overthrow. Yet, were England linked with France by a treaty offering sufficient guarantee of mutual security, the freeing of the adventurer would work no great mischief against the state.

Following the death of Gustavus Adolphus in 1632, Richelieu saw the necessity of France's entering directly into the wars in Germany if Austria were not to become preponderant in central Europe, where through family alliance with the Hapsburgs of Spain she would constitute a formidable danger to France. To secure France's northern flank during the conflict, he looked to England for diplomatic assurances. If possible, Richelieu wanted an offensive-defensive alliance with England, but failing that he hoped at least to acquire military levies from England and to have the English navy defend the northern coast of France against Spanish raiders.[2] Charles I, on the other hand, hoped by diplomatic

1. *MSS Français 15993*, fols. 64, 65.
2. *Ibid.*, fol. 58.

94

negotiations with France to obtain a promise that the Palatinate would be restored to his nephew.[3] Henrietta's interest in the whole affair was very simple. She cared little about the restoration of the Palatinate except insofar as it might please her husband; she had little at stake in supporting Richelieu's diplomatic ambitions, since as a proponent of the Spanish party she had hitherto been opposed to him. She was interested only in securing the release of de Jars from prison, and to this end agreed to do what she could to promote a treaty between England and France.[4]

In November, 1635, Henrietta had sent Walter Montagu to France to promote her suit for de Jars's freedom. Richelieu was effusive in his expression of esteem for the queen, but said that he was forced to await a more favorable occasion for granting her request.[5] The queen replied with many thanks for the kindness and consideration shown her emissary, and said she hoped the minister would not forget her petition, which if granted would greatly oblige her to France.[6]

A year later the queen was still making the same request. Meantime she had done what she could to move Charles to accept a French treaty, as indeed the French ambassador, Santerre, had assured the government in France. When in September, 1636, the king was at Oatlands, Henrietta told Santerre that she would go there to convince her husband in France's favor. In order to receive her report on how the king was inclined in his relations with France, the ambassador was to meet her at Windsor after the court moved there in the course of its annual progress.[7] Her report was everything that Santerre might have wished to hear. The king would soon allow troops for French service to be raised in England, would restore French ships seized in maritime areas

3. *Ibid.*, fol. 68.
4. *Ibid.*, fol. 74.
5. Armand J. du Plessis, Duke of Richelieu, Cardinal, *Lettres, Instructions Diplomatiques et Papiers d'État* (8 vols., ed. Denis M. L. Avenel [*Collection de Documents Inédits*], Paris, 1853–77), V, 353–355 (referred to hereafter as Richelieu, *Lettres*).
6. *MSS Français 15993*, fol. 79.
7. *Ibid.*, fol. 166.

to which Britain made exclusive claim, and would lend assistance with the Royal Navy.[8]

Not long afterward, Henrietta asked Santerre when the time would be right for freeing de Jars.[9] Whenever Henrietta set about some business, she could be doggedly persistent. "The Queen always reproaches me for the refusal made concerning the Chevalier de Jars," wrote the weary ambassador.[10] Nevertheless, he was well pleased with Henrietta's efforts in fulfilling her part of the bargain—so much so as to advise his home government to comply with the queen's wish and release the chevalier. But Richelieu, intent upon exploiting the value of his prisoner to the utmost, refused to act upon Santerre's advice.[11] The haggling over a treaty dragged on until internal disturbances rendered England insignificant in international politics and gave Henrietta concerns overshadowing her solicitation for a former servant and favorite.[12]

The Chevalier de Jars was not the only friend in whose behalf the queen was lending her influence. In a dispatch to Bouthilier, the French foreign secretary, Santerre wrote that Henrietta was championing Francis Cottington for the office of Lord High Treasurer, made vacant by the death of Lord Portland.[13] In opposition to Cottington was Archbishop Laud, who proposed William Juxon, Bishop of London, for the position. Cottington and Laud had fallen into personal differences as joint administrators of the office while it was still in commission.[14] Indisputable as was the queen's support of Cottington, she probably did not play a dominant role in his candidature. Cottington had long been an official at the court and had been employed in many offices and missions, so by experience and ability he was not a weak aspirant for the office and was competent in fighting his own battles. Even so, the queen's

8. *Ibid.*, fol. 170.
9. *Ibid.*, fol. 186.
10. *Ibid.*, fol. 188.
11. *Ibid.*, fol. 178.
12. *Ibid.*, fols. 227, 228.
13. *Ibid.*, fol. 193.
14. "Francis Cottington," *D.N.B.*, XII, 294.

influence was not to be ignored. Writing to Thomas Wentworth, Lord Deputy of Ireland, shortly before the king made his appointment to the office of Lord High Treasurer, Archbishop Laud declared he believed that because of the queen's support Cottington would be the successful candidate for the position.[15] As it happened, the king chose Bishop Juxon, being influenced in his choice by the personal merits Juxon could bring to the office. Juxon, he knew, was incorruptible in his honesty, had no enemies around the court, and possessed no family for whom he might be tempted to sequester royal income.[16]

If Henrietta had failed to obtain the appointment of her own candidate for the office of treasurer, she was not greatly disturbed that she did not rule her husband in all matters. Unlike her mother, she did not seek to domineer. She enjoyed being the wife of England's king and found diversion from official concerns in sharing life and experiences with him.

In April, 1636, Their Majesties visited the asylum at Bedlam. Such was the pastime of those days when, mental derangement being little understood, the insane found scant sympathy and were taken as objects of amusement. A later age might wonder at the morbid interest of Their Majesties in visiting the "mad folk," by whom, a wag commented, "they were madly entertained." The visit proved not so amusing when the foul language of some of the inmates shocked royal sensibilities.[17]

In contrast to the visit at the asylum was the journey the king and queen made to Oxford University toward the end of their summer's progress.[18] The particular occasion for their going there was Laud's visit made in his capacity as Primate of All England. Their Majesties were met two miles outside the city of Oxford by a delegation of townsmen, masters, and students in the robes and

15. William Laud, Archbishop of Canterbury, *Works* (7 vols., ed. James Bliss, Oxford, 1854–60), VII, 230.

16. "William Juxon," *D.N.B.*, XXX, 233–237.

17. Thomas Birch, *The Court and Times of Charles I* (2 vols., London, 1848), II, 244.

18. Laud, *Works*, V, 148–154.

regalia of their offices. The vice-chancellor extended official greetings in a lengthy speech, after which the king and queen were taken to lodgings at Christchurch, where they did not enter until they had listened to another speech delivered before the door of the college. That evening the royal party was entertained with a play, *Passions Calmed or the Settling of the Floating Island*, presented by students of Christchurch. One spectator said it was the worst production he had ever witnessed upon the stage except for one he had seen enacted by students at Cambridge. The following day honorary degrees were conferred in the Convocation House. Among those conferred the M.A. degree was the king's nephew Prince Rupert, who was at that time sojourning at the court in England. Rupert's brother Louis, Prince of the Palatinate, being the titular ruler of a sovereign state and nominal head of the University of Heidelberg, was given the courtesy of naming his own choice of candidates for a degree.[19]

Charles utilized what time remained to him after attending official functions to look about the colleges. He seems to have been much interested in the library at St. John's College, a part of which was of new construction. There is nothing to indicate that the queen showed a like interest, perhaps because such curiosity was considered outside a woman's orbit of concern. However, her favorite form of amusement, the stage, was fully indulged, for on the evening of the second day the royal entourage witnessed two more plays, *The Hospital of Lovers* and *The Royal Slave*. The second of these productions, elaborately staged with scenery and costumes designed by Inigo Jones, elicited such enthusiastic response that the queen asked to borrow the costumes and stage effects for the production of the play at her own court.

About a month after the visit to Oxford the queen was at Oatlands. Here news reached her that a madman, Robert Carr, the brother of one of the gentlemen of the bedchamber, had stolen

19. *Calendar of State Papers, Domestic Series, of the Reign of Charles I, 1625–1649* (23 vols., ed. John Bruce and others, London, 1858–97), 1636–37, p. 114 (referred to hereafter as *Cal. S. P. Dom.*).

away from his place of confinement with the intention of killing the king. On hearing of this the queen was "so agitated as [*sic*] her lace had to be cut to give her more breath";[20] nor did her emotional upset subside until two days later when Charles came to her. The king came the more willingly since his wife was again "very visibly with child"[21] and was experiencing more discomfort than was usual with her.

In August, 1636, the pope's representative to the queen finally arrived from Rome.[22] He was George Con, the younger son of a Scottish nobleman. Con had all of the qualities that Panzani had recommended for a person filling his position; he was young (about thirty), affable, handsome, tactful, of refined manners, at ease around women, and a capable linguist. He brought gifts to distribute at the court. Pope Urban VIII sent the queen a cross composed of clusters of diamonds arranged in the form of bees, the symbol of the Barberini family, to which he belonged. On examining this present, the king, who appreciated works of art, asked his wife, "Is it possible, my heart, that the pope has given you this?" Henrietta answered that he had. "I am very glad of it," continued Charles, "because I shall change the opinion I have hereto held that the priests of Rome are always ready to take, but never to give anything away."[23]

Con intended a more fundamental change of Charles's opinion before returning to Rome. The envoy aimed at nothing less than gaining England for Catholicism through the conversion of Charles.[24] In this effort the queen's assistance was taken for granted and was indispensable if Charles was to be won for Rome. Indeed, it appeared there were factors favoring Con's purpose. He was well liked by the king,[25] and Laud's reforms in the

---

20. Birch, *Court and Times of Charles I*, II, 250.

21. *Calendar of State Papers, Venice* (38 vols., ed. Allen B. Hinds and others, London, 1864–1940), XXIV, 77 (referred to hereafter as *Cal. S. P. Ven.*).

22. *Ibid.*, p. 39.

23. *Ibid.*, p. 70.

24. *Ibid.*, p. 69.

25. Letter of F. Barberini to G. Panzani, Feb. 27, 1636, *Roman Transcripts* (Public Record Office, London).

established church seemed to bring Anglicanism nearer to Catholic ritual.

Con's presence in England was not much noticed during the first few months of his residence. At first he obscured himself by remaining close to the queen and her circle.[26] Realizing the envoy's presence to be a concession which the king had made out of consideration for his wife, Laud ignored Con as earlier he had ignored Panzani. The Protestants who might have objected were too busy denouncing Laud's leadership in the established church, for they as well as many Catholics believed Laud was slowly Romanizing the Anglican Church to bring about a final union under the pope.[27] One of those who suspected Laud of papistical tendencies declared: ". . . I can honor and esteem a virtuous or learned Papist, who, being educated in that religion, supposeth it to be truth. But for men to call themselves Protestants, as Bishop Laud, Bishop Wren, and their wicked adherents, to swallow up the preferments of our Church, to inveigh against Popery in word only, and in the main to project and plot the ruin of the truth and the Gospel . . . this my soul abhors as the highest step of wickedness and of prevarication against God and His honour."[28]

In December, 1636, the queen's new chapel at Somerset House was completed and opened to public worship. Henrietta had laid the cornerstone for this structure, built upon the site of what had formerly been tennis courts, in September of 1632.[29] Catholics at the queen's court evidently sought to entice English people by the sheer beauty of the chapel, a feature usually lacking or underemphasized in Protestant churches of that day. The skill of the

26. *Cal. S. P. Ven.*, XXIV, 92.

27. Peter Heylin, *Cyprianus Anglicus: The History of the Life and Death of William Laud* (London, 1671), pp. 203, 310.

28. Sir Simonds D'Ewes, *Autobiography and Correspondence* (2 vols., ed. James Orchard Halliwell, London, 1845), II, 113–114. Puritan in belief and habit, Sir Simonds D'Ewes (1602–50) made his greatest contribution to posterity in tirelessly collecting documents pertaining to English history. He threw in his lot with Parliament at the beginning of the Civil War, signed the Covenant in 1643, and was expelled from Parliament by Pride's Purge in 1648.

29. Birch, *Court and Times of Charles I*, II, 176.

noted artist and sculptor François Dieussart, who had come to England on commission for a nobleman, was employed to construct a device styled "the Ascent to Heaven" for the display of the Sacrament. Four pillars, around which clustered the light of four hundred candles, supported a large canopy, and spiraling upward toward the canopy were figures of angels, prophets, saints, and doves, which through some art appeared to be suspended in the air. Beneath the canopy was the altar on which was the Sacrament. At the first mass in the new chapel—the first high pontifical mass held in England for the past hundred years—the building was jammed with worshipers. Suddenly, at the beginning of the mass, a curtain closing the apse parted to reveal the especially devised display, while from hidden parts of the church came the voices of the choir, making it seem as if the song were issuing from the figures of angels above the altar. The effect, wrote one of the Capuchin monks, was breathtaking.[30]

For three days and nights the chapel was visited by a constant stream of worshipers, including some English Catholics who had not been to church for many years. Among others impressed by the display was the king, who said he had never seen anything so beautiful. Finally, on the third night he ordered the doors closed, but the decorations were to remain until Christmas. Until that time, mass was held continuously from six in the morning until noon, and penitents had to wait two to three hours to have a turn in the confessional.[31]

Among a certain group of English people, especially those who consorted at the court or who wished to do so, Catholicism was beginning to be considered fashionable. The living quarters of the queen's Capuchins were opened occasionally for public visit. To impress the austerity of their order upon the minds of the English, the Capuchins removed during these visits what few ameni-

30. Cyprien de Gamache, *Memoirs of the Mission in England of the Capuchin Friars of the Province of Paris, from the Year 1630 to 1669* (in vol. II, 293–501, of Birch, *Court and Times of Charles I*), pp. 311–314.

31. Isaac Disraeli, *Commentaries on the Life and Reign of Charles I* (2 vols., ed. and rev. B. Disraeli, London, 1851), I, 217–218.

ties, such as pillows, they actually did enjoy.[32] No less an honor was accorded to them than the visit of Their Majesties, who did not disdain to share the monks' coarse food at supper.[33]

During the year following the opening of the chapel, the Catholic clergy at the court proselytized with a freedom and audacity that were surprising to onlookers. "The Catholics are no longer hated or persecuted with the old severity,"[34] wrote the Venetian ambassador in a dispatch to his home government. In conferences with the queen, Con urged her to play upon the affections of her husband to exact even greater concessions for Catholics, and said the pope hoped through her gracious influence for the conversion of all England.[35] The king assured Con that the Oath of Allegiance was not meant in any way to impinge upon the spiritual authority of the pope. However, he could hardly be expected to alter the wording of the oath in a way that would be pleasing to Rome, since any change would require a meeting of Parliament for its authorization.[36]

Even the queen's almoner, made bishop of the French diocese of Angoulême in 1636, proselytized with an ardor that went beyond the bound of his natural courage. Hitherto subdued in his activity in behalf of the Church, he now laid aside circumspection so far as to openly frequent the houses of Protestants, where he disputed against Protestantism in upholding the tenets of the Catholic faith. In his own house he gathered secular and regular priests for secret conferences to promote the increase of the faith in England.[37]

Besides the king's connivance, which was entrusted to the care of the queen, the Catholic clergy also relied upon what they believed to be the friendly disposition of Laud as a basis for their optimism. Laud's attitude in the religious controversy seems to

32. Gamache, *Memoirs*, p. 310.
33. *Cal. S. P. Ven.*, XXIV, 120.
34. *Ibid.*, p. 217.
35. Letter of G. Con to S. Antonio Ferragali, April 9, 1637, *Roman Transcripts*.
36. *Cal. S. P. Ven.*, XXIV, 149.
37. *Ibid.*, p. 150.

have been little understood. Because he had ordered the erecting of stone altars in the churches, adorned church walls with images, and caused auricular confession to be advocated from pulpits, the Catholics as well as the Puritans supposed him to be veering toward Rome.[38] Others thought his sympathy toward Catholicism arose out of a wish to destroy the Puritans.[39] His biographer believed his reforms were intended to facilitate the transition of Catholics to the Anglican Church.[40] Few supposed that he had the sincere intention of bringing the established church nearer what he believed to be the practices of the early Christian church and of introducing uniformity and order into the worship of England.

Laud was no Romanist, even if he did pretend to ignore the liberties which the king allowed his wife in religious matters. Having twice refused the offer of a cardinalate in 1633, Laud wrote in his diary, "Something dwells within me which will not suffer me to accept that till Rome be other than it is."[41] Although privately disapproving the freedom allowed Catholics at the court, he did not feel himself strong enough to challenge the queen and her party. In 1637 he wrote Thomas Wentworth that he feared the growing strength of the queen and her followers, although he believed the Earl of Holland, one of the queen's coterie, had lost status with the king.[42]

The missionary zeal of Catholics finally led to a flare-up when the Countess of Newport, one of the social leaders at the court, became a convert. Returning from a play in Drury Lane one evening, she stopped at Somerset House, where one of the Capuchins received her into the Church. On hearing of this event, her husband, the Earl of Newport, flew into a passion. He went forthwith to Lambeth Palace to complain to the archbishop, and named George Con, Walter Montagu, and Sir Tobie Matthew, an English Jesuit, as the principal persons instrumental in bringing about the

38. *Ibid.*, p. 217.
39. *Ibid.*, p. 151.
40. Heylin, *Cyprianus Anglicus*, p. 391.
41. Laud, *Works*, III, 219.
42. *Ibid.*, VII, 34.

subversion of his wife's religion. At the council meeting on the day following Newport's visit, Laud presented the grievance of the injured earl and desired that Montagu be banished from the court and that Matthew be brought before the Court of High Commission. As for Signor Con, the primate knew not how he came to England or what he did there and therefore would say nothing of him.[43] In truth, neither Montagu nor Matthew had much to do with the conversion, which was the work of the countess's sister, Lady Porter, and of Signor Con, but the archbishop hesitated to attack Con for fear of offending the queen.[44] There were reports that Laud secretly asked the king for the expulsion of Con from England, and in light of the queen's reaction against Laud, the reports were by no means improbable.[45] His Majesty was much disturbed over what had happened and said that steps would be taken against those responsible for the conversion. The queen was not long in finding out what had taken place in the council. She put the blame on the presumption of her Capuchins and severely scolded their rector, admonishing him not to make further attempts on other people's religion. But she could not forgive Laud, whom she met with scowls and studied aloofness.[46]

Although Laud's suggestions were not put into effect, the affair centering around Lady Newport had received too much publicity to be ignored by the council. Accordingly, a proclamation to prevent the recurrence of Catholic conversions was prepared. The original order in council against Catholic indoctrination directed Secretary Windebank and the attorney general to review all laws passed during Charles's reign against priests and to put the laws

43. Thomas Wentworth, Earl of Strafford, *Letters and Dispatches* (2 vols., ed. William Knowler, London, 1739), II, 128. It might have been chagrin over his wife's conversion that made Mountjoy Blount, Earl of Newport (1597?–1666), an uncertain supporter of the king during the Civil War. Although he seems never to have had any thought of taking up arms against his king, by whom he had been favored with lucrative offices and important assignments, he was hostile to the court. *D.N.B.*, V, 249–252.

44. *Ibid.*, p. 251.

45. Heylin, *Cyprianus Anglicus*, pp. 337–338; *Cal. S. P. Ven.*, XXIV, 319.

46. Laud, *Works*, VII, 380.

into execution.[47] This decree, dated October 22, 1637, was printed but never published. The queen was doing what she could to prevent the issuing of a decree.[48] Whatever the intensity of her efforts or the extent of her influence, the order as finally published on December 20 was so mild as to fail of the original purpose. It declared that Catholic priests had taken advantage of the king's clemency toward them to make converts at the court, and that if such presumption did not cease, the laws would be invoked against them. Nothing was said against Catholics worshiping in their own faith, nor was any measure to be taken against past violations, but only a warning was given against further attempts to disseminate the Catholic religion. The decree itself was an open admission that the laws were not being enforced and was also a flagrant concurrence in the violation of the laws.[49] At any rate, Henrietta seemed to be pleased with the final outcome of the whole controversy, for Laud noted in his diary that she was again speaking to him, and commented that after a long conversation he and the queen had "parted fair."[50]

Although the king gave in to his wife in reducing the severity of the decree against Catholic proselytizing, he had good reason to please his subjects in this matter, for already a rebellion was arising out of religious conflict in his northern kingdom of Scotland. To unify religious practices throughout his kingdoms, he had decided at the instigation of Laud to make the Scots conform to episcopacy. In August, 1637, a new service book prescribing the form of worship to be followed in the churches of Scotland had been introduced at the Cathedral of St. Giles in Edinburgh. Since the religious innovations offended the Presbyterian faith of the Scottish people, the result had been an immediate upsurge of protest among all classes of the nation. Vowing to maintain Presbyterianism, the Scots had drawn up the National Covenant, and had found sympathetic ears in England when they charged Laud

47. *Cal. S. P. Dom.*, 1637, pp. 491–492.
48. *Cal. S. P. Ven.*, XXIV, 359.
49. John Rushworth, *Historical Collections* (8 vols., London, 1721–22), II, 453.
50. Laud, *Works*, III, 230.

with attempting to lead England back to Catholicism so that he might himself obtain a high office in the Roman Church.[51]

Before the prayer book had been introduced into the Scottish churches, the king had brought a copy of it to the queen in order that she might see how nearly the form of service prescribed therein approached the ritual of her own religion. Whether Henrietta was favorably impressed by the prayer book is doubtful, but she was later to explain to Madame de Motteville that the king and Laud were attempting to transform religion in Scotland and England for its easy fusion into Catholicism.[52]

Certainly the queen was not satisfied with the policies of the king's servants on religious matters. Besides her rift with Laud, she had differences with Wentworth, Lord Deputy of Ireland, concerning a petition she made in behalf of Catholics under his jurisdiction. In October, 1638, she asked that St. Patrick's Purgatory in Ulster be restored as a shrine to which Irish Catholics could repair. Wentworth in his reply explained that St. Patrick's had been closed to Catholics by a previous governor, and that since Scottish Protestants had colonized the country surrounding the shrine, it would provoke trouble to have Catholics traveling through the area on pilgrimage.[53]

There were those persons at court, including Holland and Jermyn, who to gain advantage for themselves were ready to seize upon any displeasure the queen might find in Wentworth. Wentworth, however, was a formidable adversary who struck in the manner of Richelieu against his opposition. The only way to defeat Wentworth was to destroy him before he took the initiative. Late in 1638 there was a move at the court to bring suit against Wentworth for his ill treatment of Sir Piers Crosby, one of the Lord Deputy's opponents in the Irish council. Believing Holland and Jermyn to be among the instigators of this proposal, the Lord Deputy on December 10 wrote the king asking that the two fa-

51. *Cal. S. P. Ven.*, XXIV, 359.
52. Françoise Bertaut, Madame de Motteville, *Mémoires sur Anne d'Autriche et Sa Cour* (4 vols., ed. M. F. Riaux, Paris, n.d.), I, 190.
53. Strafford, *Letters*, II, 221–222.

vorites of the queen be questioned in Star Chamber for their part in the intrigue to ruin him. Luckily for the culprits, the queen's intercession was enough to save them from the person whom the king considered his ablest and most loyal servant.[54]

Meanwhile, during 1638, the rebellion in Scotland had grown apace. In April the queen pleaded with the king to satisfy the demands of the Scots in order to avoid a civil war. The king replied tenderly, begging her not to alarm herself and assuring her that when he wished he could reduce those subjects to obedience as usual.[55] The Duke of Hamilton was sent to Scotland as the king's commissioner to settle differences over religion.[56] The Assembly of the Kirk met in November. Of the clergy who convened in the Assembly, Hamilton wrote the king that there was "not oune goune amongst the Wholl Companie," but that there were "manie swords and manie more daguers (most of them having left the guns and pistoles in their lodgings)."[57] The disagreement between the king and the Scots was too deep to be settled by compromise. When the Assembly voted bishops to be illegal in Scotland, Hamilton declared the meeting dissolved, but the members refused to disperse. Confronted with the open defiance of his Scottish subjects, Charles continued to collect military supplies preparatory to subjugating his northern kingdom by force.[58]

The king already had enough trouble on his hands when in October, 1638, the queen mother, Marie de Medici, landed in England. He did not wish her presence at his court, and though in the previous year he had expressly told her not to come to England, he

54. *Ibid.*, p. 258; Laud, *Works*, VII, 512.

55. *Cal. S. P. Ven.*, XXIV, 395.

56. Gilbert Burnet, *The Memoirs of the Lives and Actions of James and William, Dukes of Hamilton and Castleherald* (London, 1677), pp. 50, 54. Although sharing in the favors that Charles I dispensed and acting as the king's chief counsel in Scottish affairs, James Hamilton, Duke of Hamilton (1606–49), was at times a dubious supporter of his benefactor. In the end, however, he remained loyal, fighting for the king in Scotland and suffering execution at the hands of Parliament in 1649.

57. *The Hamilton Papers* (ed. Samuel Rawson Gardiner [The Camden Society], Westminster, 1880), p. 59.

58. *Ibid.*, pp. 63, 65.

ultimately surrendered to the entreaties his wife made in behalf of her mother.[59] The people of England no less than the king were displeased by her coming, because they knew her to be a source of trouble wherever she went.[60] Making the best of an unpleasant obligation, Charles behaved with filial duty, going twenty-five miles outside London to greet and welcome his mother-in-law.[61] The queen, because of her advanced stage of pregnancy, had to await her mother's arrival in London. In contrast to Charles, she was overjoyed at the prospect of again seeing her mother after a thirteen-year separation, and sumptuously furnished apartments at St. James's for the dowager's residence.[62]

Out of courtesy to Their Majesties the members of the court and the foreign ambassadors resident in London went to St. James's to pay their respects. Still the great lady, Marie de Medici received visitors with a hauteur that did nothing to make her visit more pleasing in the country where she was a guest. When the royal council called on her, she did not rise from her chair to receive the members, replying to their address in only a few words, and toward the higher nobility of the realm she was also sparing of her courtesies.[63]

Marie de Medici was the more unwelcome in England because of the burden her maintenance placed on the treasury, which was already overtaxed by the necessity of providing arms against the Scots. Furthermore, Marie de Medici had imposed upon the king's hospitality by bringing with her a suite of six hundred servants. To quiet complaint in the council, the queen said that the cost of her mother's support would be met by the government of France. The final settlement made upon the dowager for her maintenance while in England was an immediate grant of £5,000 and £3,000 for each month thereafter.[64]

59. Laud, *Works*, VII, 406; *Cal. S. P. Ven.*, XXIV, 449.
60. Rushworth, *Historical Collections*, II, 724.
61. *Cal. S. P. Ven.*, XXIV, 468.
62. Hermann Ferrero, *Lettres de Henriette-Marie à Sa Soeur Christine* (Rome, 1881), p. 54; *Cal. S. P. Ven.*, XXIV, 463.
63. *Ibid.*, p. 471.
64. *Ibid.*

On her arrival, Marie de Medici found she was not the only refugee from France dependent on the royal largesse, for the Duchess of Chevreuse had come from Spain during the preceding April. Exiled by Richelieu's government, Madame de Chevreuse had been living in Spain after the defeat of Chateauneuf and his cabal in 1633. On first arriving in England, she spoke of a short stay before going on to Flanders, but she was received by Henrietta with such hospitality and gladness that she postponed her departure indefinitely. The queen was lavish in her bestowal of attention and honor on this girlhood friend—so much so as to assign the duchess living quarters at Whitehall Palace. She treated her with such familiarity that even on formal occasions the duchess was permitted to remain seated in the queen's presence. When after a few months the council cut off the allowance granted the adventuress, Madame de Chevreuse became wholly dependent upon the charity of the queen, who was most willing to provide for her guest.[65]

Charles was personally fond of Madame de Chevreuse, but her visit and the queen mother's encumbered his affairs at a time when his attention was needed for quelling the Scottish insurrection. On March 27, 1639, he left London to join his reluctant army at York preparatory to the invasion of Scotland.[66] Before his departure he directed the council to make weekly reports concerning state business to the queen.

While the king was absent in the north, the queen was busy attending her own means of raising money in support of the expedition against the Scots. She called on all English Catholics to make a contribution to the king's war chest in consideration of the clemency they had enjoyed under his rule. Leading Catholics from the counties of England convened in London, where they were addressed to this purpose by Signor Con.[67] Each delegate was given

65. *Ibid.*, pp. 404, 406, 410, 414, 446.
66. Burnet, *Memoirs of Hamilton and Castleherald*, p. 116; *Cal. S. P. Ven.*, XXIV, 525.
67. Rushworth, *Historical Collections*, II, 820–821; Mary Anne Everett Green, *Letters of Queen Henrietta Maria* (London, 1857), pp. 24–25.

letters that he was to circulate among Catholics of his area, who upon learning of the king's need were to make their pledges of contribution. "It is sufficiently already known to every one the extraordinary Graces and Protections we owe the Queen's Majesty," stated the letters, "to whose favorable Intercession we must ascribe the Moderation we live under. . . ."[68]

The queen could hardly have done anything more injurious to the welfare of Catholics in England—or indeed to the interest of Charles and herself—than she did in soliciting her coreligionists for a special assessment. Catholicism was an outlawed religion in England, and Englishmen were still fearful of what they conceived to be Catholic encroachment against the nation's interests. The memories of Queen Mary and the Spanish Armada were by no means obliterated.

The Catholics of England were not unaware of the risk they took in paying the contribution. From Berkshire came a petition asking the queen's protection for one of the collectors of money, who had a suit brought against him in the king's court by an informer against recusants.[69] In addition to the queen's appeal there was also circulated among Catholics a letter, probably spurious, purporting to be addressed from the pope to the papal envoy in England. In this letter the pope advised Catholics to have nothing to do with raising money for the Scottish wars and to display no aversion to a meeting of Parliament.[70] It is not at all impossible that the letter was written and circulated by Catholics who wished to counter the unfavorable publicity which the queen's appeal gave to Catholicism in England and to reduce the amount of money given in assistance for royal arms.

68. Rushworth, *Historical Collections*, II, 822.
69. *MSS Clar. S. P. 1231*, fol. 92.
70. Rushworth, *Historical Collections*, II, 821. It does not seem very probable that the pope would have made any representations favorable to a ruling body that had enacted laws against Catholics. Of course we can only conjecture who wrote the letter. In a note of explanation, Rushworth adds that a copy of it was given to him by a Mr. Audley but that he had never verified the pretensions under which the letter circulated. The donor might have been the Hugh Audley listed in *D.N.B.*, II, 249.

Meanwhile, in the north, Charles's ill-provided and disaffected army halted before Scottish forces along the border. After Lord Holland at the head of a body of troops made a cautious foray into Scotland, from which he quickly retreated, the Scots sent representations for a peace, and a temporary treaty was concluded at Berwick.[71]

The king was back in London by August, 1639—in time to greet the new papal envoy, Count Rossetti, and to bid farewell to the ailing Con, who left for Rome.[72] Charles returned not to peace but to the preparation of another expedition against Scotland. Lord Traquair, now the king's deputy in Scotland, consented to a meeting of the Scottish parliament, although the king had not previously given his consent thereto. When the Scottish parliament convened in the fall of 1639, it soon fell into disagreement with the king. Charles ordered it prorogued until June of the next year, but the members refused to obey his command and continued to make laws for Scotland. Thereupon both sides began arming for a renewal of the conflict.[73]

Much as Charles regretted to do so, he at last called for the convening of a parliament in Westminster. After an interval of eleven years, during which he had refused to issue writs for the election of an English parliament, he was now constrained to do so as the only means of providing adequate revenue to pay for the raising of an army. Even the best of the king's counselors, Thomas Wentworth, who had recently returned from Ireland, could think of no expedient sufficient to pay for the war other than new taxes, which required the consent of Parliament. The parliament which met in April, 1640, insisted upon redress of its grievances before granting money, whereas the king promised to hear the members'

71. Burnet, *Memoirs of Hamilton and Castleherald*, pp. 131–141.
72. *Historical Manuscripts Commission, Fourth Report* (London, 1874), p. 294.
73. Burnet, *Memoirs of Hamilton and Castleherald*, pp. 148, 161. Sir John Stewart, Earl of Traquair (d. 1659), was descended from an illegitimate branch of the ruling family in Scotland. Feeling no strong personal commitment to either episcopacy or Presbyterianism, he would have been willing to forget the whole controversy. Though he fought with the Royalists in the Civil War, he was distrusted by both sides in the conflict. *D.N.B.*, LIV, 326–328.

petitions only after grants had been made for his army. Neither side would surrender to the other, and on May 5 the parliament was dissolved after only five weeks' duration.

Henrietta, in contrast to her attitude of the previous year, urged the king to stand firm against the Scots, although he might be hard pressed to provide the material means of carrying on a war.[74] She promised that money would be coming from Rome, a hope in which she was encouraged by the pope's envoy, Rossetti. She had made representations to Rome for aid, promising the king would grant religious freedom for English Catholics in exchange for assistance. The reply to her appeal was received in a letter from Cardinal Barberini to Rossetti in June, 1640. The pope promised monetary assistance to the limit of his resources and even agreed to send an army of six to eight thousand men if one condition were met: that Charles become a Catholic.[75] Such an unrealistic proposal was impossible for Charles to consider. His personal feelings on the matter apart, England certainly would not have tolerated a Catholic king.

Events that finally led to civil war developed with quickening tempo. Extraordinary means of providing revenue having proved insufficient, the king's army remained undersupplied and mutinous. The Scots took advantage of English military weakness by invading northern England and occupying Newcastle. They could have marched on to London had they wished to do so, but too cunning to inflict such injury on English pride, they chose instead to send the king an address asking for peace. The king called a council of peers to convene at York, where a truce was signed agreeing that the Scottish forces would be paid £850 for each day they were in occupation of English soil. Thereupon, a group of twelve English peers framed a petition asking that Parliament be called to redress grievances, among which was listed "The great Increase of Popery, and imploying Popish Recusants, and others ill affected

74. *Cal. S. P. Ven.*, XXV, 52.
75. Letter to Count Rossetti, June 30, 1640, *Roman Transcripts*.

to Religion in Places of Power and Trust."[76] In London the populace was jubilant over the victory of the Scottish army, for they considered it in effect a victory of the English people over the king. Finally Charles gave way and called a new parliament to convene on November 3, 1640.

During the weeks preceding the convening of Parliament, the doubtful loyalty of some of the king's servants gave cause for anxiety at the court. The Duke of Hamilton, leader of the naval expedition sent to the coast of Scotland, privately declared that he would not work the ruin of his own country,[77] and Lord Holland was in communication with Richelieu, who had his agents busy in England doing what they could to agitate the unrest there.[78] Those servants of unquestioned loyalty were so hated by the people that they were becoming ineffective in the king's service, as was evident when mobs attacked Lambeth Palace with such fury that Archbishop Laud was forced to move to Somerset House for his personal safety.[79]

The queen's Capuchins and the papal envoy also appeared to be in danger. On September 7 Secretary Windebank wrote the king, who was still at York, that he thought it advisable for Rossetti to go to France and the Capuchins to be sequestered in places of safety in the country. In fact, considering that the London mobs had vented their hatred in demolishing windows, altar rails, and images in the churches, Windebank wondered how the Capuchins had escaped violence. Charles, too occupied to give close attention to Windebank's advice, replied that whatever his wife resolved to do would be satisfactory with him.[80]

About a month later the secretary, who had repeatedly used his

76. Sir Bulstrode Whitelocke, *Memorials of English Affairs during the Reign of Charles I* (London, 1732), p. 37.

77. Burnet, *Memoirs of Hamilton and Castleherald*, p. 163.

78. *MSS Français 15995*, fol. 20; Edward Hyde, Earl of Clarendon, *The History of the Rebellion and Civil Wars in England* (7 vols., Oxford, 1849), IV, 138; Whitelocke, *Memorials*, p. 32.

79. *Cal. S. P. Ven.*, XXV, 73.

80. *MSS Clar. S. P. 1421*, fol. 25.

office to obtain pardons for recusants, followed his own advice by fleeing to France. Carrying with him the queen's letter of introduction and commendation, he departed with such secrecy that several days elapsed before his absence was generally noticed.[81]

Although the support of the crown seemed to be crumbling away on all sides, the queen still maintained her courage. To be sure, she had reason to wish for domestic peace, since she now had a family of six children, the youngest born the previous July.[82] But when the honor of the person she loved was impugned, she was ready to fight in his defense. Not until after Parliament convened and the queen was subjected to the ugly threats and insinuations of that overpowering assemblage did she become alarmed over her own safety.

81. *MSS Français 15995*, fols. 164, 165.
82. Prince Henry, Duke of Gloucester, born July 8, 1640. A daughter, Catherine, born January 29, 1639, died shortly after birth.

CHAPTER V

THE QUEEN AND THE TRIBUNAL

OF THE PEOPLE

1640-42   PARLIAMENT convened on November 3, 1640. For the first time Henrietta was to be judged by the tribunal of the people, her influence not having been great enough during her early years in England to bring her seriously before the attention of Parliament. During the years of Parliament's suspension, the people could indicate their disapproval of her only by indirect and unofficial means, in pamphlets, letters, gossip, and sermons. Now that the cumulative record of the past decade could be examined, Puritan members of Parliament were ready to bring forth a long array of charges against the queen, including her protection of recusants in violation of the law, her keeping a group of priests at her court and maintenance of a chapel where English Catholics worshiped,[1] her exchange of representatives with the pope, her communications with Rome, her evil counsel imposed upon Charles, her solicitation of revenue from Catholics, her endeavors to convert ladies of high rank, and her support of the Catholic power of Spain.

1. Of course, the marriage treaty specified the queen was to be allowed priests in sufficient numbers to serve her religion, and was also to have chapels that Catholics in England would be permitted to attend by the government.

In the estimation of the majority of members in Lords and Commons, religion was no less endangered than was lawful government. To be sure, religion and politics could hardly be considered separately. During the first week of its sittings Parliament heard grievances, among which were a complaint against "Suspension of laws against them of the Popish Religion" and an accusation that the pope had a nuncio in England to execute his authority.[2]

But the one person who had to be ruined before full attention could be given to the queen's subversive connivings, and who, indeed, was to be linked with the Catholic attempt to reduce England, was Thomas Wentworth, recently made Earl of Strafford. To John Pym and other members of Parliament, Strafford personified an autocratic government determined to bend Parliament to the royal will.[3] About a week after the beginning of the session, Strafford was arrested on a charge of high treason and imprisoned in the Tower. Shortly thereafter, Commons began gathering evidence and examining witnesses in preparation for Strafford's trial.[4]

No sooner was Strafford removed from power than the clamor against Catholics swelled to proportions greatly in excess of any reaction the recusants by their numbers or importance in the nation's life could have elicited from the English people in calmer times. The king was moved to reinvoke the law excluding Catholics from residence within a ten-mile radius of London.[5] Pulpits, and to a lesser degree pamphlets, were employed to whip the populace into peaks of excitement, which though subsiding during intervals could always be reactivated whenever some crisis was at

2. Sir Bulstrode Whitelocke, *Memorials of English Affairs during the Reign of Charles I* (London, 1732), p. 38.

3. Samuel Rawson Gardiner, *History of England from the Accession of James I to the Outbreak of the Civil War, 1603–1642* (10 vols., London, 1896–99), IX, 229–230.

4. *Journals of the House of Commons*, II, 27–30 (referred to hereafter as *J. C.*); *Journals of the House of Lords*, IV, 88–89 (referred to hereafter as *J. L.*).

5. *Ibid.*, p. 85; *J. C.*, II, 24.

hand. On Tuesday, November 17, a "universal fast" was observed throughout the parishes of England, with public prayers to implore divine assistance in the time of trouble. Pulpit-pounding ministers exhorted their hearers to put down the Catholic religion and exalted the Scots as men sent by God to deliver England from her perils. These ideas found a ready hearing, for on the following Sunday a crowd of Puritans gathered outside the queen's chapel and furiously attacked the worshipers who came out following the observance of mass.[6]

In Parliament, too, the alarm was sounded against the pernicious threat of popery. Among the committees formed in Commons at the beginning of the session was one to investigate the effectiveness of the laws against recusancy and other aspects of Catholicism in England. On December 1 this committee made its first report,[7] which confirmed the suspicions of the hearers. Upon examination of the records of only two prisons, Newgate and the Clink, it was learned that sixty-four priests had been released in one year, some by privy signet and others by warrants of the lords of the council, but most by warrants from Secretary Windebank. Brief questioning of three clerks employed in the royal courts revealed that within the previous seven or eight years, seventy-four letters of grace had been granted to Catholics in London, usually upon request of a foreign ambassador or of the queen mother, Marie de Medici; and here again Windebank, having issued twenty-nine warrants under his own hand, had been especially active. Only one priest had been discharged under the king's hand, and this by misrepresentation, for His Majesty had been told the priest was only indicted whereas in fact he had been convicted of high treason. Of course, the investigation on which the committee reported was

6. *Calendar of State Papers, Venice* (38 vols., ed. Allen B. Hinds and others, London, 1864–1940), XXV, 97 (referred to hereafter as *Cal. S. P. Ven.*).

7. *J. C.*, II, 41; *The Journal of Sir Simonds D'Ewes from the Beginning of the Long Parliament to the Opening of the Trial of the Earl of Strafford* (ed. Wallace Notestein, New Haven, 1923), p. 89 (referred to hereafter as D'Ewes, *Journal of the Long Parliament*).

made at random and was by no means exhaustive, but it did indicate that laws against recusancy had been largely subverted by officers at the court.

If the queen's name was not specifically mentioned in the report, it was nevertheless believed that she lent her influence to the undermining of the laws. And though it was hardly feasible to rid England of her papalistic queen, the next best measure could be taken in removing all other Catholics from the court. Not long after the committee report on recusancy, Parliament asked the queen to dismiss her Catholic servants. The queen's will stiffened against this request as it had many years before when she was deprived of her Catholic friends. If she dismissed her Catholic servants, she said, she would also dismiss her Protestant ones and then provide herself with a new staff, all of whom would be Catholic.[8] This was a brave speech, but Parliament wore a grim face. The queen, realizing she had defied a people of firm resolution, advised the pope's envoy, Rossetti, to leave England. As if to match the bravery of the queen, Rossetti begged to be allowed to stay, secretly intending to find safety with a French or Venetian ambassador if his courage were put to the test.[9] Although Rossetti's departure was postponed, Catholics in England probably would have been better off had he left the country.

Distressed as she was by the encompassing hate against her and her religion, Henrietta's suffering was made doubly poignant by a loss within her family. On December 6 her three-year-old daughter, Anne, died. Henrietta had already lost two children, one being stillborn and the other dying shortly after birth, but this was the first child she had to give up after its personality had formed and infused her heart. The queen's grief, according to the Venetian ambassador, was intense.[10]

Deep though her sorrow was, the queen had to overcome it to

8. *Cal. S. P. Ven.*, XXV, 103.
9. *MSS Français 15995*, fol. 168.
10. *Cal. S. P. Ven.*, XXV, 106.

give attention to other concerns which pressed upon her. With her eldest daughter, nine-year-old Princess Mary, she was concerned in quite another way. Since the preceding January, the Prince of Orange had been trying to negotiate a marriage between his son and Princess Mary.[11] Neither the king nor the queen was flattered by Orange's overtures, for his was not a crowned head and they planned a better match for Mary, intending her for the heir to the Spanish throne. In fact, Charles misunderstood the initial proposal, never supposing Frederick Henry would presume to ask for the eldest daughter, but rather for the second one, Princess Elizabeth.[12] Orange insisted upon having Mary, saying that her more mature years would better suit the necessity of producing an heir as soon as possible. The best the pretentious prince could do, however, was to reach an agreement on a marriage between his fourteen-year-old son and Charles's second daughter, then only five years of age.[13]

But the prince had not given up his hope of having the eldest daughter, an ambition in which he was seconded by the French, who had no wish to see the ruling houses of Spain and England linked by marriage, and also to some extent by Marie de Medici.[14] By January of 1641, Orange knew the King of England had come down a bit in the world, and negotiations were reopened. Charles, badly in need of help against his rebellious subjects, thought that through marriage he could obtain a timely alliance with the Netherlands. In February, 1641, a marriage treaty promising Princess Mary to Orange's son was concluded.[15]

Parliament, if not greatly concerned about the marriage, was not displeased that a Protestant match had been arranged for the daughter of England.[16] In other ways Parliament was far from

11. Guillaume Groen van Prinsterer, *Archives ou Correspondence Inédit de la Maison d'Orange Nassau* (4 vols., Utrecht, 1859), III, 159–160 (referred to hereafter as Prinsterer, *Archives*).

12. *Ibid.*, p. 170.

13. *Ibid.*, pp. 190, 191, 198–199, 212, 243–245.

14. *Cal. S. P. Ven.*, XXV, 52.

15. Prinsterer, *Archives*, III, 306, 322–323, 338–342, 353–354.

16. Whitelocke, *Memorials*, p. 40.

pleased with Charles's stand on religious matters. The king had recently reprieved one Goodman, a Jesuit condemned to be executed for high treason, and the members as well as people in the city of London attributed this act of mercy to the queen's intercession.[17] Parliament informed the king that the people were much offended by the reprieve of Goodman, and, so the Venetian ambassador wrote his government, "threatened the Queen with greater ill."[18] Attention was again given to the committee on recusants, which reported that Goodman had twice before been imprisoned and released, and told of priests and Jesuits walking forth boldly at midday.[19] The House of Commons heard testimony of a Mrs. Anne Hussey against an Irish priest, O'Conner, who was accused of conspiring to raise a Catholic army in Ireland and of personally plotting the murder of the king.[20]

In addition, the queen's letters of appeal for Catholic contribution were taken into consideration. Sir Simonds D'Ewes, speaking on the subject of the queen's letters to the Catholics, said she had represented the war against the Scots as one undertaken in behalf of Catholicism, "as if these motives had proceeded from her contrarie to what the King had declared; and that this warre did tend to the advancement of Poperie."[21] Walter Montagu was called to appear before the bar of Commons to tell what he knew of the levy exacted from Catholics. He said that he met with others to discuss means for raising money and that collectors were appointed for each county, but that he was unaware that Con had been the instigator of the assessment, although the meetings had been held in Con's house. Sir Kenelm Digby also stood before Commons, talking at length but in substance saying little. Asked in what capacity Con had been employed at the court, a question that evoked dark suspicions in England, Digby replied that Con had been sent by the pope to perform such offices touching religion as Her Majesty

17. D'Ewes, *Journal of the Long Parliament*, p. 279.
18. *Cal. S. P. Ven.*, XXV, 119.
19. D'Ewes, *Journal of the Long Parliament*, p. 290.
20. *Ibid.*, p. 287.
21. *Ibid.*, p. 291.

might require and to present the queen's wishes to the pope from time to time.[22]

In these inquiries Parliament had been unable to find anyone who admitted knowing much about the activities of Catholics at the queen's court, but just enough had been revealed to excite its fears beyond what a full exposé could have done. The specter lurked in what remained hidden. The king was reminded of the statute of 27 Elizabeth I, declaring that priests ordained by authority in Rome and resident in England were ipso facto traitors to the state, and was further informed that "Priests and Jesuits swarm in this Kingdom."[23]

The pressure of both houses, especially when they began to bring the queen under purview of their censure, was enough to cause the king to retract his reprieve of Goodman. In a speech delivered to the members assembled in the Banqueting Hall, the king declared that being pressed to give way, and being unwilling to persist in causing discontent which his mercy might produce, he remitted Goodman's case to the care of Parliament.[24] The queen, too, tried to appease Parliament by sending to Commons her letter of explanation and apology for the Catholic assessment. She begged a woman's ignorance as her excuse. She did not know she was doing anything wrong in asking the Catholics for money. She merely thought herself to be following the example of other of His Majesty's loyal subjects who were forward in helping their king. And then she added demurely that thenceforth she would be more cautious and do nothing except what might stand with the established laws of the country.[25] One can imagine a dour Puritan member stirring impatiently in his seat while the letter was being

22. *Ibid.*, pp. 295, 302; John Rushworth, *Historical Collections* (8 vols., London, 1721–22), IV, 164. Sir Kenelm Digby (1603–68) became acquainted with Charles while the latter was in Madrid wooing the infanta, and was almost immediately taken into Charles's household. As a Catholic, Digby helped raise money among his coreligionists in England to support Charles's military campaign against the Scots. *D.N.B.*, XV, 60–66.

23. Rushworth, *Historical Collections*, III, 1332, 1334.

24. *J. L.*, IV, 151.

25. *J. C.*, II, 78; Rushworth, *Historical Collections*, III, 823–824.

read before the House of Commons. (What was this, a little girl's trick?) When Sir Simonds D'Ewes moved a vote of thanks to the queen for her letter, not one voice was raised to second him.[26] Perhaps some of the members were aware that at the time she sent her letter, she was writing to Richelieu in request for money to be used against them, or, as did the Venetian ambassador, that she was appealing to the pope for 500,000 crowns to be used for the defense of Catholicism in England.[27]

Henrietta took the adamantine attitude of Parliament as an ominous sign. Already she was thinking of leaving England to escape the coming wrath. The Dutch ambassador had notified his government of the queen's intention of going to France for her health and of her wish that the marriage of her daughter be solemnized before her departure.[28] Richelieu in reply to her application said the king her brother would not approve her repairing to France, whereupon the queen then began to speak of Ireland as a place of refuge.[29]

The threats against the queen became more intense as the trial of Strafford dragged on through the weeks of the following spring. The proceedings began on March 23, 1641. The king and queen were present during many of the sessions, sitting in a loggia that was provided for them in Westminster Hall, where the trial was held.[30] By their presence they sought to indicate their sympathy for the defendant and to bolster his courage. Henrietta was tardy in recognizing this loyal servant who had been willing to give his all to maintain the king's prerogative. Several years later, after she had fled from the storm in England, she was to tell a confidant that though Strafford was not handsome, he was pleasing enough

26. D'Ewes, *Journal of the Long Parliament*, p. 325; *Harl. MSS 1219*, fol. 104.

27. Charles, Comte de Baillon, *Lettres de Henriette-Marie, Reine d'Angleterre* (Paris, 1877), p. 361; *Cal. S. P. Ven.*, XXV, 117; D'Ewes, *Journal of the Long Parliament*, p. 324.

28. Prinsterer, *Archives*, III, 353.

29. *Cal. S. P. Ven.*, XXV, 127.

30. Françoise Bertaut, Madame de Motteville, *Mémoires sur Anne d'Autriche et Sa Cour* (4 vols., ed. M. F. Riaux, Paris, n.d.), I, 196–197; *Cal. S. P. Ven.*, XXV, 138.

as a person, and that he had the prettiest hands she had ever seen.[31] Henrietta was much influenced in her opinion by the superficialities of outward appearance.

But now aware that Strafford was her husband's best friend, she did what she could to save him. Although Henrietta did not appear to be especially interested in political matters or to be adept at political scheming, she was always ready to connive in the interest of someone she considered a friend, and often the subjects of her concern were persons of political importance. During the time of the trial, she held secret nocturnal meetings with leaders of Parliament in an attempt to win them to Strafford's support. As she later related these experiences, she met the "*mechans*," or opposition leaders, at the bottom of a secret stairway leading from the room occupied by one of her maids of honor, who at that time was away in the country. She made her passage to the rendezvous in greatest secrecy, her way down the dark stairs lighted only by the flambeau that she carried. There is no evidence to indicate she persuaded any of those whom she interviewed to change sides, although she might have had some influence on George Digby, who, after having been one of the strongest prosecutors of Strafford, became his staunch supporter when it was dangerous to speak in behalf of the defendant.[32]

Another means of aiding Strafford and asserting the king's authority was offered in proposals by two separate groups of army officers to march upon London with their forces. These forces were

31. Motteville, *Mémoires*, I, 196.

32. *Ibid.*, pp. 196–197; *The Memoirs of Edmund Ludlow* (2 vols., ed. C. H. Firth, Oxford, 1894), I, 18 (referred to hereafter as Ludlow, *Memoirs*); *Manuscripts of Earl Cowper, Historical Manuscripts Commission, Twelfth Report* (London, 1888), part I, p. 272. That Henrietta did hold such secret conferences was very much in keeping with her character, but the circumstances as she recounted them to Madame de Motteville do seem too dramatic. It is difficult to believe, as Henrietta recounted, that she undertook these trysts without escort.

George Digby, Earl of Bristol (1612–77), was the oldest son and heir of the English ambassador in Madrid at the time Charles and Buckingham journeyed to Spain. Although a Royalist, Digby was slow to forget what he considered grievances he had suffered at the court, and was really too mercurial to be of much use to the king during the wars. *D.N.B.*, XV, 52–55.

the remnants of the army which had been sent on the second expedition against the Scots, and not having been disbanded, were still garrisoned in Yorkshire. The inception of the military conspiracy arose out of the chagrin of younger army officers over the payment of Scottish occupation forces around Newcastle, while their own salaries remained long in arrears.[33] Two distinct plots were formed, one under a cabal consisting of Henry Wilmot, Algernon Percy, and Jack Ashburnham, and the other under the leadership of George Goring. The inevitable conflict between these two factions became apparent when Wilmot revealed his plans to the king, and Goring confidentially informed the queen of his scheme. Obviously the ambitions of the two groups, neither of which knew of the other's intrigue, had to be coordinated and brought into common purpose. As a mediator to join the two conspiracies, Their Majesties chose Henry Jermyn, the queen's confidant and master of horse. At first the queen had misgivings about employing Jermyn in so dangerous a task, for if the two factions fell into quarrel and the plots were revealed, Jermyn's involvement would deprive her of his services at a time when he was about the only trustworthy servant she had remaining with her. But the king would hear of no change in plans, and Jermyn was dispatched on his errand of conciliation.[34]

33. Bartholomew Warburton, *Memoirs of Prince Rupert and the Cavaliers* (3 vols., London, 1849), I, 193–194 (referred to hereafter as Warburton, *Prince Rupert and the Cavaliers*); Whitelocke, *Memorials*, p. 46.

34. Motteville, *Mémoires*, I, 197–199; Rushworth, *Historical Collections*, IV, 255–257. All of the men involved in this double plot could be classified generally as Cavaliers. Among them, Henry Wilmot, Earl of Rochester (1612–58), as the king's master of horse, was probably most often in Charles's company during the years of the Civil War. A Cavalier who never defected, Wilmot nevertheless was not liked by Charles I, though he became a trusted adviser to Charles II. (*D.N.B.*, LXII, 61–63.) Few of the Cavaliers had been favored more by their king than had Algernon Percy, Duke of Northumberland (1602–68), through whose support Charles hoped to keep much of the north on the Royalist side. Gradually, however, Percy gave his allegiance to Parliament and became the guardian of Charles's younger children as long as they were in Parliament's keeping. (*D.N.B.*, XLIV, 385–390.) John Ashburnham (1603–71) began his career at court as a protégé of Buckingham. He and Dr. Hudson were the king's sole attendants when Charles

Jermyn was almost certain to fail in his attempt to bring about harmony. The plotters with whom he had to deal were Cavaliers, a hot-blooded and proud group ambitious for their own advancement and very sensitive on points of personal honor. Perhaps Goring was the most obstinate and self-centered of the lot. He was a soldier of fortune with a streak of cruelty in his soul and was motivated by a desire for self-gain. When in the settlement between the two parties it became apparent to Goring that he would not get as much as he hoped for, and when the complexity of the scheme made its success doubtful, he blandly informed Pym's followers of the conspiracy.[35] Pym chose not to publicize the army plot immediately, but to await the opportune moment a few weeks later to inform Parliament.[36]

Amid the fears and anxieties over attacks on the queen's religion, the trial of Strafford, the challenge to royal authority, and the army plot, young William of Orange arrived in England on April 19 for his marriage to Princess Mary.[37] From all descriptions, the prince was a fine, well-tutored lad of fifteen, whose personal qualities soon won the approbation of the king.[38] The prince found his child bride a more captivating creature than he had expected, despite the fact that she was recovering from a fever. "At first we were a little sober in one anothers company," he wrote his father, "but now we are very informal and relaxed; I find her much pret-

---

set forth to surrender himself to the Scottish army in 1646. (*D.N.B.*, II, 162–163.) Starting as a gentleman pensioner at the court of Queen Elizabeth, George Goring, Earl of Norwich (1583–1663), later attracted James I's attention as a wit and buffoon. Offices, monopolies, and various favors were granted him, but what affluence he owed to the king he sacrificed in the Royalist cause during the wars. Sometime master of horse to the queen, he later accompanied her to Holland to help her raise money, and in 1643 was sent on embassy to Paris for the purpose of negotiating a loan. (*D.N.B.*, XXII, 245–250.)

35. Sir Philip Warwick, *Memoirs of the Reign of Charles I* (London, 1702), pp. 197–198; *Cal. S. P. Ven.*, XXV, 142; Warburton, *Prince Rupert and the Cavaliers*, I, 197–199.

36. *J. C.*, II, 135.

37. Prinsterer, *Archives*, III, 434.

38. *Cal. S. P. Ven.*, XXV, 147n.

tier than the paintings. I love her deeply, and I believe she loves me, too."[39] Owing to political conditions in England, the marriage ceremony was simple in the extreme, with none of the festivity that ordinarily would have been observed. The queen viewed the Protestant wedding service from a latticed recess in the chapel.[40] On the afternoon of the wedding day the prince promenaded in Hyde Park with the queen, Princess Mary, and Mary's brothers the Prince of Wales and the Duke of York.[41] At least it was still safe for members of the royal family to venture into the palace gardens, as it was not a few days later. That evening the marriage was formally consummated. The Prince of Wales called at young William's room to conduct the groom, dressed in nightclothes, to the bed of his wife. In Mary's room members of the court pressed around the bed to witness the proceedings. The queen, who had already put her daughter to bed, stood at one side of the bedstead. On the other side was the king, who parted the curtains to permit the young Prince of Orange to kiss his bride on the forehead. The formality of consummation consisted in having the prince place his uncovered leg against the leg of his bride. When the coverlet was pulled back, a trick was discovered, for the princess's chemise reached to her ankles. Thereupon the queen's dwarf, Geoffrey Hudson, produced a pair of shears to cut the garment, and general merriment over the incident ensued among those crowded into the room.[42]

But a grimmer business overshadowed the rites of Hymen. Only a few blocks away from the palace in which the marriage had taken place, Parliament considered the fate of Strafford, who still stood trial for his life. Pym and his followers, having become doubtful of success in carrying through the impeachment, had moved an act of attainder against the king's loyal minister. On the day following the wedding, London mobs clamored at the door

39. Prinsterer, *Archives*, III, 460–461.
40. *Ibid.*, p. 454.
41. *Ibid.*, p. 462.
42. *Ibid.*, pp. 455–456.

of Commons for the condemnation of Strafford. Two days later, on May 5, Pym unveiled the army plot to Parliament.[43] Except for Goring, who in reward for his informing had been made governor of the fortress at Portsmouth, all of those involved in the conspiracy were forced to take flight, including the queen's favorite, Henry Jermyn.[44]

The public fear and anger over what was presented as national betrayal mounted to a frenzy. Now anything could be believed; dark rumors of new plottings were readily manufactured and fell upon receptive ears. The King of France, it was reported, stood ready to sail with an army from Dieppe to bring about the subjugation of Parliament. Commons, as if to authenticate this story, sent four commissioners to Portsmouth to investigate the defenses there and to supervise the strengthening of the fortifications against attack.[45] The bill of attainder having by now passed the lower house, crowds milled about the hall of Lords shouting for justice and for Strafford's head.[46] On Friday, May 8, the Lords acceded to these demands, and the crowds moved on the palace of Whitehall. Only the king's signature stood between Strafford and death. This was Charles's darkest hour. Charles owed much to Strafford and had promised he would never consent to the execution of his minister, but as he sat in the council chamber he could hear the muffled tumult of the crowd, which threatened to storm the palace if their wish was not met. He was torn between fidelity to his friend and love for his wife, who would hardly survive if the maddened and uncontrollable crowd broke the barriers of the palace walls. This terror was not imagined. Even foreign ambassadors of Catholic countries lived in fear for their lives and wished to be called away from England.[47] The king and queen precipitately planned flight to Portsmouth but were dissuaded from going by an official of the

43. *J. L.*, IV, 236.
44. Motteville, *Mémoires*, I, 199.
45. *Cal. S. P. Ven.*, XXV, 150.
46. Edward Hyde, Earl of Clarendon, *The History of the Rebellion and Civil Wars in England* (7 vols., Oxford, 1849), I, 359.
47. *Cal. S. P. Ven.*, XXV, 152.

French embassy.[48] When Parliament warned the king and queen not to depart from their palace, Henrietta defiantly replied that she was a daughter of Henry IV and did not know how to flee.[49] Yet the possibility of his doughty little queen's being massacred by the rabble must have been too much for Charles to bear. On the morning of May 9 his resolution broke, and he signed the bill of attainder.

These were beclouded days for the queen. It was she, the public assumed, who had been responsible for the threat of French invasion. As if intimidation were not enough, they sought to make life unendurable for her by impugning her morals, saying that she wished to go to France in order to be with her lover, Jermyn, who had somewhat of a reputation with women.[50]

During the two months following the death of Strafford, the pressure of the revolutionary party upon the queen slackened, since Parliament was occupied with the exclusion of bishops from government office and with other measures to solidify the gains made over the power of monarchy. Nevertheless, the houses did not ignore what took place at Whitehall Palace. In June indignation was expressed in Parliament because Rossetti had not left the kingdom. The envoy was called to appear before the bar of Commons, whereupon he took refuge in the Venetian embassy and shortly afterward left for France.

The queen proposed to follow Rossetti's example in July when the king announced that he would soon depart for Scotland to bring about settlement between himself and his northern subjects. Plans for a trip to the Continent had been forming in the queen's mind since the beginning of the year, and now that her husband was to be absent, she was determined not to remain alone in the unfriendly atmosphere of London.[51] In addition, there was the excuse of escorting her daughter Mary to Holland. The Dutch strongly insisted the girl be permitted to come to her husband's country so

48. *Ibid.*, p. 151.
49. *Ibid.*, p. 149.
50. *Ibid.*, pp. 150, 163.
51. Prinsterer, *Archives*, III, 353.

that she might learn the Dutch language and customs. Even while crowds had milled about the palace in demand for Strafford's death, the Dutch ambassador had tried to persuade the queen to consent to the girl's immediate departure, but Henrietta had refused his request.[52] Giving neither her fear of Parliament nor her desire to escort Mary to Holland as reason for going to the Continent, Henrietta informed Parliament that her excuse was the very proper one of health; she wished to go to France in order to take a course of the waters at Spa.[53]

The queen's explanation did not carry much conviction in Parliament—especially when it was learned she intended to take with her a quantity of plate and jewelry far in excess of what her journey demanded. A committee was appointed to look into the queen's proposed voyage. Since Pym, John Hampden, and Sir Henry Vane were among those appointed, the findings of the committee were hardly to be to the queen's liking. The elderly Dr. Theodore Mayerne, personal physician to the queen, was called upon by the committee to give testimony concerning her health. Mayerne said the queen's indisposition was due to her state of mind, not to physical causes, and that the waters of Spa could do her no good except in a psychic way. Parliament petitioned the king asking that the queen not leave England, since departure at such a time would be a dishonor to the nation, and expressed a wish to do all in its power to ease the queen's condition.[54] Henrietta had to remain, but she answered Parliament with a letter of biting irony and double meaning. "I give many thanks to both Houses of Parliament," she wrote, "for their great Care of my Health, and their Affection to me; hoping I shall see the Effect of it."[55]

52. *Ibid.*, p. 458.

53. *Manuscripts of Earl Cowper*, part I, p. 289.

54. Mary Anne Everett Green, *Letters of Queen Henrietta Maria* (London, 1857), p. 41; Prinsterer, *Archives*, III, 489; John Pym, "The Reasons of the House of Commons to Stay the Queenes Going into Holland" (London, 1641), pp. 1–8; *J. C.*, II, 210–213; Frances Verney, *Memoirs of the Verney Family* (4 vols., New York, 1892–99), II, 22–23.

55. *J. C.*, II, 215.

The king left for Scotland on August 12, 1641.[56] Insofar as was possible, the queen was to act in his stead in executing the laws. When, a few weeks later, Secretary Edward Nicholas wrote the king to inquire about a general act of oblivion designed to exculpate those persons involved in the army plot, the king told his servant to consult the queen, since she knew his wishes concerning the matter.[57]

With the king's departure also came that of the queen mother, although she had to wait in Dover several months before obtaining passage across the Channel.[58] Charles had had to cut off the old queen's allowance in the preceding February. To maintain herself, Marie de Medici sold her plate and horses and other possessions until she was reduced to what for her seemed the last extremity.[59] Whimpering in fear before the contumely of the Puritan-minded mobs of London, the elderly lady had for several months been negotiating for permission to travel through the Netherlands in passage to Cologne.[60] Parliament finally became impatient of her stay and asked her to get out of England as soon as possible.

With her husband and mother gone, her advisers fled, and herself forced to remain in England by a hostile government, Henrietta's spirits were at their nadir. From the highest summit of happiness, she wrote her sister Christine, she had fallen into the depths of despair. The king was deprived of power, the poor Catholics were persecuted, the priests were executed, the royal servants were exiled, and her attendants and she were living like prisoners. Christine, it was true, had known adversity, but she had always

56. Gilbert Burnet, *The Memoirs of the Lives and Actions of James and William, Dukes of Hamilton and Castleherald* (London, 1677), p. 184 (referred to hereafter as Burnet, *Memoirs of Hamilton and Castleherald*).

57. *The Private Correspondence between Charles I and His Secretary of State, Sir Edward Nicholas* (in vol. II, part 2, of *Memoirs Illustrative of the Life and Writings of Sir John Evelyn* [2 vols., ed. William Bray, London, 1819]), pp. 1, 8–9 (referred to hereafter as *Correspondence between Charles I and Sir Edward Nicholas*).

58. *Ibid.*, n. 12.

59. *MSS Français 15995*, fol. 180.

60. *Ibid.*, fols. 186, 187, 189; Prinsterer, *Archives*, III, 475; *Cal. S. P. Ven.*, XXV, 176.

been able to fight her way out. The hopelessness of Henrietta's condition was that she was powerless to bestir herself against her enemies. If only she could do something! But no room for action was left; her only choice was to wait helplessly before the onrush of public violence.[61]

Nevertheless, she was determined not to remain in London to suffer the affront of the populace during her husband's absence. She and her children went to Oatlands, one of the royal estates, to remain until the king's return. Even here she did not escape the insolence of the Protestants, for Parliament sent the Earl of Holland, now out of favor with the queen and a supporter of those who opposed her, to ask that Prince Charles be moved from her company and taken to the palace of Richmond, where he would be under the care of the Marquis of Hertford. This step was urged, the queen was informed, out of fear not that she would endanger the prince's religion but that those about her might endeavor to instruct him in the Catholic beliefs. Reluctantly, the queen agreed that after the prince had stayed to celebrate the birthday of one of his sisters, he should go to Richmond.[62]

It was also during Henrietta's stay at Oatlands that she was confronted with a scheme to frighten her into an attempt to flee from England. Just who was behind this trick or whether it was really a serious undertaking is difficult to say, although Henrietta attributed it to the intrigue of some of her enemies in Parliament. Be that as it may, a "gentleman" living not far from Oatlands informed the queen he had received secret instructions to have a

61. Hermann Ferrero, *Lettres de Henriette-Marie à Sa Soeur Christine* (Rome, 1881), pp. 58–59.

62. *Manuscripts of Lord Montagu of Beaulieu, Historical Manuscripts Commission Report* (London, 1900), p. 132; *J. C.*, II, 303; Motteville, *Mémoires*, I, 203. William Seymour, first Marquis and second Earl of Hertford (1588–1660), was too scholarly in temperament to spend his time at court, where he gained little recognition until the meeting of the Long Parliament. When, however, the troubles between Parliament and monarch became serious, he was too important for the king to ignore. In 1641 he was made governor of the Prince of Wales and subsequently fought with the Royalist forces. Allowed after the military defeat of the Royalists to compound for his estates, he seems to have been little molested during the time of the Commonwealth. *D.N.B.*, LI, 333–335.

group of armed horsemen mounted and ready at midnight in a nearby forest, where he would receive definite orders for further action. Faced with a tangible danger, the queen could act with consummate courage. She told the informer to ignore the orders which he had shown her, and she hastily summoned from London those officers she felt she could trust. Simultaneously she dispatched a message to Goring, whom she believed to have won back into her following, to have relays of horses held in readiness in the event she found it necessary to flee to Portsmouth. She armed such men as were available at Oatlands, even the boys who worked in the kitchen, with what crude weapons were at hand. As the appointed hour of midnight approached, the queen walked watchfully, but without much fear, up and down one of the paths of the gardens. Midnight passed, nothing happened, and finally darkness faded before the dawn, putting an end to the queen's anticipation.[63]

The incident at Oatlands could hardly have been taken as an indication that the widespread animosity toward the queen was an empty threat. To members of Parliament the Catholic queen appeared to be an obstacle to understanding between the king and his people. "Popery," Secretary Nicholas warned the king, "hath and doth (more than anything) prejudice yor Matie in the esteeme and affection of yor people, whose love I humbly conceave to be soe much yor Majesties interest, as it ought to be preserved and reteyned by yor Matie by all possible means. . . ."[64]

On Monday, November 1, the worst suspicions against popery seemed confirmed. That morning when the House of Commons convened, it was announced that three lords of the council with something to announce to the members waited outside the doors.

63. Motteville, *Mémoires*, I, 202–204.
64. *Correspondence between Charles I and Sir Edward Nicholas*, p. 21. Sir Edward Nicholas (1593–1669) was a bureaucrat who occupied a number of offices under the crown before being appointed secretary of state to Charles I. After the king went to the Scottish army, Nicholas was given permission by Parliament to go abroad. Charles II appears never to have relied upon him as much as had his father, and Henrietta felt a deep dislike for the secretary. *D.N.B.*, XL, 422–426.

On being admitted into the hall, the lords read letters they had received the day before telling of the outbreak of rebellion in Ireland and of the slaughter of Protestants there. After the lords left, the hearers sat as if stunned. No one spoke for several minutes.[65] Rather than view the uprising as a reaction of Irish Catholics, who had long smarted under English dominance, the House of Commons conceived it to be a vast conspiracy emanating from England and having the queen and her cohorts among its contrivers.[66] Contrary to constitutional precedence, Parliament set about raising an army to be sent to Ireland and appointing its officers without consulting the king, who was still in Scotland.[67] Clearly, in the minds of the members, this whole business issued from the evil counselors of the king; henceforth Parliament must choose his advisers. Measures against Catholics were to be prosecuted with a new vigor.[68] Credence was given to the fantastic tale of one Thomas Beal, a tailor, who said he had overheard a plot by papists who planned the murder of one hundred and eight members of Parliament.[69] Father Philip was called to testify before Commons, and was imprisoned when he refused to take oath on the King James Version of the Bible.[70] In the lower house a declaration was drawn up, to which the queen was to be required to subscribe, asserting "detestation of the execrable and pernicious Catholic conspiracy," but the peers refused to let her be embarrassed in this manner before the Catholics of the world.[71] "The odium of all was thrown upon the papists, because the generality of the nation

---

65. Clarendon, *History of the Rebellion*, I, 423–424; *Calendar of State Papers, Domestic Series, of the Reign of Charles I, 1625–1649* (23 vols., ed. John Bruce and others, London, 1858–97), 1641–43, p. 156 (referred to hereafter as *Cal. S. P. Dom.*).

66. *Manuscripts of Lord Montagu of Beaulieu*, pp. 133–134; *Cal. S. P. Ven.*, XXV, 241.

67. Thomas Carte, *The Life of James, Duke of Ormonde* (6 vols., Oxford, 1851), II, 7–17 (referred to hereafter as Carte, *Ormonde*).

68. *Correspondence between Charles I and Sir Edward Nicholas*, pp. 62, 69.

69. *Cal. S. P. Dom.*, 1641–43, p. 168.

70. *Cal. S. P. Ven.*, XXV, 241–242.

71. Carte, *Ormonde*, II, 34.

in their abhorrence of popery, would readily swallow anything that was suggested to the prejudice of that sect. . . ."[72] The queen stood almost alone in this deluge of hate and panic. Wishing to communicate with her husband, she plaintively appealed to Secretary Nicholas: "I am so ill provided with persons I dare trust, that at this instant I have no person that I dare send. Pray do what you can to help me, if little Will Murray cannot go, to send this letter."[73] She appealed to a servant who himself quaked before the fury of public panic and who feared to appear too zealous in the king's service.

But even the fear of popery could not blind the populace of London to the fact that Parliament was at times an exacting master. Besides, Parliament appeared to have overreached its authority in its exactions from the king. The houses had had their demands satisfied during the past twelve months, and now it was time to slacken the progress of the revolution. There was still affection in the hearts of the English people for the institution of monarchy. During October and November, London made ready to show it had not lost all confidence in the king, preparing a gala celebration to welcome him on his return from Scotland. Secretary Nicholas instructed the king by letter to show himself gracious to the people on making his entry to London, "by speaking a short word now and then" as he passed among them to encourage them in their affections to his royal person.[74]

The king, having reached settlement with the Scots on matters relating to church and government, started his return to London about the middle of November. Traveling through northern England, he was received with acclaim on all sides. So gladdened were the people to have their king back in the country that the mayor

72. *Ibid.*, p. 13.

73. Green, *Letters of Henrietta Maria*, p. 44. William Murray, Earl of Dysart (1600?–51), was taken by his uncle to court when a boy and educated along with Prince Charles, who became his intimate friend. Mostly he served Charles and Henrietta as a mediator in their negotiations with the Scots. It was said that he became more reticent and discreet in speech when drunk, which was frequently his condition. *D.N.B.*, XXIX, 406–408.

74. *Correspondence between Charles I and Sir Edward Nicholas*, p. 35.

of York in delivering his address of welcome was moved to declare, ". . . our wives conceive with joy."[75] The queen met her husband at Theobalds, a country seat twelve miles north of London,[76] and Charles made his entry into the city on November 25. He and the Prince of Wales rode on horseback through the decorated streets, while the queen followed not far behind them in a carriage. Magistrates and guilds lined the way to the Guildhall, where the royal party was banqueted. In token of response to the splendid reception, the king made the mayor a baronet and knighted three aldermen. Following the reception, the king and queen went to Hampton Court, where they intended to spend the winter, but when a delegation from London went there and petitioned them to remain nearer to the city because of the stimulation their presence would give to business, they agreed to make the palace of Whitehall their residence during the winter months.[77]

The popular demonstration occasioned by the king's return disturbed his enemies in Parliament. On December 2 Commons passed by a narrow margin a long list of grievances known as the Grand Remonstrance, which in effect constituted an indictment of the king for violations enumerated in the document.

The king, on the other hand, was mistaken in thinking the show of popular esteem for him was a license to strike back at Parliament with impunity. When he attempted to supplant the governor of the Tower, who the spring before had refused to accept a body of troops he had sent to garrison the prison, his hand was stayed by an uprising of the apprentices of the city. Encouraged by this success, the apprentices descended with arms upon Parliament late in December to demand that bishops be forever excluded from government. They behaved in an insolent and violent manner, entering the halls and stopping for a time all deliberations there. They scoffed at the armed bands of London called out to quell the tumult, since they knew this military organization

75. Warburton, *Prince Rupert and the Cavaliers*, II, 203.
76. *Cal. S. P. Ven.*, XXV, 254.
77. "The Triumph of King Charles," *The Harleian Miscellany* (12 vols., London, 1808–11), V, 86–103; *Cal. S. P. Dom.*, 1641–43, pp. 167, 177–178, 192.

to be composed largely of their masters, who had encouraged them to march on Parliament in the first place.[78]

The king realized the move from the halls of Parliament to Whitehall Palace was but a short one, and in anticipation of a possible raid by the mob, he formed a corps of guards to protect his own household. For the king to increase any armed force at his command touched Parliament to the quick. As a countermove, they sent a delegation of fifty members to the king to ask that Parliament also be given a guard. If polite in his response, the king was noncommittal on the point of their request. The delegation of fifty and some other members of Parliament met unofficially in the Guildhall as a sort of junto to form policy for the two houses. The queen, they believed, was behind the rebuff they had received.[79] Outside the Guildhall, the more ignorant citizenry supposed this meeting portended some dire threat to Parliament. The city teemed with rumors that Sir John Winter, the queen's secretary, was in communication with Owen O'Neill, leader of the Irish rebels in Ulster, and it was said a Catholic army stood ready in the ports of southern Ireland to descend upon Lancashire.[80] The conference within the Guildhall resulted in a resolution to accuse the queen of conspiring against the public liberty and of secret intelligence with the rebels in Ireland.[81]

Charles was not long in hearing of the proposal to bring charges of treason in Parliament against his wife. Charles might have endured much, but Parliament had now struck where it hurt most. He moved with consummate determination and no doubt with a deep feeling of anger against this new threat. Believing the animosity toward his wife to be instigated by certain leaders, he had the attorney general prepare articles of accusation charging five members of the House of Commons and one member of the House of Lords with high treason. At the same time officers were

78. *Cal. S. P. Ven.*, XXV, 271–272.
79. *Ibid.*, p. 275.
80. *Manuscripts of Lord Montagu of Beaulieu*, p. 140.
81. *Cal. S. P. Ven.*, XXV, 276.

sent to the houses of the accused to seal all their papers. But rather than turn the five members over to the king as the articles demanded, the lower house replied that it would assume custody of those indicted and would stand as surety for their persons. Within the walls of the Commons hall, the king's move was denounced as a libel against parliamentary leaders, and the sealing of members' papers was declared a breach of their privilege.[82] The king took a desperate step against this defiance of his orders. With a small group of guards he went from Whitehall Palace to where Commons was in session personally to seize the five members. Only to Henrietta did he reveal his intention of entering the House of Commons. Just before setting out for this purpose, he embraced his wife and told her that in another hour he hoped to be master of his kingdom. After his departure the queen anxiously counted the minutes. An hour passed. At that moment the Countess of Carlisle, one of Henrietta's closest associates, entered the room in which she awaited her husband's return. Unable to contain her anxiety any longer, she said to Lady Carlisle, "Rejoice, for at this hour, I hope the King is master of this country, and that so-and-so are without doubt under arrest."[83] The countess displayed no inquietude over this news, but found excuse to leave almost immediately and dispatched a message to Pym, the principal person accused, with whom she had been in secret correspondence and with whom her relations were said to have been more than friendly. Meanwhile, the king had been detained on his way by petitioners, poor people who took the opportunity of a chance meeting to press some appeal or other. To avoid giving suspicion he stopped to hear them. On entering the House of Commons, he found that those he had come to apprehend had fled.[84]

Just how soon the queen realized her mistake is uncertain, but when she did become aware of it she withheld nothing from the king, and he on his part did not scold her for her thoughtless

82. Rushworth, *Historical Collections*, IV, 473–474.
83. Motteville, *Mémoires*, I, 207.
84. *Ibid.*, pp. 205–208.

act. It might well have been that even without Lady Carlisle's note the members of Commons had some presentiment of the king's intentions, for on the morning of the day the seizure was attempted, some of the king's bodyguard had been seen opening boxes of ammunition.[85]

The next day the king spoke before a meeting of members of Parliament assembled in the Guildhall. He assured them that those persons he had attempted to seize would be given a fair trial, that popery would be exterminated, and that the established church would be restored to as it had been in the days of Queen Elizabeth. But his assurances were not enough to overcome the distrust resulting from his entry into the House of Commons in violation of the privileges of that body. Londoners would not surrender those members of Parliament who had taken refuge within the walls of the city. The city itself was put in a state of war, and merchants dolefully closed their shops for three days. As the king rode away from the Guildhall following his speech, shouts of "privileges of Parliament" were heard from the citizens gathered on the street.[86]

Under pretense that His Majesty had been treacherously misinformed regarding the threat against his wife, Parliament started an investigation to learn who had fomented the rumor. A committee was sent to the queen to inquire where she had heard of such a plot. Probably fearing to expose her informer, the queen had to retract. "Upon better recollection of myself," she said in a letter to Parliament, "I do confess and acknowledge to have been mistaken, upon what was delivered me upon Discourse from some Member of the House of Commons; and am most heartily sorry for it; beseeching, with all humility, the pardon of the honorable House of Commons, for that my great mistake."[87]

Parliament had clearly overborne the king, and when crowds appeared before Whitehall carrying clubs and placards bearing

85. Warwick, *Memoirs*, p. 225n.
86. *Manuscripts of Lord Montagu of Beaulieu*, p. 141.
87. *J. C.*, II, 388, 399.

the word "liberty,"[88] Their Majesties resolved to quit London for a place of greater safety. They departed so suddenly that the mansion at Hampton Court could not be prepared for them before their arrival, making it necessary for the royal family to share a common bed on the first night of their stay there. From Hampton Court they moved on to the more distant safety of Windsor Castle.[89]

About this time Lord George Digby, who had absented himself from Parliament because of fear resulting from his defense of Strafford and his strong support of the king, fled to Holland.[90] Likewise, the queen made preparation for her own departure, offering the necessity of escorting her daughter Mary to Holland as reason for her going. This time Parliament did not object to her proposals, because it was thought that with the queen removed, the king would be exempt from her counsel and hence more amenable to the direction of Parliament.[91]

From Holland, however, the Prince of Orange wrote the Dutch ambassador in England to oppose Henrietta's visit by all possible means.[92] Ever since the marriage, Orange had been insisting that Mary be sent to him, but he did not wish the mother to come with her. In August of 1641 he had even attempted through appeal to Parliament to obtain an order for Mary's departure without the queen's escort.[93]

The king planned to accompany his wife to the coast and then to go to York, where the people were loyal to him. Even before the queen's departure, he directed the Earl of Newcastle to seize Hull, where there was a store of arms which had been collected for the campaign against the Scots. Coinciding with Newcastle's arrival before Hull was that of Sir John Hotham, who had been

88. Motteville, *Mémoires*, I, 207.
89. Ludlow, *Memoirs*, I, 26; *Cal. S. P. Ven.*, XXV, 281.
90. Rushworth, *Historical Collections*, IV, 554–555.
91. Prinsterer, *Archives*, IV, 7, 26.
92. *Ibid.*, III, 490–491; IV, 18–19.
93. *Ibid.*, III, 494.

sent by Parliament to assume command of the port. The mayor of the city, being confronted with such conflicting demands, refused to admit either envoy and sent a message to Parliament asking for further instructions.[94]

Thus matters stood when on February 19, 1642, Parliament presented to the king a declaration of grievances decrying the fact that "Priests, Jesuits, and Papists have powerful influence upon the Queen who is permitted to intermeddle with great affairs of state . . ." and suggesting as remedy that all priests and other Catholics be removed from employment about the queen's person; furthermore, that the king not entertain any advice from his wife.[95] These demands by way of remedy violated the marriage treaty with France, and from the queen's standpoint made her further residence in England impossible so long as Parliament was ascendant.

As a further impetus to the queen's flight, Parliament intercepted a letter sent from George Digby and, much against the king's objections, opened the missive to learn its contents. In this letter Digby said the Prince of Orange was willing to give aid against Parliament and advised the king to retire to a fortified place. Parliament thereupon declared Digby a traitor.[96] Insomuch as the letter had been dispatched to Henrietta, the implications in Parliament's reaction were clear.

Preparations for the queen's departure proceeded rapidly. "Things are done in such post-haste," wrote a royal servant to Sir John Pennington, commander of the ships which were to carry the queen across the Channel, "that I never heard of the like for the

94. *Ibid.*, IV, 18–19; Motteville, *Mémoires*, I, 208; *Cal. S. P. Ven.*, XXV, 284. For one who had spent lavishly to entertain the king and then had lost a fortune in fighting for his defense, William Cavendish, Earl and later Duke of Newcastle (1592–1676), appears to have received little compensation, unless the title of duke, conferred in 1665, is considered adequate recompense. Until the Scottish invasion, he held the county of York for the Royalists. Returning from exile after the restoration, he spent most of his time building up his estates and pursuing his equestrian interests. *D.N.B.*, IX, 364–369.

95. *J. C.*, II, 443–445.

96. *Ibid.*, pp. 432, 438, 439, 442–443; Green, *Letters of Henrietta Maria*, pp. 46–47.

voyage of persons of so great dignity."[97] The plan was for the queen to go from Windsor to Greenwich, from there to Rochester, on to Canterbury, and finally to Dover, where she was to embark. The queen took with her some of the crown jewels and all of the personal jewelry belonging to her and her husband. Only a few people of high rank were to accompany her to Holland: of the ladies, only the Duchess of Richmond, Lady Denbigh, and Lady Roxburgh, and of the lords, Arundel and Goring.[98]

At last the day of the queen's departure, February 23, 1642, arrived. "His Majesty," wrote the Venetian ambassador to England, "accompanied his wife as far as the shore, and did not know how to tear himself away from her, conversing with her in sweet discourse and affectionate embraces, nor would they restrain their tears, moving all those who were present."[99] As the ship bearing Henrietta to Holland moved out to sea, Charles rode along the water's edge waving his hat in farewell to his wife's response from the ship's railing, until finally the bellied sails dimmed into the distance, and the queen set her face against new trials and new dangers.[100]

97. Prinsterer, *Archives*, IV, 13; *Cal. S. P. Dom.*, 1641–43, p. 283.

98. Green, *Letters of Henrietta Maria*, p. 50. An unfailing supporter of Charles I, Henry Howard, Earl of Arundel (1608–52), had held various judicial and administrative offices in the northern counties. He voted against the attainder of Strafford and joined Charles in York soon after the royal standard had been raised near Nottingham in 1642. *D.N.B.*, XXVIII, 3.

99. *Cal. S. P. Ven.*, XXVI, 5.

100. Motteville, *Mémoires*, I, 208.

CHAPTER VI

NEW TRIALS, NEW DANGERS

1642-44 [ornament] THE Prince of Orange and his wife were present to welcome the queen when she landed at Brill on the first day of March, 1642.[1] Although Orange had told his ambassadors in London to oppose her coming in all ways possible, he performed his duty arising out of family relationship with an outward show of gladness. Orange had sent a fleet under Admiral van Tromp to escort her across the Channel, and after she landed the prince regaled her with what munificence his means allowed. Even so, the reception was modest for a queen of England, and the reluctance with which the prince welcomed her was indicated by complaints he made to his subjects concerning the cost of entertaining the queen.[2]

The prince received some recompense for the inconvenience of Henrietta's visit in at last having his daughter-in-law with him, as he had insisted for the past half-year. After remaining a few weeks longer in her mother's keeping, Princess Mary went to Orange's court to begin her training in the customs and language

1. *Calendar of State Papers, Venice* (38 vols., ed. Allen B. Hinds and others, London, 1864–1940), XXVI, 5 (referred to hereafter as *Cal. S. P. Ven.*).

2. Guillaume Groen van Prinsterer, *Archives ou Correspondence Inédit de la Maison d'Orange Nassau* (4 vols., Utrecht, 1859), IV, 29–30 (referred to hereafter as Prinsterer, *Archives*); *Cal. S. P. Ven.*, XXVI, 13.

of the Dutch, while her husband remained under the care and instruction of his tutors. So delighted had Orange been to gain this fair prize for his son that the marriage had been performed without definite arrangement as to dowry or living accommodations for the bride, and in view of Charles's circumstances these matters would have to wait many a day for final settlement.[3]

Although the Prince of Orange had put on a good front in receiving the queen, the burghers did not hide their objection to her presence in Holland. They cared little for what happened to monarchy in England and feared that the queen's continued sojourn in their country would bring trouble between them and the English parliament. Being themselves Protestant, they were not inclined to welcome a Catholic queen against the wishes of her Protestant subjects.[4] Unaccustomed to royalty, they made no show of obeisance before her, but greeted her as a fellow townsman without removing their hats in her presence and often seated themselves when conversing with her. There were instances when a Hollander, not knowing quite how to act before a queen, would merely stare at her and then walk away without saying a word.[5] If not really pleased with Dutch manners, the queen was highly amused by some of the incidents in her meetings with Hollanders. An Englishman who observed the feeling of the Dutch toward Henrietta's arrival wrote from Holland, "I verily thinke the Queen as the matter stands, will not trouble them long heere, and that yee shall have her in England yet a good while before Easter."[6]

Henrietta had more serious business in Holland than to visit Orange's court. Finding the hope of immediate aid from the prince to be delusive, a hope even more remote now that Princess Mary had been brought to Holland, the queen moved from The Hague

3. *Calendar of State Papers, Domestic Series, of the Reign of Charles I, 1625–1649* (23 vols., ed. John Bruce and others, London, 1858–97), 1641–43, p. 296 (referred to hereafter as *Cal. S. P. Dom.*).

4. *Cal. S. P. Ven.*, XXVI, 21.

5. Françoise Bertaut, Madame de Motteville, *Mémoires sur Anne d'Autriche et Sa Cour* (4 vols., ed. M. F. Riaux, Paris, n.d.), I, 209.

6. Henry Ellis, *Original Letters* (12 vols. in 3 series, London, 1824–46), ser. 2, III, 295.

to Breda, from which place she intended to superintend the sale and pawn of the jewels she had brought with her to raise money for the king. The pawning of the crown jewels proved difficult, since Parliament issued a notice that they had been taken from England without authorization. Hence brokers were uncertain over the security with which those jewels were offered. Henrietta wrote to the king requesting a special warrant for pawning the great collar of rubies. The personal jewelry belonging to Their Majesties was readily accepted, although the prices offered at the sale of these valuables equaled about half their real worth. Charles's pearl buttons were sold and the queen's own gold chain as well. It must have wrenched the queen's heart to part with these possessions, each carrying with it a token of love with which it was given and holding precious memories resulting from long years of ownership. "You cannot imagine how pretty your pearls were," she wrote to Charles of the buttons, "when they were taken out of the gold settings and made into a chain."[7] She placed her large chain and cross in pawn. Having little thought for personal attachments to the jewelry but looking only for profit, the shrewd, calculating dealers with whom she bargained struck a feeling of revulsion in the queen. "You may judge how," she informed her husband, "when they know we want money, they keep their foot on our throat."[8]

Besides trying to supply the king with money, Henrietta also attempted to advise him in his relations with Parliament. During the spring of 1642 she repeatedly urged him to seize Hull, a port through which military supplies for Royalist armies could be sent from Holland. During the first month of her stay in Holland she insisted this course of action be taken immediately, or if the king could not obtain Hull, he should secure Berwick or Newcastle, to which places she could send arms.[9] Charles replied that since it was considered expedient to let Parliament commit the first act of

7. *Harl. MSS 7379*, fol. 86.
8. *Ibid.*
9. *Ibid.*, fol. 16.

open hostility, he had been advised not to attempt the seizure of Hull. This advice the queen could not understand. Had Parliament not already committed the first act of aggression in placing its own followers in control of the city? She upbraided him for his lack of decision. "Delays have always ruined you," she stormed. "You are beginning again your old game of yielding everything."[10] By his failure to take positive action, Charles made her journey to the Netherlands appear ridiculous. And later, in May, she wrote, "My whole hope lies in your firmness and constancy, and when I hear anything to the contrary, I am mad."[11] Henrietta's lack of patience over her husband's indecision was aggravated by her own physical infirmities throughout these months, as indicated in the closing line of the same letter: "I have such a bad toothache I hardly know what I am doing." When ultimately Charles had to concede the loss of Hull to Parliament, the queen's retort was not so violent as her letters of warning might have led him to expect. "If you had not delayed this going to Hull so long as you did," she said with resignation, "I think that you would not have lost your magazine."[12]

Another issue which called forth strong remonstrance from the queen was the demand that the king grant Parliament control over appointment of officers in the militia. Charles was so firmly opposed on this issue that he hardly needed the queen to bolster his resolution. True, he did agree to allow Parliament power over the militia in England during the year he proposed to be in Ireland for the quelling of the Irish rebellion, but he resolutely refused any further incursion upon the crown's control over the army.[13] Nevertheless, the queen could not feel sure of her husband's determination. "Courage," she admonished him. "I have never had so much; it is a good augury."[14] Were Charles to allow the army to be sub-

10. Charles, Comte de Baillon, *Lettres de Henriette-Marie, Reine d'Angleterre* (Paris, 1877), pp. 372–373.

11. Mary Anne Everett Green, *Letters of Queen Henrietta Maria* (London, 1857), p. 63.

12. *Ibid.*, p. 80.

13. John Rushworth, *Historical Collections* (8 vols., London, 1721–22), IV, 518–519, 544–546.

14. Baillon, *Lettres de Henriette-Marie*, p. 382.

ject to Parliament, she could not think of returning to England, for her husband would no longer be able to protect her against her enemies, who she believed were determined to destroy her. In such an event she likely would find retreat in a convent.

Not long after arriving in Holland, she had looked to France as a place of possible refuge.[15] In answer to her request for asylum in the event she could not return to England, Richelieu, though not refusing her admission to the country, tried to discourage her coming by showing surprise that she could think of abandoning the Catholics in England.[16] The caution of the French government toward Henrietta's request arose out of a desire to avoid offense to Parliament. However, a few weeks following the receipt of Richelieu's letter, the French ambassador in England informed Parliament that the French king, Louis XIII, could not turn his sister away should she wish to return to the land of her birth.[17]

State policy in the Netherlands was guided by a similar policy of neutrality regarding the differences between king and Parliament in England. Although reluctant to give the king material aid, the Prince of Orange tried to show concern for the Royalist cause and at the same time to assert the neutral position of the Netherlands by sending ambassadors to act as mediators in the conflict. Henrietta advised Charles to accept the services of the mediators if it were agreed that the initial negotiations would be carried out in secret and with a chosen few of Parliament; then, should it appear Parliament sincerely wished to mediate, the further proceedings could be publicized.[18]

When the ambassadors approached Parliament on the subject

15. Green, *Letters of Henrietta Maria*, p. 80.

16. Armand J. du Plessis, Duke of Richelieu, Cardinal, *Lettres, Instructions Diplomatiques et Papiers d'État* (8 vols., ed. Denis M. L. Avenel [*Collection de Documents Inédits*], Paris, 1853–77), VI, 305 (referred to hereafter as Richelieu, *Lettres*).

17. *Manuscripts of Lord Montagu of Beaulieu, Historical Manuscripts Commission Report* (London, 1900), p. 152.

18. *Harl. MSS* 7379, fol. 67. Before departing for England, the Dutch ambassadors took formal leave of the queen. Henrietta was much amused when one of the envoys, assuming her dwarf, Geoffrey Hudson, to be the Prince of Wales, kissed the midget's hand. Baillon, *Lettres de Henriette-Marie*, p. 375.

of mediation, they were informed that the members preferred to have the queen act as their mediatrix with the king on the basis of His Majesty's offer of control over the militia for one year.[19] The response of Parliament was probably a political tactic intended to embarrass the queen, for in her letters to Charles she was absolutely opposed to any parliamentary authority over appointment of officers in the militia, and would entertain negotiations for a settlement only when Parliament was willing to become obedient to the king.[20]

By the summer of 1642 the queen had acquired a sufficient sum of money through the sale and pawn of jewelry to purchase arms and ammunition for Charles's use. Her letter of June 4 informed him she had six cannons, a hundred barrels of powder, two hundred pairs of pistols and carbines, and ten thousand pieces of money ready for shipment. Procuring the cannons had caused considerable difficulty. They were supplied by the Prince of Orange, although whether as a gift or by purchase was not specified. When the queen applied to Orange's secretary, the prince then being in the field with his own armies, she was allowed only four cannons rather than the six the prince had promised. Not until Lord Heenvliet, the former Dutch ambassador to England, consulted Orange was the matter straightened out to the satisfaction of Henrietta, who had taken umbrage over the secretary's niggardliness.[21]

In a letter of July 14 she proposed to send ten "loads" of powder, some pistols, thirty thousand pieces of money, one thousand saddles, five hundred carbines, and two hundred firelocks.[22] Whether these stores represented an augmentation of those described in the letter of June 4 is indefinite, for Henrietta was not systematic in enumerating the supplies she gathered, and there was nothing to indicate that a shipment had already been dispatched. It is certain, however, that the articles mentioned in her

19. *Cal. S. P. Ven.*, XXVI, 40, 47.
20. Green, *Letters of Henrietta Maria*, p. 77.
21. Prinsterer, *Archives*, IV, 38.
22. *Harl. MSS 7379*, fol. 50.

second letter were not sent until Prince Rupert sailed for England about July 21. In a letter of that date the queen said she was sending twenty thousand pieces of money instead of the thirty thousand previously mentioned.[23] In a message of September 9, in which she summed up her contribution to the king during the summer of 1642, she added to what she had listed in July a thousand each of muskets, pistols, and swords.[24] But Prince Rupert, along with the arms he carried with him, was forced back to Trexel by unfavorable weather and Parliamentary ships.[25] When early in August Rupert set out for England a second time, Henrietta sent with him the arms and ammunition already acquired and added to the consignment one thousand saddles, although the monetary contribution was reduced to eight thousand pieces.[26] The Venetian ambassador in England, writing of Rupert's landing at Newcastle, said the king's nephew brought with him a supply of arms,[27] but the queen's letter of September 9 stated that the "little ship" in which the arms were loaded was forced to return to the Netherlands.[28] The only other shipment of any size to be sent from the Netherlands evidently sailed in October. The queen's account of its contents was so confused that it is impossible to be certain of just how much was shipped, although five thousand muskets and eight to ten thousand pieces of money would appear to be a safe estimate.[29]

Because the English navy adhered to Parliament, only a small fraction of what Henrietta sent from the Netherlands actually got through to the king, and after October she attempted no more shipments until her return to England the following spring. Edward Hyde said that only one shipload of supplies reached the king

23. Baillon, *Lettres de Henriette-Marie*, p. 392. Henrietta did not give the denomination of the money she sent.

24. *Harl. MSS 7379*, fol. 69.

25. *Journals of the House of Lords*, V, 181–182, 199 (referred to hereafter as *J. L.*); *Cal. S. P. Ven.*, XXVI, 103.

26. *Harl. MSS 7379*, fols. 69, 75.

27. *Cal. S. P. Ven.*, XXVI, 142.

28. *Harl. MSS 7379*, fol. 69.

29. *Ibid.*, fol. 37.

after the vessel carrying the stores was forced by Parliamentary ships to flee into the Humber River, where it ran aground and Royalist forces recovered the cargo. This ship, the *Providence,* was probably one of those that sailed with the last shipment in October, for the Venetian ambassador in one of his dispatches of that month mentioned a shipload of munitions being received by the king, but he said the vessel put in at Newcastle rather than the Humber River.[30] The *Providence* carried a cargo of two hundred barrels of powder, between two and three thousand muskets, pistols, and carbines, and seven or eight field pieces.[31] This, then, was all besides some money that the queen was able to get through to Charles during her stay in Holland.

No authoritative or official record exists of the total amount of money raised by the queen in her husband's cause during the time she was in Holland. Miss Strickland's estimate of £2,000,000 certainly appears too high a figure.[32] Perhaps Madame de Motteville's assertion that Henrietta supplied enough money to arm four thousand men was a little nearer the truth, depending on what was considered necessary for the arming of a soldier.[33] Among papers later seized from George Digby was a sheet totaling the sum raised from loans and from pawn of jewelry at 1,281,700 guilders, or about £128,700,[34] which hardly denigrates the result of Henrietta's efforts, since Warburton estimates the English equivalent to have been £106,000.[35] But of the money and arms supplied, only the boatload mentioned above actually reached the armies with the

30. *Cal. S. P. Ven.,* XXVI, 189. At other times he mentions altogether four ships sent from Holland being seized by the Parliamentary navy; see pp. 103, 109, 178.

31. Edward Hyde, Earl of Clarendon, *The History of the Rebellion and Civil Wars in England* (7 vols., Oxford, 1849), II, 254–255, 294, 373; Bartholomew Warburton, *Memoirs of Prince Rupert and the Cavaliers* (3 vols., London, 1849), I, 300–301n.

32. Agnes Strickland, *Lives of the Queens of England* (8 vols., Boston, 1860), VIII, 73 .

33. Motteville, *Mémoires,* I, 209.

34. *The Lord George Digby's Cabinet* (London, 1646), p. 44.

35. Warburton, *Prince Rupert and the Cavaliers,* I, 283. See note on coinage, p. ix.

king. As will be seen, what Henrietta brought with her on her return to England was distributed among the Earl of Newcastle's forces in York. Even with more exact figures and records, therefore, the conclusion would be about the same as from the scattered and unsystematized accounts that do exist: the total amount of the queen's contribution from Holland, although helpful, was not enough to alter the fortunes of the war, while the munitions she directly supplied to the king were almost negligible.

This conclusion is not to belittle the efforts Henrietta was making to uphold her husband against Parliament, for she carried on her work under great handicap. She was extremely unhappy in the Netherlands. There were times when she must have felt that not even her love for Charles and her own stout courage could support her. "I do not doubt you sympathize with me," she wrote to her sister Christine, "but if you actually knew my unhappiness as it really is, you would pity me even more."[36] To Charles she wrote of suffering from pain in her eyes, which she thought might have resulted from too much crying.[37] In July she was further saddened by the death of her mother,[38] and to this sorrow was added the emotional anxiety she felt over the welfare of the children she had left in England. Oppressed as she was by these personal concerns, she still had to supervise the business of procuring money, purchasing munitions, and preparing shipments. The merchants with whom she dealt, seeing how urgent was her need for the supplies she bought, exacted high prices from her, and attempts to mulct the queen were not wanting.[39] Without the counsel and help of Jermyn, Finch, and Windebank, she told the king, she could not have continued her endeavors.[40] But more essential for her

36. Hermann Ferrero, *Lettres de Henriette-Marie à Sa Soeur Christine* (Rome, 1881), p. 61 (referred to hereafter as Ferrero, *Lettres à Christine*).

37. *Harl. MSS 7379*, fol. 47.

38. *Ibid.*, fol. 88.

39. *Manuscripts of J. Eliot Hodgkin, Historical Manuscripts Commission, Fifteenth Report* (London, 1897), Appendix, part 2, pp. 98–99.

40. Baillon, *Lettres de Henriette-Marie*, p. 394. A bigoted supporter of royal power, Sir John Finch, Baron Finch of Fordwich (1584–1660), was the speaker of

spirit, indeed the motivating factor behind all her actions, was her love for her husband, as she expressed it in a letter to him: "I must confess a truth about my weakness; that although I have no doubt of your affection for me, yet I am not sorry to see by your letters, the pretty things you have put in them upon the small services that I render you where I am. Their being agreeable to you, is a greater pleasure to me than I can express, and if anything could increase my affection and zeal in your service, that would do it—for you know I like to be praised—but it is impossible to be increased." [41]

She did not cease to solicit the Prince of Orange for his direct intervention in support of the Royalists against Parliament, but Frederick Henry dissembled. When Windebank's plea brought little response from the prince, Henrietta sent George Digby to him in renewal of her supplication. Orange avowed his determination to help the queen, saying he would have done so earlier had Windebank's apparent indifference not caused him to think that the queen did not seriously expect aid. [42] "It is necessary to do the impossible for the king and queen," he blustered, "for the possible is too little." [43] He did give the queen a small sum of money—about 30,000 guilders [44]—and held out promises of much more if he were

the House of Commons who in 1629 was held down in his chair until that body had passed resolutions repugnant to the king. Appointed chief justice of Common Pleas in 1633, he became notorious for the severity of his sentences, as when in 1637 he ordered the remainder of William Prynne's ears, which already had been clipped, to be severed closer to his head. Impeached by the Long Parliament late in 1640, Finch sought exile in Holland, after which event he was no longer important in political affairs, though he did remain on friendly terms with Henrietta Maria. D.N.B., XIX, 14–17.

41. Green, *Letters of Henrietta Maria*, p. 89.
42. *Cal. S. P. Ven.*, XXVI, 94; Baillon, *Lettres de Henriette-Marie*, p. 394.
43. *Ibid.*, p. 402.
44. *Harl. MSS 7379*, fol. 50. Whatever the Prince of Orange gave or loaned to the queen appears to have been paid back, as indicated in George Digby's papers seized three years later, following the battle of Sherburn. As recorded in Digby's accounts, the prince was returned 300,000 guilders, which was ten times the amount contributed to Royalist arms according to the queen's letter. It is probable that the Prince of Orange was compensated for paying off some of the queen's debts incurred in Holland, since he had at various times offered to furnish surety for loans she obtained from certain bankers at The Hague. Considering the

given a contract for marriage between his daughter and the Prince of Wales.[45]

Disappointed by the response of the prince, wearied by the haggling over arrangements for loans, and thoroughly disliked by the Dutch people, Henrietta longed to return to her husband and children. Her wish was brought nearer to possibility when on August 12 Charles raised his battle standard at Nottingham, thereby signifying the final break between king and Parliament. They were now at war, which removed the likelihood of an accommodation between them as the queen so much feared. By the last week of August she wrote Charles of her happiness to think that she would leave Holland soon, and on the last day of the month she sent a letter asking him where she should disembark in England.[46]

Her hopes for a speedy departure received a setback when news reached her that means were being sought to bring accord between the warring parties in England. In a letter of September 10 she reminded Charles of his promise that he would never make peace with Parliament without her knowledge and consent, and closed her letter by saying that if he reached an agreement allowing the continued existence of the present parliament, she would never return to England.[47] Simultaneously with her warning to Charles, she sent her former almoner, the Bishop of Angoulême, who had been visiting her in the Netherlands, to obtain permission for her entry into France.[48] On this occasion Richelieu was more definite in his answer than he had been during the preceding spring. If possible, he advised, Henrietta should return to England, but failing that she would be welcomed in France, where a pension would be provided for her needs.[49]

---

unpopularity of the Royalist cause in Holland and the fact that Dutch armies were still engaged against the Spanish Netherlands, Orange can hardly be censured for failing to go to the rescue of King Charles. See *George Digby's Cabinet*, p. 44.

45. *Cal. S. P. Ven.*, XXVI, 131.
46. *Harl. MSS 7379*, fols. 14, 27.
47. *Ibid.*, fol. 36.
48. *Ibid.*, fol. 76; *Cal. S. P. Ven.*, XXVI, 164.
49. Richelieu, *Lettres*, VII, 136–137.

Having received so encouraging a reply, Henrietta began to look with more favor upon France as a place of retreat. Even after Charles had assured her that no treaty would be concluded with Parliament, she wrote in glowing terms of the services she could render him if allowed to go to France, whereas if she returned to England she might encumber his affairs, since it was difficult for women to travel with an army. Persons high in the service of the French king, and above all the king himself, urged her to come to France. Nevertheless, if Charles wanted her to return to England, she would obey his orders.[50] Evidently Charles wished his wife with him rather than in France, for during October Henrietta in her correspondence with him repeatedly inquired where she should land.[51]

Among her other letters of this month were several intended as a ruse to cause trouble for John Pym. "I received yesterday a letter from Pym," she wrote on October 6, "by which he sends me word that I am offended with him, because he has not had a letter from me for a long time. I beg you tell him that this is not the case, and that I am as much his friend as ever." And again, on October 29: "As to the thirty thousand pieces which Pym sends me word have been promised a long time ago, and not sent, you will also be shown how they have been employed most usefully for your service."[52] The purpose of these letters was too apparent to cause Pym any embarrassment before Parliament.

Parliament, on the other hand, had been causing the queen distress in Holland and had thereby increased her desire to leave the country. Late in August, Walter Strickland was sent as ambassador from Parliament to the Netherlands. Henrietta was furious in her protestation to any recognition being given him. "If I do not go crazy, it will be a great miracle," she wrote to Charles in comment upon the incident.[53] At first Strickland was refused a hearing

50. *Egerton MSS 2619*, fol. 9; *Harl. MSS 7379*, fol. 76.
51. *Ibid.*, fol. 37; *Harl. MSS 6988*, fol. 163.
52. *Harl. MSS 7379*, fols. 38, 39.
53. *Ibid.*, fol. 79.

by the Estates, or legislative body, on the excuse that his credentials were not in proper order. But among the people of the Netherlands, and especially among the strong municipal administrations, Strickland received a ready welcome.[54] He appealed to the religious sentiments of the people in order to gain support, asking that the Dutch free the English from tyranny in matters of religion, as earlier during the reign of Elizabeth the English had fought for religious liberty in the Netherlands. "It is the Jesuitical faction here [in England]," his instructions declared, "that hath corrupted the Counsels of our King, the Consciences of the greater part of our Clergy, which hath plotted so many mischievous designs to destroy the Parliament, and still endeavoreth to destroy the Parliament. . . ."[55] The Prince of Orange tried to quiet the queen's anger by telling her that Strickland was of such low social origin he should not be taken seriously in political matters. Nevertheless, if not officially recognized as the English ambassador, Strickland was permitted to state his case before a committee of the Estates,[56] and in November the Estates voted that no more arms or men were to be sent from the Netherlands to serve the Royalist cause in England. Loopholes were readily found in this new law, and except for the efforts of some burgomasters, no serious attempt was made to enforce it, despite the continued protests of Parliament.[57]

In addition to the annoyance caused by Strickland's presence in Holland, the queen was troubled by rumors coming from England. So tenuous was her means of communication with Charles that weeks passed without word from him. A poor woman employed for the queen's intelligence service in Portsmouth reported that a plot had been formed to seize the king;[58] again, the king was said to be dead and the Prince of Wales a prisoner, and there were men who avowed they had touched the dead body of Prince Rupert.

54. *Cal. S. P. Ven.*, XXVI, 145, 157.
55. Rushworth, *Historical Collections*, V, 157–158.
56. Prinsterer, *Archives*, IV, 68–69.
57. *Egerton MSS 2619*, fol. 11; Rushworth, *Historical Collections*, V, 159–160.
58. *Harl. MSS 7379*, fol. 49.

As for battles, hardly a day passed without news of the Royalists' destruction.[59] In despair, the queen closed one of her letters to Charles: "I need the air of England."[60]

At last the queen set November 16 as the date of her departure,[61] but had to change her plans when the Earl of Newcastle informed her that he had been driven back to Durham by Parliamentary forces.[62] The north of England was not yet secure enough in Royalist possession to receive the queen. Meanwhile, in September, Charles had left Nottingham and marched with his army to the west of England, ultimately to make his headquarters at Oxford.[63]

There was still work for Henrietta in the Netherlands. On November 24 Cardinal Richelieu died, after having guided the diplomatic policy of France for almost two decades. His passing was looked upon as a good omen for the Royalists, since he, believing that Charles favored Spain over France, was not inclined to aid the king against Parliament.[64] Early the following year Henrietta sent Walter Montagu to France to determine whether the government there, now under the leadership of Cardinal Mazarin, would give assistance to Charles.[65]

Already, during the fall of 1642, Henrietta had attempted to negotiate for help from Denmark. She had asked Charles whether she should accept the offer of Charles Louis, deposed Elector of the Palatinate and nephew of Charles, to go to Denmark in request for a loan.[66] Before Charles could answer her question, the Danish ambassador in passing through the Netherlands on his way to England conferred with the queen. Henrietta urged Charles to treat the envoy with every consideration, and suggested that ships

59. *Ibid.*
60. *Ibid.*
61. *Cal. S. P. Ven.*, XXVI, 193.
62. *Harl. MSS 7379*, fol. 20.
63. *Cal. S. P. Dom.*, 1642, p. 389.
64. *Cal. S. P. Ven.*, XXVI, 211.
65. *Harl. MSS 7379*, fol. 86.
66. *Egerton MSS 2619*, fol. 18; *Harl. MSS 7379*, fol. 14. Frederick V, father of Charles Louis and "winter king" of Bohemia, had died in 1632.

were what was most needed from Denmark and were the form of aid that Denmark could most easily afford to give.[67] Charles seemingly did not act on her advice, for in a letter of December 29 she expressed disappointment that he had not asked the Danish king for arms, and told him that Denmark was a more likely source of assistance than either France or the Netherlands.[68]

While dealing with France and Denmark for loans, Henrietta kept her departure from Holland in preparation. During December, Newcastle's military position in the northern part of England improved somewhat with the return of his forces to York. This news caused the queen to hasten plans for her departure. On January 21, 1643, she sent her coaches to be embarked at Scheveningen, where eleven warships stood ready to transport her and her followers along with some military supplies back to England.[69] In the Netherlands everyone from the Prince of Orange and his wife down to the lowest citizens awaited her leaving with great impatience. So long had her departure been pending that when at last she set sail on February 2, the news was a welcome relief to the Netherlanders.

But the Dutch were not yet rid of Henrietta—not quite. For after having been tossed about for nine days by one of the worst storms in years, Henrietta's fleet returned to Scheveningen. "I confess," she wrote in a letter to Charles shortly after landing at Scheveningen, "that I never expected to see you again."[70] Henrietta's fears had been shared by those persons who went through the harrowing experience with her. Buffeted about on the raging sea, they made preparation for the end by consulting their confessor, and all sense of shame being eradicated by the nearness of death, shouted out their sins above the din of the storm so that their secrets fell upon ears not intended to hear them. Henrietta, who maintained her courage much better than the ladies with her, was later to laugh heartily on recalling the admissions she had

67. *Ibid.*, fol. 100.
68. *Ibid.*, fols. 12, 86.
69. *Cal. S. P. Ven.*, XXVI, 227, 230, 233.
70. *Egerton MSS 2619*, fol. 17; *Harl. MSS 7379*, fol. 62.

overheard. The disheveled party that landed at Scheveningen had had little food or sleep for more than a week, and most of them were distressingly seasick. Since the gyration of the ships had made personal sanitation impossible, much of their clothing had to be burned, and the sickest of the passengers had to be carried from the ships which had survived the storm. Among the company was a Capuchin, who, celebrating a mass of thanksgiving at the water's edge just after disembarking, was held upright by two attendants in order to carry out the observance.[71]

Nothing daunted by the loss of two of her ships, Henrietta made ready for a second attempt to reach England. Just before her second departure, one of her ships was detained by the government in the province of Holland on the excuse that the queen had obtained no license for the shipment of munitions contained in the hold of the vessel. Having experienced so many annoyances in the Netherlands, the queen's patience snapped, and she sent a stinging note of rebuke to the Estates of the Netherlands. She explained that the States General had forbidden the issuing of licenses for shipment of arms, and that such munitions as her ships carried were for their defense in passage to England. She closed her protest by reminding the Estates that this most recent inconvenience inflicted upon her was a violation of English rights existing under treaties previously concluded between England and the Netherlands.[72]

The queen again sailed for England late in February. This voyage was troubled not by tempests but by Parliamentary ships sent to intercept the queen's passage. How determined Parliamentary leaders were in their design to seize the queen was shown when Pym told the members of the House of Commons that if they would only be patient, they might have in their possession so great a prize that they could fix their own conditions in terminating the war.[73] But Henrietta's ships escaped the interceptors by cutting

71. Motteville, *Mémoires*, I, 210–211.
72. Rushworth, *Historical Collections*, V, 163; *Cal. S. P. Ven.*, XXVI, 247–248.
73. Green, *Letters of Henrietta Maria*, pp. 165–166.

sharply to the southwest after having made an attempt to reach Newcastle, and touched the coast at Bridlington Bay.

On the first night after reaching land, Henrietta slept in a cottage near the quay where her boats were moored. Early the next morning the Parliamentary fleet, having discovered the eluders, entered the bay and began firing upon the ships anchored there. Since the house in which Henrietta rested was near the targets of the attack, she was forced to rise from her bed and to flee in such clothes as she could hastily gather about her to the dubious safety of a ditch behind the nearby village. As she hurried for shelter, cannon shot striking the ground sprayed dirt over her, and a soldier about twenty paces away was shot dead. When the receding tide forced the large Parliamentary ships to withdraw seaward, the attack ended without having inflicted damage on the munitions contained in the holds of the vessels moored in the harbor.[74]

Henrietta had no sooner reached England than she began to dispense to the Duke of Newcastle's armies those supplies she had intended for Charles's forces. From Bridlington Bay she wrote the king that she had given up half of the stock of a thousand saddles to troopers in the vicinity where she disembarked.[75] Newcastle had, of course, rushed several units of foot and cavalry to the place of landing in order to protect the queen and the supplies she had brought with her.

After being detained at Bridlington Bay for a little more than a week by difficulty in obtaining wagons to transport the store of munitions, Henrietta went to York, where she was greeted by the gentry of the surrounding shire.[76] Here also some of the Scottish peers visited her and conferred on problems relating to the king's affairs in Scotland. The Duke of Hamilton and the Marquis of Montrose represented two entirely different policies regarding Scotland, although both were supporters of the king's authority there. Montrose, who had originally signed the National Covenant

74. *Harl. MSS 7379*, fol. 78.
75. *Ibid.*, fol. 81.
76. Green, *Letters of Henrietta Maria*, p. 186.

but who afterward became the most valiant champion of monarchy in Scotland, warned Henrietta that the factious nobility of that country would almost certainly join with Parliament in time, and asked for £10,000 to raise an army with which he proposed to put down all of the king's enemies in the northern kingdom. Hamilton, while not denying that there was much opposition to the king, advised a policy of peace, saying he could stir up so much internal strife as the king's viceroy in Scotland that the Scots would be too busy to think of alliance with Parliament. With regard to Scottish affairs, the queen acted entirely upon the instruction of the king, who decided to follow the policy recommended by Hamilton.[77]

Among other visitors to the queen at York was Sir Hugh Cholmley, governor of the port of Scarborough under Parliamentary command. Cholmley had opposed the king for what he considered royal encroachment upon the rights of Parliament, but found himself in unpleasant company when the rebellion became largely a Puritan movement, for he was certainly no Puritan. Wishing to transfer his allegiance back to the king, Cholmley told the queen he would surrender Scarborough to her if she agreed she would do nothing to deter the king from fulfilling his promises to maintain the government of England as constitutionally established, and if she would not prevent her husband from making a peace. Having the queen's assent to his conditions, Cholmley returned to Scarborough, and after some vicissitudes that town became a royal garrison.[78]

77. Gilbert Burnet, *The Memoirs of the Lives and Actions of James and William, Dukes of Hamilton and Castleherald* (London, 1677), p. 212; Mark Napier, *The Life and Times of Montrose* (Edinburgh, 1840), pp. 228–230, 238–239; Robert Baillie, *Letters and Journals* (3 vols., Edinburgh, 1842), II, 73. One of the earliest supporters of the National Covenant in Scotland, James Graham, first Marquis and fifth Earl of Montrose (1612–54), later turned against the covenanters. He disliked Presbyterian ministers even more than Anglican bishops, and he resented the overbearing power of the great nobility—the Hamiltons and the Argylls—who were among the chief defenders of Presbyterianism. The king was slow to trust him, and in fact did not do so until after the Scots had joined with the Parliamentary army. As leader of the Royalist forces in Scotland, Montrose proved to be the ablest strategist among Charles's generals.

78. *MSS Clar. S. P. 1669*, pp. 8–11; Baillon, *Lettres de Henriette-Marie,*

From Oxford came news of other negotiations between the Royalist and Parliamentary factions. Ever since the outbreak of hostilities, there had been intermittent attempts by one party or the other to bring about a settlement. Now, when the king's military fortunes appeared to be in the ascendant, Parliament presented an offer for a cessation of hostilities, looking forward to peace. Upon receiving the articles of cessation from Parliament, Charles wrote his wife that while he had no intention of coming to an agreement with Parliament on the basis of the terms presented, he would feign an attempt to negotiate in order to gain time and to cast odium upon his enemies as the fomenters of war.[79] Charles's design was ruined when his letter was intercepted and published by Parliament. That the queen never received his writing explains her letter of March 30, 1643, in which she warned Charles against a compromise allowing the continuance of the parliament then in session. "And for my particular," she wrote, "if you make a peace and disband your army before there is an end to this perpetual Parliament, I am absolutely resolved to go into France, not being willing to fall again into the hands of these people, being well assured that if the power remains with them, it will not be well for me in England."[80]

To a considerable number of members in Parliament, especially in the House of Lords, who earnestly desired peace, the queen appeared to be the greatest obstruction to an understanding between the king and his people.[81] Certainly the queen had many enemies even prior to her return from Holland, but now the mounting enmity against her was indicated when Parliament appointed a committee of three to take with them a body of troops for the purpose of seizing the Capuchins and defacing the queen's chapel. After breaking down the doors of the chapel, the soldiers smashed

---

p. 461. On one occasion Charles personally told Sir Hugh Cholmley (1600–59) that if he did not desist in his resistance to royal policies, he would have him hanged. *D.N.B.*, X, 268–269.

79. Green, *Letters of Henrietta Maria*, p. 174.
80. *The Works of Charles I* (2 vols., Aberdeen, Scotland, 1766), I, 294.
81. Green, *Letters of Henrietta Maria*, p. 178n.

the altar, broke images, burned ornaments and books, and carried off the Capuchins, who, after being placed in custody of the French ambassador, were transported to France.[82]

The queen had an opportunity to reprieve herself in the view of Parliament when, early in May, Pym and other leaders sent a messenger asking her to prevail upon her husband to accept terms already advanced for a cessation of fighting. They promised that during the time she was in communication with the king, their armies would make no move against the Royalists. Evidently the peace party in Parliament did not realize how strongly Henrietta was opposed to them. Of one point she was certain: never a peace unless the Long Parliament was first abolished. The most peacefully inclined member of Parliament could not accept such a condition. Taking care not to reveal her adamantine opposition to any settlement with Parliament, Henrietta agreed to write Charles in support of the offer of a cessation, but her real purpose was to take advantage of the promised truce to transport to Oxford a shipment of gunpowder which Charles desperately needed. By the time Pym realized the trick she had played, the powder had reached Charles, and the Parliamentary general, the Earl of Essex, had missed an opportunity of taking Oxford.[83]

In the House of Commons there were members who were more violent in their opposition to the queen than was Pym, and the culmination of their distrust was expressed in June when the lower

82. *Journals of the House of Commons*, III, 24 (referred to hereafter as *J. C.*); *Cal. S. P. Ven.*, XXVI, 262; Cyprien de Gamache, *Memoirs of the Mission in England of the Capuchin Friars of the Province of Paris, from the Year 1630 to 1669* (in vol. II, 293–501, of Thomas Birch, *The Court and Times of Charles I* [2 vols., London, 1848]), pp. 352–353 (referred to hereafter as Gamache, *Memoirs*).

83. *Harl. MSS 7379*, fol. 85; Samuel Rawson Gardiner, *History of the Great Civil War, 1642–1649* (4 vols., London, 1894), I, 133–134. Robert Devereaux, Earl of Essex (1591–1646), was the son of that Earl of Essex who had been Elizabeth's favorite and who was beheaded for treason late in the queen's reign. The younger Essex suffered calumny at the court when his wife was taken from him by Robert Carr, the beloved protégé of James I. Although filling a number of military appointments before the outbreak of the Civil War, Essex had done little or no actual fighting. When the Long Parliament convened in 1640, he threw in his lot with the king's opponents and in 1642 was made general of the Parliamentary army. *D.N.B.*, XIV, 440–443.

house voted the impeachment of the queen on a charge of high treason.[84] To escape the question of the doubtful legality of such an accusation against a queen of England, Parliament maintained that having never been ceremoniously enthroned, Henrietta was subject to the law as was any other English citizen. Since the formality of the law required the name and rank of the accused, some difficulty was had in avoiding the name of Bourbon, a name which Parliament for diplomatic reasons had no wish to offend.[85]

The queen was not greatly concerned over her impeachment in Commons. To her the issue seemed drawn and could result only in her own annihilation or that of Parliament. In the meantime she had been occupied with characteristic ardor in furthering Newcastle's struggle to bring all of Yorkshire under Royalist control.

Thomas Fairfax had been driven into Leeds, where he was surrounded on all sides by Newcastle's forces. If Newcastle took Leeds, all of Yorkshire except Hull would be his, and he could then proceed against Bradford and Manchester for the winning of Lancashire, where the Earl of Derby was hard pressed by Parliamentary armies.[86] Henrietta became so occupied with the war in northern England that from time to time she gave Newcastle those military supplies intended for Charles's forces around Oxford.[87] On May 27 she wrote Charles that she wanted to stay in Yorkshire

84. *J. C.*, III, 98, 139.

85. *Cal. S. P. Ven.*, XXVI, 280.

86. *Ibid.*, p. 240; *Harl. MSS* 7379, fol. 5. Thomas, Lord Fairfax (1612–71), held high commands in the Parliamentary army during the Civil War. It was he who led the Parliamentary army which defeated the king's military power. As one of the judges who tried Charles I for treason in 1649, he attempted to exercise a restraining influence. (*D.N.B.*, XVIII, 141–149.) On the outbreak of the Civil War, James Stanley, Earl of Derby (1607–51), who had taken no part in the meetings of the Long Parliament, ardently gave his energy and resources to providing arms and fighting for the king. After the defeat of the Royalists in northern England, he withdrew to the Isle of Man, where he would have been relatively safe from the retribution of Parliament had he not joined Charles II and the Scots in 1651 to restore monarchy in England. He was with Charles II at the battle of Worcester, and after that crushing defeat, wandered with him to southern England in flight before Parliamentary pursuers. Caught by the enemy, he was executed as a traitor. (*D.N.B.*, LIV, 71–73.)

87. *Harl. MSS* 7379, fols. 5, 17; Baillon, *Lettres de Henriette-Marie*, pp. 475–476.

until the fall of Leeds, which was then being besieged by New-castle.[88] She was forced to dispense with the last of her military stores to arm a regiment in compliance with Newcastle's request, but exacted a promise that those troops she had armed would be permitted to go with her whenever she went to her husband. She explained to Charles that she felt compelled to relinquish the last of her arms, for otherwise if any misfortune happened before Leeds, she would receive the blame. Instead of a store of munitions, she said, she would furnish Charles a well-supplied army in the north and would bring to Oxford a little army fully equipped.[89] She hoped to place those units which remained with her at York under the command of Jermyn and to send them into Lincolnshire to clear that area of Parliamentary troops, but this design was foiled when Fairfax, having broken out of Leeds, captured the town of Wakefield, thereby making York vulnerable to attack from the south.[90]

Immersed in the broils and uncertainties of war, the queen kept her spirits high and her pen busy in soliciting aid from foreign powers. She wrote Newcastle that if he had good news concerning the likelihood of aid from Denmark, she had similar news from France.[91] Indeed, the government in France had never seemed so favorably inclined to help the king.[92] She advised Charles to trade the Shetland Islands and the Orkneys off the coast of Scotland to the King of Denmark in exchange for war materials, but to with-hold transfer of the islands until he had been fully restored to power in order to keep the agreement a secret from the Scots, who would deeply resent such disposition of their territory.[93] When the Marquis of Montrose wrote the queen a letter of reproach blaming the bad condition of the king's affairs in Scotland on her refusal to follow the advice he had given during the conference at York, she

88. *Ibid.*, p. 490.
89. *Harl. MSS 7379*, fols. 5, 10.
90. *Ibid.*, fol. 62.
91. *Harl. MSS 6988*, fol. 145.
92. *Cal. S. P. Ven.*, XXVI, 278.
93. *Harl. MSS 7379*, fol. 62.

glibly replied that the Scottish nobility should not fight so much among themselves and tried to soothe Montrose by telling him that he would soon be plentifully supplied with arms from Denmark, although in truth she had not sufficient basis to make such a promise.[94] So that no effort would be spared in the attempt to obtain foreign aid, she also kept open communications with the Prince of Orange. There was a possibility of help from Orange if he could see some advantage for himself in giving aid to the Royalist armies. Henrietta held out the hope of marriage between Prince Charles and the daughter of Orange. In a letter of May 30 she told Orange that the king had given her full power to deal for a marriage, but that all negotiations must be kept completely secret from Parliament.[95]

Henrietta's part in the Yorkshire campaign was soon to end, although hardly before the extent of Royalist success in that county had been achieved. In answer to Henrietta's letter of May 27, Charles demanded that she start immediately for Oxford. In the same letter he also ordered Newcastle to bring his army to Oxford, which was in danger of siege by Essex. The consternation caused in Yorkshire by Charles's command that the whole of the Royalist army in the county be transferred to Oxford can be imagined when even the queen's proposal to take the small fraction of troops she had armed stirred up local jealousy and provoked charges that Yorkshire, where Royalist arms up to that time had been most successful, was being deprived of forces in order to hold Oxford. The queen among others was caught up in this feeling of local patriotism and pride in what had been achieved in Yorkshire, and told Newcastle that he did not need to give any attention to the king's directive.[96]

So far as she was personally concerned, the queen did obey her husband's wish. On June 27 she wrote him from Newark, her principal stopping place, located approximately halfway between

94. Green, *Letters of Henrietta Maria*, p. 217.
95. Prinsterer, *Archives*, IV, 100–101.
96. *Harl. MSS 6988*, fol. 145.

York and Oxford. The queen described the forces she would bring with her to Oxford as consisting of three thousand foot, two thousand cavalry, and six cannons, all under the command of Henry Jermyn, and having the queen herself, or "her she-generalissima," in charge of the baggage train. Of her own forces, she was leaving behind in Yorkshire two thousand foot soldiers, arms for five hundred more, and twenty companies of horses for the defense of Nottinghamshire.[97]

Henrietta proposed to remain in Newark for at least two days in hope that the younger Hotham, who lately had escaped imprisonment at the hands of Parliament, would surrender Hull and Lincoln to her.[98] The Hothams, father and son, had for several months past been negotiating the betrayal of the posts they held to the Royalists.[99] Their plot discovered, they were both seized and imprisoned. Before the escaped Captain Hotham could carry through his intrigue, he was again apprehended, and Hull remained in control of Parliamentary forces—the only stronghold in Yorkshire still possessed by Parliament.[100]

Setting out from Newark on July 3, Henrietta and her army went by way of Ashby-de-la-Zouch, Croxall, Walsol, and King's Norton to Stratford-on-Avon, where they were met by Prince Rupert and his cavalry on July 11. On July 13 Henrietta reached Keinton, near to which, at the foot of Edgehill, took place the happy meeting with Charles and her two eldest sons, from whom she had been separated for sixteen months. Their Majesties slept that night at Wroxton and next day went on to Woodstock, where

97. Green, *Letters of Henrietta Maria*, p. 222. In her concern over the winning of Yorkshire, it appears the queen actually did the Royalist cause a disservice, although had she been of another mind, she probably could not have made Newcastle obey the king's order to concentrate Royalist forces in the west. A Royalist victory in the areas near the Scottish border could hardly have any other result than to bring the Scots into the war on the side of Parliament, and because of concern over provincial security, the king's armies could not coordinate their efforts for the common purpose of a victory over Parliament.

98. *Ibid.*, p. 221.

99. Baillon, *Lettres de Henriette-Marie*, p. 472.

100. Rushworth, *Historical Collections*, V, 275.

they remained a short time until the disappearance of symptoms of plague permitted their entry into Oxford.[101]

Even at Oxford the queen continued to be interested in military operations in Yorkshire. She seemed to look upon the fight in the north as particularly her war. A month after reaching Oxford, she wrote Newcastle that the king had asked her to convey his order directing the earl to march into Suffolk, Norfolk, or Huntingdon-shire. "I answered him," she assured Newcastle, "that you were a better judge than he of that, and that I should not do it. The truth is they envy your army."[102] Henrietta failed to realize that Charles wished Newcastle to keep Cromwell occupied in the eastern counties while the king's forces were besieging Gloucester, the stronghold which hindered the march of Royalist armies against London.[103] Apparently Newcastle did not respond to the queen's letters, or did not respond often enough to please her, for about a week later she wrote him, saying, "It is a long time since we heard Yorkshire spoken about. I must scold you a little for not sending oftener."[104] And again, on October 7, she complained, "It is so long since I received tidings from you." In this same writing she offered him his former office of tutor to Prince Charles, which was soon to fall vacant, along with two other offices that she did not specify, and closed by saying, "I have nothing so much in my thoughts as to show you and all the world the esteem in which I hold you. If I had chosen to act ceremoniously, I should have had this written to you by another, but that is all very well only where there is no esteem, such as I have for you and as this is written with frankness, I request a reply of the same."[105]

101. Green, *Letters of Henrietta Maria*, pp. 223–224.

102. *Harl. MSS 6988*, fol. 152.

103. Sir Philip Warwick, *Memoirs of the Reign of Charles I* (London, 1702), p. 290.

104. *Harl. MSS 6988*, fol. 155.

105. *Ibid.*, fol. 158. Henrietta's coquettish manner in her letters to Newcastle might lead one to suspect her of being amorously drawn to him had she not been deeply devoted to her husband. Her behavior is difficult to explain unless we remember that she was a Frenchwoman in an age when flirtations, harmless or otherwise, were a part of court etiquette and that she embraced friendships with

Another carry-over from the events and developments of the summer was the high hope of assistance from France. The meaning of these promises became clearer when in October Mazarin sent the Count of Harcourt to mediate between the king and Parliament. The extent of Harcourt's commitments in support of the king was evidently to be conditioned by the offers Charles would make to assist France in her fight against Spain. Cardinal Mazarin wished to recruit soldiers in Ireland, where a year's cessation of arms had been concluded on September 15, 1643, and to have English naval support in the event of Charles's restoration to power.[106] Mazarin's letters to Harcourt were more concerned with obtaining the release of Walter Montagu, who, coming in the train of Harcourt, was discovered in the disguise he had assumed and was imprisoned by Parliament.[107] At first Mazarin told Harcourt to try to obtain Montagu's freedom but not to endanger relations with Parliament by enlarging upon the affair. His later letters were much more insistent upon the point as being a matter which personally concerned the queen regent of France, Anne of Austria.[108]

Charles had sufficient reason to wish mediation. The danger of invasion from the north became much more acute when on September 22, 1643, the House of Commons and Assembly of Divines swore to the Covenant, thus fulfilling the requisites for Scottish participation in the war on the side of Parliament.[109] Following the failure of Harcourt's mission, the king took the advice of his friends in London to write the mayor, aldermen, and people

enthusiasm. Also, it could have been that she tried to sweeten the cantankerous spirit of Newcastle, whose rancor toward others repeatedly called for her offices of appeasement. Baillon, *Lettres de Henriette-Marie*, pp. 475-476; *Harl. MSS 6988*, fol. 172.

106. Cardinal de Mazarin, *Lettres* (9 vols., ed. P. A. Chéruel [Collection de Documents Inédits], Paris, 1872-1906), I, 343-345, 393-394; *Cal. S. P. Ven.*, XXVII, 4.

107. Rushworth, *Historical Collections*, V, 579-580; Green, *Letters of Henrietta Maria*, p. 233.

108. Mazarin, *Lettres*, I, 421-423, 448-449, 460-461, 539; *Cal. S. P. Ven.*, XXVII, 30. Louis XIII had died on May 4, 1643, leaving a small son who assumed the title of Louis XIV.

109. Rushworth, *Historical Collections*, V, 472-474, 475.

of the city a letter in which His Majesty told them he was ready to consider any petitions they might wish to present to him, and implied that he would give satisfaction on questions of religion. This step was undertaken with the intention of bringing about division between Parliament and the city, where it was believed the houses were becoming unpopular.[110]

It was still supposed at the court in Oxford that, Harcourt's efforts having achieved nothing, France would be forthcoming with arms and munitions to reinstate Charles in his former position. From Paris, Lord Goring, who had been sent as Royalist ambassador to France, informed Henrietta that Mazarin determinedly avowed his intentions of helping the King of England to the limit of France's ability, now that mediation talks had broken down. Goring wished to know the form of aid he should request once Mazarin got around to the business of fulfilling his promises.[111]

If Mazarin were to rescue Charles, his help would have to be timely, for on January 15, 1644, the Scottish army crossed the Tweed into Northumberland.[112] In this emergency the king had a more certain friend in the Marquis of Montrose, who, being then in Oxford, was dispatched to Scotland as governor general to raise forces and carry on the war there in the king's behalf.[113]

Last-minute efforts were undertaken on the Royalist side to bring about a cessation of hostilities before the foray of the Scots. For the purpose of searching out a means to peace, Charles on January 22 convened those members of Parliament who had followed him to Oxford. An address sent to the houses at Westminster brought no result, for Charles still refused to recognize them as a true parliament, and unless they were so considered, they pro-

110. *Ibid.*, pp. 379, 380–381.
111. *J. L.*, VI, 375–376.
112. Rushworth, *Historical Collections*, V, 498.
113. Napier, *Life and Times of Montrose*, pp. 243–244. The Duke of Hamilton had in December fled from Scotland to Oxford. Here he was imprisoned, not only for his failure to prevent the Scots from joining Parliament, but also for suspicion of having deceitfully fomented unrest against the king in Scotland, with the hope that he could enhance his own position as a result of unsettled circumstances. Burnet, *Memoirs of Hamilton and Castleherald*, pp. 253–270.

tested, they had no authority to deal with him; nor would the king on his part be bound by any agreement with them.[114] On February 10 Henrietta wrote Newcastle that the French ambassador to England, de Gressy, had proposed to act as go-between in negotiating an accommodation between the warring parties. "I write to ask you whether this might be in accord with your condition in the north," she continued, "for unless it is, there will be no truce; or it will be asked only for this place, for in truth the King's army needs it."[115]

Caught between the Scots on the north and Fairfax's army on the south, Newcastle had as much reason to desire peace as anyone involved in the hostilities. The queen continued sending her letters to feed Newcastle's courage for the oncoming contest. "If you beat the Scots," she said in a writing of March 15, "our affairs are in good order, for our forces are considerable," and added that since Yorkshire was in good hands, she believed there was nothing to fear from Scotland. But then in a postscript to this letter came a doleful bit of information: "Since writing the above we have news that Sir Thomas Fairfax marches towards you to join the Scots. If the Scots pass the river Tees, I fear there is no remedy, and all is lost."[116]

Great as was the danger to Royalist arms, the queen had to divert her attention to personal concerns as the winter wore into spring. In February, 1644, she wrote her sister Christine that she was pregnant but knew not where to find safety in the war-torn country.[117] Certainly Oxford, now under threat of siege, was no place for the birth of her child. The queen must have felt very insecure at times, for England was an unhappy ground and seemed not to want her. Was there any escaping the fact she was a Frenchwoman born?

114. Rushworth, *Historical Collections*, V, 560, 566–567, 570–571.
115. *Harl. MSS 6988*, fol. 168.
116. Baillon, *Lettres de Henriette-Marie*, pp. 504–505.
117. Ferrero, *Lettres à Christine*, p. 62.

CHAPTER VII

FLIGHT TO FRANCE

1644-46 THE coming of spring brought with it renewal of military campaigning, and the gathering of Parliamentary forces along the approaches to Oxford
increased the threat of siege. Henrietta, now far advanced in pregnancy, could no longer delay her departure. The king accompanied
her on her way some distance south of Oxford to the town of
Abingdon, where husband and wife bade one another farewell—a
farewell which, as fate decreed, was to last forever.[1]

Before leaving Oxford the queen had been suffering from an
illness which was believed to be rheumatic fever, and the joltings
incidental to travel only intensified her pain. On reaching Bath
she stopped for one day in hope that the rest would ease her suffering, but her "rheum," as she described it, continued to increase.[2]
From Bath the queen had intended to go to Bristol, but then decided in favor of the more southerly port of Exeter. From here she
wrote Dr. Theodore Mayerne in London to come to her if he were
able, and Charles seconded her request with a short note of his own.

1. Mary Anne Everett Green, *Letters of Queen Henrietta Maria* (London,
1857), p. 239.
2. "The King's Cabinet Opened," *The Harleian Miscellany* (12 vols., London,
1808-11), V, 537-538; Robert Baillie, *Letters and Journals* (3 vols., Edinburgh,
1842), II, 168.

"Mayerne, for the love of me," he begged, "go to my wife."[3] Dr. Mayerne, now over seventy years old, at first sent written instructions for treatment of Henrietta's illness. Being too much the physician, however, to refuse the plea of the little queen whom he had so often attended, he finally made the journey to Exeter despite the frailties of his own ripe years.[4]

The queen regent of France had not hesitated to offer sympathy and comfort to her distressed sister-in-law. When Henrietta applied for permission to go to France, Queen Anne sent not only a hospitable invitation but also money, linens, and her own *sage femme*, Madame Perone. In reflection of Anne's selflessness, Henrietta sent most of the money to Charles, keeping only what she needed for minimum expenses.[5]

The symptoms of her illness becoming more pronounced, Henrietta did not think she would survive; nor for that matter did Dr. Mayerne. In a letter written to Charles just before her lying-in, she spoke of having excruciating pains that were "too severe to be experienced or understood by any except those who have suffered them."[6] Following the birth of her child, a girl, on June 16, 1644, she applied to the Parliamentary general, Essex, for a safe conduct to Bath, where, she believed, the mineral waters might ease her suffering. In response to M. de Sabran, the French envoy through whom the request was made, Essex said he not only would give the queen a safe conduct but also would escort her to London, where she might have the best advice and means of restoring her health.[7]

As Essex's armies approached Exeter, Henrietta informed Charles of her decision to go to Falmouth and from there to escape

3. Henry Ellis, *Original Letters* (12 vols. in 3 series, London, 1824-46), ser. 2, III, 315-316; Green, *Letters of Henrietta Maria*, p. 243.

4. *Calendar of State Papers, Venice* (38 vols., ed. Allen B. Hinds and others, London, 1864-1940), XXVII, 95, 107 (referred to hereafter as *Cal. S. P. Ven.*).

5. Françoise Bertaut, Madame de Motteville, *Mémoires sur Anne d'Autriche et Sa Cour* (4 vols., ed. M. F. Riaux, Paris, n.d.), I, 212.

6. *Harl. MSS 7379*, fol. 93; Baillie, *Letters*, II, 213-214.

7. John Rushworth, *Historical Collections* (8 vols., London, 1721-22), V, 684; *Cal. S. P. Ven.*, XXVII, 116.

to France. In the same letter she described the symptoms of her suffering in vivid detail. She told of "a seizure of paralysis in the legs and all over the body," and continued: ". . . it seems as though my bowels and stomach weighed more than a hundred pounds, and as though I was so tightly squeezed in the region of the heart, that I was suffocating; and at times I am like a person poisoned. I can scarcely stir, and am doubled up. This same weight is also upon my back; one of my arms has no feeling, and my legs and knees are colder than ice. This disease has risen to my head, I can not see with one eye."[8]

Leaving her infant daughter behind in the care of a trusted governess, the queen went to Pendennis Castle near the port of Falmouth. A Cornish gentleman who saw her as she was departing from Exeter described her as "the woefullest spectacle my eyes yet ever looked on; the most worne and weake pitiful creature in the world, the poore Queene, shifting for one hour's liffe longer."[9] At Falmouth there was debate as to whether the queen should venture the seas, for just off the harbor rode three ships of the Parliamentary navy ready to intercept her passage. But as the French commander sent to bring her to France warned, delay would only increase the naval guard, and Henrietta determined to run the risk. On the night before sailing she sent a touching declaration of her love to Charles: "I am giving the strongest proof of love that I can give; I am hazarding my life, that I may not incommode your affairs. Adieu, my dear heart. If I die, believe that you will lose a person who has never been other than entirely yours, and who by her affection has deserved that you should not forget her."[10]

Putting out of the harbor, the queen's ships sailed directly toward those of Parliament. Thinking the approaching fleet meant to offer battle, the Parliamentary officers opened fire, but the aim

8. *Harl. MSS 7379*, fol. 98; *Additional MSS 18981*, fol. 180.
9. Richard Polwhele, *Traditions and Recollections* (2 vols., London, 1826), I, 17; *Calendar of State Papers, Domestic Series, of the Reign of Charles I, 1625–1649* (23 vols., ed. John Bruce and others, London, 1858–97), 1644, p. 318 (referred to hereafter as *Cal. S. P. Dom.*); *Cal. S. P. Ven.*, XXVII, 117, 123.
10. *Harl. MSS 7379*, fol. 96.

was high. Henrietta directed the captain of her ship that rather than permit its seizure by the enemy, he should fire the magazine in the hold. Suddenly the outbound vessels turned sharply and, gaining the wind, outdistanced their pursuers.[11]

Driven to the coast of Brittany where rocky reefs prevented close approach to the beach, the queen was rowed from her ship in a small boat and was forced to clamber over coastal boulders before setting foot on land. The people of the region received the sick queen with much kindness, offering her the accommodation of a little stone cottage typical of the province in which she landed. The nobility of the area, hearing of the plight of this youngest child of Henry the Great, hastened to offer their carriages to convey her to the old royal watering place of Bourbon. In Paris, whither Henry Jermyn had been dispatched to give notice of Henrietta's arrival, the French queen was soon to provide the refugee an immediate grant of money and assurances of a yearly pension.[12]

The trip to Bourbon, occupying almost all the month of August and attended with ceremonials in nearly every important town through which the queen and her entourage passed, must have taxed her endurance to the limit. By the time she reached Bourbon, she could walk only with the aid of a person supporting her on either side. During most of September she drank the waters and took the baths. Whether or not the waters helped her, her condition, while far from good, did improve somewhat, and at last she began to hope she would not die. A numbness still pervaded her whole body, and the rash that resembled measles did not seem to diminish, but her head was somewhat relieved and her stomach was not so swollen as it had been.[13]

11. Cardinal de Mazarin, *Lettres* (9 vols., ed. P. A. Chéruel [*Collection de Documents Inédits*], Paris, 1872–1906), II, 21; Cyprien de Gamache, *Memoirs of the Mission in England of the Capuchin Friars of the Province of Paris, from the Year 1630 to 1669* (in vol. II, 293–501, of Thomas Birch, *The Court and Times of Charles I* [2 vols., London, 1848]), p. 360 (referred to hereafter as Gamache, *Memoirs*); *Cal. S. P. Dom.*, 1644, p. 356.

12. Motteville, *Mémoires*, I, 185, 213, 222.

13. *Harl. MSS 7379*, fols. 90, 92, 99; *Memoirs Illustrative of the Life and Writ-*

Going on to Paris, the queen was detained at Nevers for another month by the development of an abscess. Her breasts had to be lanced, and doctors sent from Paris prescribed the drinking of ass's milk.[14] It was not until early in November that she reached her destination. On the way from Nevers she was accompanied by her younger brother, Gaston, and outside Paris, near the faubourg St. Jacques, she was met by the queen regent, Anne, whom she had not seen for almost twenty years. After the embraces of greeting, Henrietta entered the French queen's carriage to ride to the Louvre, which had been made ready for the royal guest and which was to be her home for the next sixteen years. Paris, officially and publicly, was generous in its welcome to the exiled queen, giving her every honor and consideration due a person of her rank. The pitiable condition of the queen touched the feelings of those who beheld her. Drawn and emaciated, the beauty for which she had been famed was gone, though enough remained of the celebrated features—especially the lively eyes and well-shaped nose—to make her appearance pleasing.[15]

Although Henrietta was a long way from recovery of her health, which was never again restored to its former condition, she could hardly spare herself the luxury of convalescence. She had escaped death to help her husband regain the position he had once held, and this end was to be effected by an armed invasion of England to release the king from the bonds of his own people. During the next four years Henrietta was engaged in a series of complicated negotiations directed toward the procurement of armies for the invasion of England in behalf of the Royalist cause.

Before the queen had left Exeter, Dr. Stephen Goffe, a person

---

ings of Sir John Evelyn (2 vols., ed. William Bray, London, 1819), I, 64 (referred to hereafter as Evelyn, *Memoirs*).

14. Hermann Ferrero, *Lettres de Henriette-Marie à Sa Soeur Christine* (Rome, 1881), p. 64 (referred to hereafter as Ferrero, *Lettres à Christine*); Green, *Letters of Henrietta Maria*, p. 259.

15. *Mémoires de Mlle. de Montpensier* (4 vols., ed. A. Chéruel, Paris, n.d.), I, 98–100 (referred to hereafter as Montpensier, *Mémoires*); Ferrero, *Lettres à Christine*, p. 66; *Cal. S. P. Ven.*, XXVII, 150–151, 153; Motteville, *Mémoires*, I, 223.

whose obscurity made his employment less publicized, was handed instructions for talks with the Prince of Orange concerning a marriage between Prince Charles and the daughter of Orange. Through the fall and winter of 1643–44, the possibility of a match had continued to be held out to Frederick Henry in the letters Jermyn had dispatched to him. According to Goffe's instructions, the principal requirement for the conclusion of a marriage contract with the House of Orange was the formation of an offensive-defensive alliance, which the Netherlands would join along with France and England. In addition, the Prince of Orange was asked to furnish sea transport for two thousand horse and four thousand foot from France to England.[16]

There was one great miscalculation in this scheme of obtaining aid through marriage: it was assumed that Mazarin would furnish the men and horses for the invading army. Goring, who as ambassador to Paris was in a better position to estimate Mazarin's willingness to help, could have told the queen that she had little to expect from the French minister.[17] Jermyn was likewise convinced when he went to Paris following the queen's landing in Brittany, but he thought the promise of Dutch shipping should be obtained in case soldiers did turn up somewhere.[18] In truth, Mazarin was highly pleased with conditions as they were in England so long as neither side won a clear victory. To have England immured from international politics by internal strife ridded him of a potential

16. Guillaume Groen van Prinsterer, *Archives ou Correspondence Inédit de la Maison d'Orange Nassau* (4 vols., Utrecht, 1859), IV, 99–100, 102–104 (referred to hereafter as Prinsterer, *Archives*). Stephen Goffe (1605–81), who on several occasions served as a Royalist agent, was educated at Merton College and St. Alban's Hall, Oxford (B.S. 1624, M.A. 1627), and later attended the University of Leyden. After returning from the Continent about 1638, he was made one of Charles I's chaplains and, largely upon the king's insistence, procured a D.D. Following the establishment of the Commonwealth, Goffe changed his religion for that of Rome. Having entered the Congregation of the French Oratory, he later became a chaplain to Henrietta Maria. His brother, Col. William Goffe, was one of the regicides. See Raymond Phineas Stearns, *Congregationalism in the Dutch Netherlands* (Chicago, 1940), p. 43n; also *D.N.B.*, XXII, 69–70.

17. *Cal. S. P. Dom.*, 1644, p. 259.

18. *Ibid.*, p. 402; Prinsterer, *Archives*, IV, 108–109.

threat on his northern flank while France proceeded to defeat Austria and Spain on the Continent. Besides, Mazarin no less than Richelieu had memories of Stuart favoritism to Spain.[19]

Henrietta would not concede that all hope of succor from France was exhausted until she had herself talked with the minister. Mazarin could not see her upon her arrival in Paris, begging the excuse of an illness which rendered him unable to converse on matters of business.[20] But, in the end, Henrietta's communication with him yielded no more fruitful result than had the appeals of Jermyn; however much France might wish to help, she was so busily engaged elsewhere that she could spare no soldiers. Mazarin did suggest that Henrietta try to employ the mercenaries led by the Duke of Lorraine, and said that France would supply money for the hire of those forces. Not only would Charles thereby be aided, but France would be relieved of an old enemy who had always fought on the side of Spain.[21] Whether Mazarin seriously meant his suggestion concerning the employment of Lorraine's army or merely hoped to keep the queen busy negotiating on the matter is questionable, but if he did not mean it, Henrietta was the last person to whom the suggestion should have been made, for once having a purpose in mind she bent all her will and energies to its fulfillment.[22]

In a letter explaining to Charles why France was unable to send him an army, Henrietta also wrote that all he might wish for almost certainly would be given by the Catholics in Ireland if the king satisfied their demands, and that she would send conditions for Irish assistance as soon as she acquired their terms.[23] Evidently

19. *Cal. S. P. Ven.*, XXVII, 143.
20. *Harl. MSS 7379*, fol. 43.
21. *Harl. MSS 6988*, fols. 30, 45.
22. The French envoy, M. de Sabran, who had been sent to England after Harcourt's failure to effect a settlement between king and Parliament, told Charles that France was following a policy of neutrality toward the civil struggles in England. Charles perceived that Mazarin was not deeply concerned about Royalist fortunes but would follow a course which he considered advantageous to France. *Cal. S. P. Dom.*, 1644–45, p. 59.
23. *Harl. MSS 6988*, fol. 30.

the queen had fallen in with a plan suggested by Father Hertogan, the representative in Paris for the Supreme Council of the Confederate Irish. Hertogan was trying to get powers for settling of affairs in Ireland placed in Henrietta as representative of the English king, and to have the queen regent of France act as bargainer for the rebellious Irish. As soon as these powers were conferred, the French queen was to send arms and ammunition to Ireland. As a basis for the negotiations between the queens, it was to be understood that, granted satisfactory peace terms, the Irish would send ten thousand men to England for the king's service—not, however, until all "enemies" (meaning the Protestants) in Ulster and such others as Hertogan privately included were first driven from Ireland. Hertogan probably intended little less than the total destruction of the king's authority in Ireland, for he specified that land holdings there were to be owned only by Catholics. Actually, he was hardly more clear in his design than the queen was perspicacious in detecting the dangers in it for the king. Hertogan implied to the Supreme Council that the English queen favored his proposals even so far as to tell Mazarin that England would have to be saved through the aid of the Irish.[24]

Meanwhile, in England, as a result of the defeat of Newcastle and Prince Rupert at the battle of Marston Moor, the Royalists had lost Yorkshire, to the winning of which Henrietta had given her interest and energies. Early in December, 1644, the king sent the Duke of Richmond and the Earl of Southampton to London with offers to treat for a peace with Parliament. In order to obtain permission for his emissaries' passage to London, Charles was forced to recognize the bodies at Westminster as a parliament.[25]

Perhaps it was dread over his wife's reaction to this concession which explained his reticence toward her during the month of December. The queen complained bitterly that she had no letters,

24. Thomas Carte, *The Life of James, Duke of Ormonde* (6 vols., Oxford, 1851), VI, 215–216, 217 (referred to hereafter as Carte, *Ormonde*).

25. *Calendar of Clarendon State Papers* (3 vols., ed. O. Ogle, W. Dunn Macray, and W. H. Bliss, Oxford, 1872–76), I, 253, 254 (referred to hereafter as *Cal. Clar. S. P.*).

saying that news from him was necessary if she were to combat the rumors circulated in Paris by the rebels, and that since she regularly received dispatches from Secretary Nicholas, surely Charles also could write her.[26] Her remonstrance against the recognition of Parliament, of which she learned through sources other than Charles, was not violent, although she was disappointed that her husband had not taken her into his confidence regarding the matter.[27] When finally Charles did write his wife, he revealed himself to be as slippery as ever. The title of Parliament, he explained, did not mean recognition of the houses as in fact a parliament, but was merely a formality prerequisite for the opening of peace talks. Besides, if but one additional member of his council other than himself and Secretary Nicholas had opposed the move, he would never have acknowledged the title of Parliament. He felt constrained to open relations with the rebels because of the insistence of some of his own followers who were weary of war.[28] On this point he was borne out by Parliamentary commissioners, who reported a great longing for peace among many Royalists at Oxford and who attributed the obstruction to such a policy in the Royalist camp to the "queen's party."[29]

The conferences, held at Uxbridge, began late in January, 1645. The topics to be discussed were the ordering of church government, control of the militia, and settlement of the rebellion in Ireland.[30] No sooner had discussions opened than Charles began to talk of

26. Green, *Letters of Henrietta Maria*, pp. 274–275.

27. Charles, Comte de Baillon, *Lettres de Henriette-Marie, Reine d'Angleterre* (Paris, 1877), pp. 529–530.

28. "The King's Cabinet Opened," *Harleian Miscellany*, V, 519; *The Private Correspondence between Charles I and His Secretary of State, Sir Edward Nicholas* (in vol. II, part 2, of *Memoirs Illustrative of the Life and Writings of Sir John Evelyn* [2 vols., ed. William Bray, London, 1819]), pp. 90–91 (referred to hereafter as *Correspondence between Charles I and Sir Edward Nicholas*); Green, *Letters of Henrietta Maria*, p. 278; *The Works of Charles I* (2 vols., Aberdeen, Scotland, 1766), I, 301; Rushworth, *Historical Collections*, V, 888.

29. Baillie, *Letters*, II, 244.

30. *Works of Charles I*, I, 309–310; "The King's Cabinet Opened," *Harleian Miscellany*, V, 534–535.

going in person to London, where the popular clamor in his behalf, coupled with the divisions he believed must inevitably ensue between Presbyterians and Independents over differences relating to peace terms, might enable him to gain the upper hand.[31] The queen warned him against going to London unless Parliament were dissolved, for if his design did not work, he would be seized and held a prisoner.[32] Charles tried to cozen the Irish into coming to terms with him, saying that if acceptable terms were offered to him at Uxbridge, he might in turn agree to place Irish affairs under control of Parliament, from whom the Irish could expect far less leniency than from their king.[33] Again the queen sent her admonition against the way in which he endeavored to profit from the peace talks. Were he to offer the betrayal of his Irish subjects, she said, and were the negotiations ultimately to fail, he could no longer depend on aid from the Irish or the Catholics when their support would be most needed.[34] Hardly had the meetings begun at Uxbridge than Charles wrote his wife he did not intend the negotiations to lead to a peace, or not to more than a truce at best, and that she should so notify the French queen.[35] The meetings dragged on until the close of February, with nothing gained for the Royalists. The queen, whose thinking was far less convoluted than Charles's tortuous processes, concluded her comment on the Uxbridge negotiations by remarking, "It seems to me, cunning is no longer of any avail."[36]

While the negotiations spun themselves out at Uxbridge, the queen had again taken up the idea of foreign alliances to acquire military support for the king. Acting upon Mazarin's advice concerning the hire of Lorraine's army, Henrietta was delighted to

31. *Ibid.*, pp. 524–525; *Works of Charles I*, I, 299–300.
32. *Ibid.*, pp. 304–305.
33. Rushworth, *Historical Collections*, V, 924.
34. Baillon, *Lettres de Henriette-Marie*, pp. 530–531; *Works of Charles I*, I, 299–300.
35. Rushworth, *Historical Collections*, V, 890, 892; *Works of Charles I*, I, 307.
36. *Ibid.*, pp. 314–315; Green, *Letters of Henrietta Maria*, p. 285.

hear in January, 1645, that the duke was entirely favorable to the idea of placing his forces in the employ of King Charles.[37] Dr. Goffe, again sent to the Netherlands to continue bargaining on a marriage between Orange's daughter and the Prince of Wales, received a change in his instructions. In the first set of instructions given him on this second mission, he was directed to emphasize the formation of an offensive-defensive league and to insist upon the furnishing and transport of three thousand soldiers to England entirely at the expense of the Netherlands. The second set of instructions was fashioned upon the hope of using Lorraine's army. The question of a league was now placed last among the topics to be discussed, while the main consideration was given to the request that the Dutch navy ship Lorraine's army to England. Instead of furnishing three thousand soldiers as requested in the original commission, Orange was asked to protect Royalist shipping from the Parliamentary navy.[38]

In talking of Dutch naval assistance as a condition for the conclusion of a marriage treaty between England and the Netherlands, Goffe found the Prince of Orange skeptical about Lorraine's ability to supply the size of army he promised for transport to England. Whatever Orange's personal inclination, he was not absolute in the Netherlands, and it was certain the Estates General would never permit Lorraine's soldiers, who had long been in the service of the archenemy Spain, to march through Dutch territory and embark at Dutch ports; moreover, any Dutch shipping employed for the transport of Lorraine's army would have to be employed in the name of the King of France, since the Estates would not agree to a contract with Lorraine or the Royalists. As for a league, Orange gave his tacit approval, but passively waited for France to take the initiative and responsibility in the formation of the alliance.[39]

If Dutch ports could not be used for the embarkation of Lor-

37. "The King's Cabinet Opened," *Harleian Miscellany*, V, 539.
38. Prinsterer, *Archives*, IV, 119–120, 121, 122, 125–127; Baillon, *Lettres de Henriette-Marie*, pp. 540–541.
39. *The Lord George Digby's Cabinet* (London, 1646), pp. 12–13; Prinsterer, *Archives*, IV, 131, 132.

raine's army, there was still the possibility of having Dutch ships for the army's conveyance to England. Henrietta again turned to Mazarin, inquiring whether, having offered to pay the cost of transporting those troops, he would not also permit them to depart from the French port of Dieppe. Mazarin, whom Charles accused of being at this time in communication with the speaker of the House of Commons, refused to permit Lorraine's soldiers entry to any part of France.[40]

The likelihood of receiving Dutch shipping and naval protection was greatly reduced when in April the Netherlands sent sixty men-of-war and also transports carrying six thousand troops to aid Denmark in a war against Sweden.[41] But Henrietta never surrendered in her endeavors. There was still a possibility of hiring private shipping in Holland with the money that Mazarin promised. Toward the end of April and beginning of May, Lord Jermyn dispatched frantic appeals asking Charles for his stipulations on the detailed provisions of a marriage contract with the House of Orange. By the time these letters reached England, the king had already set out for the summer campaign, and no answer ever arrived.[42]

Indeed, the season was late to think of sending Lorraine's forces to England, but the queen had been unable to attend to such business during a part of March and most of April because of a serious recurrence of illness. When a rumor arose that Lorraine was no longer willing to take his army to England, Henrietta sent Sir Henry de Vic to confer with him. On returning early in June, the envoy said Lorraine was ready to depart for England if the queen wished to employ him.[43] Thereupon Henrietta asked Mazarin for the money he had promised for the shipping of Lorraine's mercenaries. It was doubtful that Mazarin would have fulfilled his

40. *Cal. S. P. Dom.*, 1644–45, pp. 374, 388; "The King's Cabinet Opened," *Harleian Miscellany*, V, 518.

41. *Cal. S. P. Dom.*, 1644–45, pp. 405–406.

42. *George Digby's Cabinet*, pp. 15–16, 20, 27, 28; *Cal. S. P. Dom.*, 1644–45, pp. 429, 430, 455–456; Prinsterer, *Archives*, IV, 173; *Works of Charles I*, I, 322, 324.

43. *George Digby's Cabinet*, p. 40; *Cal. S. P. Dom.*, 1644–45, p. 495.

pledge, but circumstances excused him from doing so, for a few days afterward Lorraine marched off to fight for his old employer, Spain.[44]

Besides attempting to build up an alliance and procure the shipment of Lorraine's army, Henrietta also endeavored to bring about a peace with the rebellious Irish and to enlist their services in the subjugation of England. In following out this plan the queen enlarged upon her Catholic sympathies, for without a government tolerant toward Catholicism in England, the Irish could never be secure in their religion. While Henrietta encouraged the king to reach a conclusion of hostilities with the Irish and advised him to solicit the support of Catholics,[45] the work of conducting negotiations for peace with the Confederate Irish was carried on by Charles and his viceroy in Ireland, the Marquis of Ormonde. A year's cessation of arms in Ireland had ended in September, 1644, and in December Ormonde had informed the king he could hold out against the Irish no longer than the following April unless he received supplies and men, neither of which Charles could furnish.[46] Charles wrote Ormonde that in furtherance of a peace with the Irish, he was authorized to promise the suspension of the penal laws against the Catholic religion in Ireland.[47]

44. Mazarin, *Lettres*, II, 187–188. There is some reason to suppose Henrietta was as much concerned in getting money from Mazarin as in procuring the services of Lorraine's army. In a letter of May 12, Jermyn wrote that while he did not think the negotiations with Lorraine would go through, his doubts were to be kept secret from Mazarin, since the queen might get the money to pay the cost of shipping the army on the understanding that the contract would be carried to completion. *George Digby's Cabinet*, p. 25.

45. Baillon, *Lettres de Henriette-Marie*, p. 537.

46. Carte, *Ormonde*, V, 15–16. James Butler, Earl of Ormonde (1610–88), was of an old Anglo-Irish family whose name derived from the fact that its chiefs became hereditary butlers to the lords lieutenant of Ireland. Upon the outbreak of the Irish rebellion in 1641, James Butler was made lieutenant general of the Royal Army there, somewhat later was made a marquis, and in 1644 was appointed lord lieutenant. This last honor involved him in the dilemma of negotiations between the Irish Catholics and the king. A year after the death of the king, he was driven out of Ireland by Cromwell, but he returned after the restoration to serve again for two terms as lord lieutenant. *D.N.B.*, VIII, 52–60.

47. *Cal. Clar. S. P.*, I, 258; Rushworth, *Historical Collections*, V, 925; "The King's Cabinet Opened," *Harleian Miscellany*, V, 528.

During the early months of the queen's residence in Paris, she and her followers remained in close communication with representatives of the Confederate Irish, for whom Father Hertogan was the chief agent. If we may believe Father Hertogan's story, he and the queen's officers met frequently to confer on ways of promoting the welfare of Catholics in Ireland and England. He assured the skeptical leaders of the Supreme Council in Ireland that there was no one among the queen's coterie who would do Ireland any harm and even said that Jermyn was a more loyal supporter of the Catholics than was many an Irishman. He pretended that his friendly relations with Henrietta extended to waiting on her at table, and reported he had heard her rail against Ormonde as an infidel who was never to be trusted.[48] With characteristic optimism he wrote that French aid for the rebels in Ireland was most promising. The French secretary of state had told him that France wished to be rid of the English queen and for that purpose would be willing to pay her pension to the Confederate Irish if they agreed to take her to Ireland and keep her there. While not protesting the conditions of the secretary's offer, Hertogan insisted that the Confederate Irish would require a sum greater than the amount paid to the queen. Inasmuch as Henrietta only four months before had been welcomed in France, Hertogan's claims were difficult to believe.[49]

On learning of Hertogan's duplicity, Henrietta ceased to hold him in confidence. Charles had repeatedly warned her against the Jesuit, and a month after Hertogan wrote his letter to the Supreme Council, the queen informed George Digby that Hertogan was a knave.[50]

But there were Catholics whom the queen felt she could trust. Her former almoner, the Abbot of Peron, now Bishop of Angoulême, raised a contribution of 40,000 pistoles (approximately

48. *MSS Clar. S. P. 1794*, fol. 212.
49. *Ibid.*, fol. 211.
50. Rushworth, *Historical Collections*, V, 891; *Harl. MSS 7379*, fol. 23; *Cal. S. P. Dom.*, 1644–45, p. 373; Green, *Letters of Henrietta Maria*, p. 299; *George Digby's Cabinet*, p. 9.

£36,000) among the devotees of Paris to give to the queen.[51] This was the first sizable sum of money Henrietta acquired for Charles after coming to France. Also, she prepared to send Sir Kenelm Digby to Rome to solicit money from the pope, but Digby did not start on his mission until June, 1645.[52] The king tried to give his wife a bargaining point in her appeals to Catholics by writing that if the Catholics contributed sufficiently to his restoration, he would grant toleration for Catholicism in England, although he was not specific on the amount of contribution necessary to merit fulfill-ment of his promise.[53]

By May, 1645, Ormonde's position in Dublin was becoming precarious. The king, unable to supply means of protecting his Protestant subjects there, instructed Ormonde to offer the Con-federate Irish repeal of penal laws against their religion.[54] The queen sent a letter to the Supreme Council urging its members to make a peace and telling them that Ormonde had been given full powers by the king to treat for a conclusion of hostilities.[55]

At about this time also Henrietta endorsed and sent to the king the plan of a Colonel Oliver Fitzwilliams for Irish aid upon the conclusion of a peace with the Confederates. According to terms of the plan, Fitzwilliams would raise and equip for shipment to England an army of ten thousand Irish upon being paid £10,000. The soldiers would land in Wales, where they would immediately be given one month's pay at the prevailing rates in the Royalist army. To these Irish soldiers the king would attach a body of two thousand cavalry, and all of these forces were to fight as a unit, never being separated or scattered into separate commands. Col-onel Fitzwilliams as commander in chief was to have no officers superior to him except the king and Prince Rupert.[56]

51. *Cal. S. P. Ven.*, XXVII, 175. Concerning monetary exchange values, see note on p. ix.
52. *D.N.B.*, XV, 63; *Cal. S. P. Dom.*, 1644–45, p. 546.
53. Rushworth, *Historical Collections*, V, 893; *Works of Charles I*, I, 314–315.
54. *Carte MSS*, XV, 200; *Cal. Clar. S. P.*, I, 264.
55. *The Embassy in Ireland of Monsignor G. B. Rinuccini* (tr. Anne Hutton, Dublin, 1873), p. 553 (referred to hereafter as Rinuccini, *Embassy in Ireland*).
56. *Cal. S. P. Dom.*, 1644–45, pp. 464–466; 1645–47, p. 81; *George Digby's*

Although the queen's attempts to procure assistance for Charles had been frustrated, she had been able through her private resources to secure some money and munitions. She cut the expenses of her court in Paris to the minimum in order to send to England a part of the pension she was receiving from the French government. During her first few months in Paris, she had all of the accouterments belonging to a queen—carriages, liveried servants, footmen, fine horses—but gradually these luxuries disappeared, and the queen lived with a frugality that was almost scandalous.[57] The Venetian ambassador in Paris wrote of her sending 36,000 crowns (£10,800), which, if not going very far in fulfilling Charles's needs, did represent a large sacrifice on the part of Henrietta.[58]

By the spring of 1645 the queen had received warrants from the king authorizing the sale of tin extracted from the mines of Cornwall, where a portion of the ore produced had long constituted revenue for the crown. In April the first consignment of the metal reached Holland, and Goffe was sent there to get a loan on the shipment and to put it into the hands of brokers. Upon Goffe's application, the Prince of Orange agreed to use his influence in having the cargo exempt from duties.[59] A part of the proceeds derived was applied to semiyearly payments on jewels that the queen still had in pawn.

Late in March the Dutch captain, John van Haesdonck, was dispatched to England with a cargo of military supplies consisting of 6,040 muskets, 2,000 pairs of pistols, 1,200 carbines, 150 swords, 400 shovels, 27,000 pounds of match, and 50,000 pounds of brimstone.[60] Haesdonck was to have unloaded one-half of the shipment at Exeter and Dartmouth, and then to have carried the remainder of the supply to Montrose in Scotland. Instead he put off all of the

Cabinet, pp. 49, 56; "The King's Cabinet Opened," *Harleian Miscellany*, V, 532.

57. Montpensier, *Mémoires*, I, 100.

58. *Cal. S. P. Ven.*, XXVII, 178.

59. *Cal. S. P. Dom.*, 1644-45, pp. 371, 372, 387, 469-470; *George Digby's Cabinet*, p. 10.

60. *Cal. S. P. Dom.*, 1644-45, pp. 469-470.

munitions at Pendennis Castle, because the assignment given him had proved too difficult to perform against the threat of the Parliamentary navy.[61]

The military exploits of Montrose in behalf of the king's cause in Scotland constituted the brightest part of Royalist fortunes. In an attempt to strengthen this valiant leader, Henrietta sent Sir John Cochrane to the Baltic region, where he entreated the Duke of Courland to ship his army to northern England and there join forces with Montrose. The instructions given to Cochrane really constituted a double mission, since the King of Denmark would have to be consulted for permission to transport Courland's army through Danish waters that separated the Baltic from the North Sea.[62]

Although having many irons in the fire and showing great energy in her endeavors to send help to Charles, Henrietta had been under great physical handicap all the while. In March she wrote that her health was still precarious. The numbness in her legs and arms and the feeling of drowsiness persisted, but she did manage to move about. The prolonged illness was beginning to affect her spirits, so that she became sensitive to imagined slight or injury. Believing the king to have indicated displeasure with her in one of his letters, she answered him, "Be good to me, or you will kill me. I already have enough affliction for suffering, which, without you, I could not endure; but your service enables me to surmount all."[63] In April she suffered a relapse and was extremely ill. By the middle of the following month she was much recovered except for a great "rheum" caused by the fever. What had most tormented her in her sickness, she was able to write, was the fear of dying far away from her husband.[64]

61. *Ibid.*, pp. 374, 494–495; *George Digby's Cabinet*, p. 33.

62. *Ibid.*, p. 11; *Cal. S. P. Dom.*, 1644–45, p. 387. Sir John Cochrane (d. 1650?), soldier and diplomat, was implicated in Charles's attempt to seize Pym and four other leaders of the Parliamentary party. After Henrietta fled to exile in France, he was employed in raising money for the Royalist cause in a number of the Baltic countries and in Hamburg. *D.N.B.*, XI, 162.

63. "The King's Cabinet Opened," *Harleian Miscellany*, V, 539.

64. *Harl. MSS 7379*, fol. 83; *Cal. S. P. Ven.*, XXVII, 185.

Foreign assistance for the king became more imperative with the crushing of his military power at the battle of Naseby on June 14, 1645. A concomitant misfortune was the loss of the cabinet containing his correspondence, including those letters written to him by the queen. The letters were soon published by Parliament with telling effect against the crown. Now revealed to the English people were those missives in which the queen described her efforts to engage foreign armies to invade England and fight against the king's own subjects. Because the correspondence in Charles's cabinet was not entirely complete, the case against him appeared somewhat worse than if none of the letters had been missing. The writing which would have disclosed his opposition to Hertogan's plans, for example, was not among the contents of the cabinet.[65] In a short preface to the published letters, extreme conclusions were stated concerning Henrietta's influence over her husband. Charles was represented as being little more than a puppet in the hands of the queen, whose counsels were said to be as powerful as commands.[66]

The dealings with the Confederate Irish for a treaty were greatly complicated when, late in May, Giovanni Rinuccini, Bishop of Fermo, arrived at Paris en route to Ireland, where he was being sent as the pope's nuncio.[67] Ostensibly, Rinuccini was going there to bring the Church in Ireland into conformity with the reforms established by the Council of Trent. The pope professed no intentions of infringing upon temporal authority. Yet the fact that the papacy sent a nuncio to Ireland implied recognition of the legitimacy of the Irish rebellion, for the king certainly had not been consulted concerning the entry of a legate into his domains. Shortly after arriving in Paris, Rinuccini received a letter from Innocent X in which His Holiness declared, "May it please God that the

65. *MSS Clar. S. P. 1957*, fol. 143; *Correspondence between Charles I and Sir Edward Nicholas*, pp. 105–106.

66. *George Digby's Cabinet*, p. 61; "The King's Cabinet Opened," *Harleian Miscellany*, V, 548.

67. Alphonsus Bellesheim, *The Papal Nuncio among the Irish Confederates* (tr. W. McLoughlin, Dublin, 1908), p. 7 (referred to hereafter as Bellesheim, *Papal Nuncio*).

circumstances of the times may make this enterprise similar to that of former days in conquest of the Holy Land, as indeed I esteem it not much inferior."[68] The nuncio brought £12,000 and some munitions, including 500 muskets and 2,000 pistols, in support of the Irish rebellion—a trifling contribution in consideration of the Confederates' needs and the authority that Rinuccini later pretended in Ireland.[69]

According to the pope's instructions, Rinuccini was to inform the queen that she must prevail upon Ormonde to surrender Dublin to the Irish before any consideration would be given to the pleas of Sir Kenelm Digby, who was soon to arrive in Rome. Furthermore, the queen was to move her husband to make a peace with the Irish rebels on terms specified in the instructions—terms which were about the same as those later given to Digby. The document outlining Rinuccini's mission indicated distrust of the queen. No great hope was entertained that she would comply with the pope's wishes, and Rome was much displeased that she kept Protestants in her service and allowed them to be often in her presence. Above all, Rinuccini was to prevent her going to Ireland, where it was feared her influence would impede the conclusions of a peace on Rome's terms.[70]

Henrietta and Rinuccini did not meet during the envoy's stay at Paris. The queen, who was spending the summer at her childhood home of Saint-Germain-en-Laye, was not in Paris during much of the time Rinuccini was there, but a meeting could have been arranged had other difficulties not entered in. Rinuccini's going to Ireland as nuncio, the queen contended, prejudiced her husband's sovereignty over his subjects there. She refused to grant the bishop an audience unless he agreed to uncover his head in her presence, thereby giving symbolic recognition of the king's authority. Since no regular diplomatic relationship existed between

68. Rinuccini, *Embassy in Ireland*, pp. 10, 559; Bellesheim, *Papal Nuncio*, p. 3.
69. Carte, *Ormonde*, III, 220; Bellesheim, *Papal Nuncio*, p. 11.
70. Rinuccini, *Embassy in Ireland*, intro. pp. li–lv; Bellesheim, *Papal Nuncio*, pp. 6–7.

the Papal See and the English king, Rinuccini refused to bend to the queen's demand.[71]

Henrietta did, however, apply to Mazarin to open negotiations between herself and Rinuccini for the settlement of differences in Ireland. Henrietta's purpose in corresponding with Rinuccini was to defer his going to Ireland, where there was a possibility of peace being concluded between Ormonde and the Supreme Council. She played upon the vanity of the envoy, who liked to think of himself as the one bringing about a settlement in Ireland to the credit and glory of the Church. Actually, Henrietta had no powers from the king to deal for a peace in Ireland. Evidently her ruse worked, for Rinuccini remained in Paris throughout the summer of 1645, although he later claimed that he saw through her scheme all the while.[72]

On July 16, just two days after the queen asked for an exchange of notes with the nuncio, Colonel Fitzwilliams, carrying with him the queen's approval of his propositions for supplying an Irish army to fight for the king, was dispatched to Ireland. The fulfillment of his plan depended on whether a peace was concluded between Ormonde and the Irish.[73] In England meanwhile, Sir Nicholas Crisp was visited at Exeter and Captain Haesdonck at Falmouth by Daniel O'Neill, a groom of the bedchamber, who told them to sail to Ireland, where their fleets would take aboard Fitzwilliams's army if the peace talks proved successful.[74]

71. *Ibid.*, p. 10; *Cal. S. P. Ven.*, XXVII, 194.
72. *Ibid.*, p. 192; Rinuccini, *Embassy in Ireland*, pp. 36, 565; Carte, *Ormonde*, III, 218–219.
73. *George Digby's Cabinet*, pp. 49–50.
74. *Ibid.*, p. 49. Sir Nicholas Crisp (1599?–1666) was a wealthy London merchant who profited immensely from monopolies held by grant of the crown. Elected to the Long Parliament, he was attacked in that assembly as a monopolist and collector of duties on merchandise without parliamentary grant. After joining the Royalists in Oxford, he was commissioned to outfit privateers. His ships constituted the only navy the Royalists had, and were invaluable in supplying shipping for them between England and the Continent. He fled to France upon the triumph of the Parliamentary armies, but thanks to the influence of Puritan friends he was soon able to return to England, where a large portion of his wealth had been confiscated, though a substantial amount remained in his possession. Under

In her negotiations with Rinuccini, the queen complained that Hertogan and his co-workers in Paris were attempting to use the struggle for religious freedom to withdraw Ireland from allegiance to the crown.[75] Hertogan was little less the offender in this respect than was Rinuccini, who advised the pope not to dispense any aid directly to the queen, lest the money bestowed would be squandered by her followers. Doubting the king's honesty, Rinuccini was skeptical that any agreement could be made with him. Even were a peace to be signed, he contended, Ireland would need a period of rest before entering into the war in England, where the king was so near defeat that any deferment of aid would make its arrival too late to be useful to him.[76] It might be wondered how Rinuccini expected to safeguard the Catholic religion in Ireland without having a government favorable to the faith in England. Pointing to the fact that the Earl of Tyrone, with only Ulster in his control, had been able to carry on war against Queen Elizabeth's armies for sixteen years, Rinuccini believed that once Royalist forces were displaced and Ireland united under the suzerainty of the Church, the country could repel any future invasion from England.[77]

The nuncio remained in Paris much longer than had been intended for his visit there. In a letter dated September 18, the pope reprimanded him for his tardiness in departing from France, and told him that unless he left for Ireland forthwith, he was to hand over the money and arms intended for the rebels to Father Scampari, who might put these military supplies to some good use.[78] Rinuccini made ready to leave France and, with expectation of a huge gift, asked Mazarin for the money he had promised in support of the Confederate Irish. Mazarin did grant Rinuccini the comparatively paltry sum of 25,000 livres, but continued to procras-

---

the Commonwealth he speculated in crown lands, and after the restoration again held lucrative positions in royal customs and finance. *D.N.B.*, XIII, 95–97.

75. Rinuccini, *Embassy in Ireland*, pp. 49–50.
76. *Ibid.*, pp. 39–40, 565; Bellesheim, *Papal Nuncio*, pp. 9–10.
77. Rinuccini, *Embassy in Ireland*, p. 41.
78. *Ibid.*, pp. 569–570.

tinate in fulfilling his pledge to furnish the legate transportation across the water. Ultimately Rinuccini was forced to buy a ship for his conveyance, and early in October he sailed for his destination.[79]

The queen had but little more success in dealing directly with Rome through Kenelm Digby's embassy there than in relations with the papal and Irish representatives in Paris. Kenelm Digby was perhaps one of the worst choices she could have made in her selection of an envoy to the papal court. Generous, voluble, witty, and possessing a considerable store of knowledge, he did exude a certain charm that enabled him to make acquaintances easily, but he was too impetuous and of too questionable character for the assignment given to him. On first arriving in Rome, he seemed to make a favorable impression on the pope and others who met him. It was not long, however, until his weaknesses were exposed. Innocent X, not knowing how else to explain some of Digby's extravagances, considered him slightly insane. Even more damaging to the success of the mission, Digby's sincerity in his profession of Catholicism became suspect among many officials at the papal court.[80]

The pope, contrary to advice given by Rinuccini, did send the queen a contribution of 20,000 crowns (£7,000), not so much because of Digby's persuasion as because His Holiness wished to prepare the queen for a list of proposals coming from Rome.[81] The Earl of Arundel had sent to the pope an outline of means for raising cavalry in England to join with infantry sent from Ireland. Innocent X was so favorably impressed with Arundel's offer that he enlarged upon it in a draft treaty he gave to Digby for reference to the queen. If the queen sanctioned the contents of the treaty, the pope agreed to give 100,000 crowns immediately and a like sum

79. Carte, *Ormonde*, III, 220; Bellesheim, *Papal Nuncio*, p. 11. Mazarin's grant was equal to £2,500. See note on p. ix.

80. *Private Memoirs of Sir Kenelm Digby* (London, 1827), intro. pp. xxxvi, lxvi, lxviii; *D.N.B.*, V, 968; Rinuccini, *Embassy in Ireland*, pp. 557–558; *Cal. S. P. Dom.*, 1644–45, p. 546.

81. *Ibid.*, 1645–47, p. 113. Presumably the pope paid in Roman crowns, which were worth seven shillings sterling.

for the second and third years thereafter, were the king not restored to power before that time. In substance, the terms laid down by the pope amounted to stipulations for a treaty between the king and the Irish preparatory to the employment of an Irish army in Charles's service, and also contained provisions for complete liberty of the Catholic religion in England. In English opinion, the pope was attempting to carry out a Catholic conquest of England with the connivance of the king. Had the terms relating to Ireland been granted, it was doubtful Charles could any longer have maintained his authority over the country. The first article of the pope's draft struck upon a point which the queen could not admit—the restoration of all churches and church land in Ireland. With slight modification, this was the very topic which had prevented agreement between Ormonde and delegates of the Supreme Council in their talks during the summer,[82] and to which, Ormonde knew, the king would never accede. Other parts of the treaty, insofar as it related to Ireland, specified abolishment of all penal laws, a free and independent parliament, the employment of Catholics in principal offices, and the expulsion of Scottish forces from Ulster.[83]

In Ireland, Fitzwilliams's mission had been superseded by that of the Earl of Glamorgan, who had been sent by the king. Glamorgan's main purpose was to bring an army of ten thousand men from Ireland to the aid of the king, and in furtherance of this purpose he was to facilitate negotiations for peace between Ormonde and the Confederate Irish, since the viceroy, being himself Irish, was reluctant to proceed in negotiations on some points, thinking that matters involving the question of concessions should be left

82. *Carte MSS*, XV, 198. Thomas Howard, Earl of Arundel (1586–1646), might be remembered as the owner of the first large private art collection in England. Though he sacrificed much of his wealth and fought in behalf of the king, he later grew out of sympathy with the court. Leaving England in 1642 ostensibly as escort for Henrietta Maria and her daughter Mary, he settled in Padua, where he was to die without returning to England. It was the Earl of Arundel who on one of his earlier diplomatic missions to Germany brought back with him Wenceslaus Holler, famous for his etchings of Caroline London. *D.N.B.*, XXVIII, 73–76.

83. Carte, *Ormonde*, III, 224; Rinuccini, *Embassy in Ireland*, p. 573.

to the responsibility of an Englishman.[84] And yet the evidence seems to indicate that the king intended Glamorgan to act only under the supervision and with the approval of Ormonde. To Glamorgan the only matter worth consideration was the raising of an army to save the king, for whom he was willing to stake his honor as well as the fortune he had already given to Charles. On August 26, 1645, he signed with the Supreme Council a secret treaty in which he accorded in substance most of the points of the treaty drafted by the pope (although that treaty was not yet known in Ireland), even so far as to grant churches and church lands to the Catholics.[85] Glamorgan offered as the basis for his authority in concluding such a treaty a warrant presented to him by the king on March 12, 1645. While the document was not drawn up in strictly legal form, probably out of intent on the part of the king to keep its contents secret, it empowered Glamorgan to conclude an agreement concurred in by Ormonde, and went on to state, ". . . and if upon necessity anything to be condescended unto and yet the Lord Marquis not willing to be seen therein, or not fit for us at the present publicly to own, do you endeavor to supply the same."[86]

Glamorgan's treaty was opposed by Rinuccini, who arrived in Ireland about two months after the agreement was signed. The papal nuncio assumed a lordly mien as soon as he set foot in the country. He acted as if he were in complete control of the Irish

---

84. Samuel Rawson Gardiner, "Charles I and Glamorgan," *English Historical Review* (London, 1887), II, 696. Edward Somerset, Earl of Glamorgan (1601–67), at the beginning of the Civil War was made lieutenant general in South Wales, where he was never trusted because of his Catholic religion. His treaty with the Irish Catholics was later disavowed by Charles I, who said Glamorgan had exceeded his instructions. His zeal for the Church appeared to be greater than his devotion to the king, for when the papal nuncio, Rinuccini, arrived in Ireland, he completely dominated the mind of the earl. Always interested in mechanical experiments, Glamorgan has been erroneously credited with the invention of the steam engine. *D.N.B.*, LIII, 232–237.

85. Gardiner, "Charles I and Glamorgan," p. 699; *Carte MSS*, XV, 581.

86. Gardiner, "Charles I and Glamorgan," p. 698; Carte, *Ormonde*, III, 206–211. A facsimile of the king's warrant to Glamorgan will be found between pages 686 and 687 of the *English Historical Review* (1887), II.

rebellion, and resisted any immediate agreement with either Ormonde or Glamorgan, on the excuse that a treaty should wait until the terms the pope offered Henrietta were known.[87] When informed of the treaty signed with Glamorgan, he was skeptical of its efficacy, for even if Charles approved of Glamorgan's action, Rinuccini doubted the king's power to grant the provisions without the approval of Parliament.[88]

If the queen looked to Ireland for the delivery of the king from ruin, the offices of Mazarin looked to another quarter of Charles's kingdom, Scotland, for the same end. Mazarin had hoped to maintain a balance between the contending parties in England, but after the battle of Naseby he began to realize that England under the rule of Parliament might cause him more anxiety than if controlled by the king.[89] Among the Scottish and English Presbyterians, on the other hand, there was apprehension over the growing power of the Independents resulting from the development of the New Model army and its victories in the field.[90] Mazarin sent his agent Jean de Montreuil to Scotland to see what could be done toward bringing about an accommodation between the king and his Scottish subjects.[91] About the middle of October, 1645, Sir Robert Moray started on a return mission from Scotland to France, bringing with him the Scots' terms for a treaty with the king. To get Charles's agreement to the Scottish terms, Mazarin expected to employ the queen by having her use all her power of persuasion and her influence in moving her husband to accept a treaty.[92]

Were assistance to be had from Scotland, the queen expected it would be given by Montrose rather than by the Presbyterians. Montrose led the only Royalist army that had not been defeated by

87. Rinuccini, *Embassy in Ireland*, intro. p. lxiii, p. 571.

88. Carte, *Ormonde*, III, 225.

89. Edward Hyde, Earl of Clarendon, *The History of the Rebellion and Civil Wars in England* (7 vols., Oxford, 1849), IV, 176–177.

90. *MSS Français 15994*, fols. 5, 35.

91. *Ibid.*, fol. 25.

92. *Ibid.*, fols. 55, 56, 57; Clarendon, *History of the Rebellion*, IV, 172–173.

Parliament, but to hold out against the enemy he badly needed military supplies.[93] The queen had collected £10,000 worth of arms and powder for him, and in August she applied to the Dutch to permit the passage of the boats in which the supplies were loaded.[94] In the same month, on hearing that the war between Sweden and Denmark had ended, she proposed to send an envoy to the latter country in solicitation of an army including at least five hundred horse, offering in return some of the islands off the coast of Scotland. Continuing uncertainty in relations between Denmark and Sweden, however, made the success of such a mission most unlikely.[95]

Private persons also made offers to raise forces and land them in England to fight under the Royalist banner. Late in the summer of 1645, the Duke of Bullion volunteered his own army, then fighting the Spanish on the front against Flanders. Mazarin did not believe Bullion had at his command as many troops as he caused Henrietta to believe, and also questioned where the duke would acquire money for his proposed expedition—money which France would not contribute lest offense be given to Parliament. Henrietta sent Bullion to Rome, supposing that by having an army ready at hand the pope might be induced to support the venture, although Mazarin believed money for her purpose was more likely to be had from Spain. In the end Bullion's enterprise proved as abortive as had all other private offers.[96]

The people of England received another exposé of the queen's efforts to bring about their submission by an invading force when in October the papers of Lord George Digby, secretary to the king, were captured at a relatively minor engagement near Sherburn.

93. *Additional MSS 33369*, fol. 13.
94. *Cal. S. P. Dom.*, 1645–47, p. 23; Prinsterer, *Archives*, IV, 141.
95. *George Digby's Cabinet*, pp. 41–42; *Cal. S. P. Dom.*, 1645–47, pp. 31–32.
96. *Cal. S. P. Ven.*, XXVII, 220; *Cal. Clar. S. P.*, I, 275; Mazarin, *Lettres*, II, 237. Soon after the queen arrived in France, there was an offer by a private person to lead an army against Parliament, and the Duke of Nevers also considered diverting to the queen's cause an army which he led against the Turks. *Cal. S. P. Ven.*, XXVII, 200.

In Digby's cabinet were letters pertaining to marriage negotiations directed to gaining Dutch participation in the Royalist cause, correspondence touching the engagement of Lorraine's army, communications concerning Kenelm Digby's mission to Rome, messages in reference to dealings with Fitzwilliams, and dispatches relating to requests for aid from Denmark.[97] The introduction to Digby's published papers concluded by declaring, ". . . and to make up the Messe, the Popish Irish Rebels, with their Commander in chief, the very Romish Antichrist himself is solicited and sought unto."[98]

The year's end found Charles again at Oxford. After his defeat at Naseby he had gone on a recruiting campaign into Wales and had tried to fight his way northward to join Montrose, but was stopped near Chester. In mid-September, Montrose, deserted by his Highland levies, was crushed at Philipbaugh, and in the same month Prince Rupert, somewhat treacherously it was believed, had surrendered Bristol to the besiegers.[99] The only immediate hope for help was from Ireland, although the forces intended to come from there would have to arrive before the beginning of the next year's campaign. On the last day of the year but one, Charles sent an order to the keeper of the university library at Oxford for a copy of D'Aubigny's *Histoire Universelle de 1550 jusqu'a l'An 1601*. Well might Charles have found interest in the writings of one who, having served as a soldier under Henry IV at the conclusion of France's religious wars, had undergone experiences not far removed from those of the English king.[100]

Charles did not despair of his condition. Final defeat of his hopes seemed almost inconceivable to him. Whatever the result of the contest on the field of battle, he believed, ultimately he would

97. Rushworth, *Historical Collections*, VI, 130–131; *Cal. S. P. Dom.*, 1645–47, p. 216.

98. *George Digby's Cabinet*, p. 8; *Additional MSS 33596*, fols. 15, 18.

99. *Ibid.*, fols. 17, 18; *Cal. S. P. Dom.*, 1645–47, p. 66; *Correspondence between Charles I and Sir Edward Nicholas*, pp. 111–112; *Cal. Clar. S. P.*, I, 289.

100. *Ibid.*, p. 292.

have to be restored his rightful powers, because England could not be governed without him. Besides, as God was the sure arbiter of the universe, He would not permit rebellion to prosper. Governed by such an optimistic outlook, Charles again proposed to treat personally with Parliament in London, his real aim being, as it had been a year before, to split Presbyterian and Independent and then to step into the breach and resume his former role. But Parliament, now aware of his trickery, refused any guarantee for his safety or liberty in London.[101]

Pursuant to bringing about agreement between the king and the Presbyterian faction of Parliament, Jean de Montreuil arrived in England at the beginning of January, 1646. To make the king more pliant in his attitude toward Presbyterianism, Montreuil told him the queen had assured Robert Moray that she wished her husband to reach a settlement with the Presbyterians and that she would bend every effort in influencing him to do so. Charles did not trust Montreuil—or certainly not Mazarin, on whose behest Montreuil acted. Either Montreuil was lying, Charles thought, in representing the queen's opinion to him, or his wife had been overwhelmed by the advice of those counselors around her.[102] On one resolve Charles's mind was determinedly fixed: he would not surrender church government to Presbyterianism; in Scotland he would, but in England, never.[103]

It was only by surrendering episcopacy that Charles could ever

101. *MSS Français 15994*, fols. 70, 81, 91, 99; Clarendon, *History of the Rebellion*, IV, 180; *Charles I in 1646. Letters of Charles I to Queen Henrietta Maria* (ed. J. Bruce [The Camden Society], Westminster, 1856), p. 10 (referred to hereafter as *Letters of Charles I to Henrietta in 1646*).

102. *Cal. Clar. S. P.*, I, 297; Clarendon, *History of the Rebellion*, IV, 177–178. Robert Moray (d. 1673) was of Scottish origin. Having served in the French army, he returned to England about 1642 to aid the king in his fight against Parliamentary forces. He was later engaged in conducting negotiations between Scottish and French leaders for the purpose of restoring Charles I. Much interested in chemistry, he helped to establish the Royal Society after the restoration. Pepys described Moray as "a most excellent man of reason and learning." *D.N.B.*, XXXIX, 401–402.

103. *MSS Clar. S. P.* 2099, fol. 7; Clarendon, *History of the Rebellion*, IV, 179; *Correspondence between Charles I and Sir Edward Nicholas*, p. 104; *Works of Charles I*, I, 324–326.

acquire the backing of the Scots and Presbyterians. Henrietta could not understand why Charles balked at so small a matter as Presbyterianism when episcopacy was already destroyed.[104] To so earnest a Catholic as Henrietta, the question of episcopacy or Presbyterianism seemed hardly worth the consideration, since both were heretical, but she probably would not have stressed a point she knew to be against the opinion of her husband had she not had an agreement with Mazarin on the matter. Charles, knowing that his wife placed as many strictures on religion as anyone when it concerned her personal practice, answered her, "With what patience wouldest thou give ear to him who should persuade thee, for worldly respects, to leave the communion of the Roman church for any other? Indeed, sweetheart, this is my case; for, suppose my concession in this should prove but temporary, it may palliate tho' not excuse my sin."[105] Charles begged reason of conscience, then, for his rejection of Presbyterianism.

Henrietta by no means abandoned her husband just because she could not convince him to compromise on the subject of church government. Never more ardent than when all seemed lost, she again at the beginning of the year turned to France for help. She addressed an appeal to her brother Gaston, the Duke of Orleans, so often at odds with the French court but now temporarily restored to favor, asking that he use his influence in obtaining for Charles some of the French troops held back in garrison during the winter retirement from military campaign. If granted no units from the French army, Henrietta did obtain approval for recruiting four to five thousand soldiers in Brittany and Guienne.[106]

Hearing that his wife was raising an army in France to land on the English coast by the next spring, Charles shaped his plans to complement the measures Henrietta was undertaking. From various small Royalist garrisons still holding out against Parliament,

104. *Letters of Charles I to Henrietta in 1646*, p. 6.
105. *Ibid.*, p. 19; *Additional MSS 33596*, fol. 7.
106. Green, *Letters of Henrietta Maria*, p. 309; *Cal. Clar. S. P.*, I, 299; *Cal. S. P. Ven.*, XXVII, 238; Baillie, *Letters*, II, 350.

he proposed to gather about fifteen hundred horse and one thousand foot, and with these to march into Kent, where Royalist sentiment was strong. There he intended to await the coming of the queen's army, which, on disembarking at Hastings as he had ordered, he would join with his own forces.[107] Among the queen's followers in France, plans for the shipment of an army did not seem to correspond to the king's instructions. They never spoke of debarking their soldiers anywhere other than Cornwall, where the Prince of Wales continued in command of some troops, although intentions of landing there were much discouraged by the fall of Plymouth to General Fairfax.[108] Actually, the endeavor to recruit an army in France amounted to little more than an air castle, since the queen did not have money to raise an army, and not one soldier was enlisted and equipped. Before the month of February had ended, this empty talk about a French army had largely faded away.[109]

The Catholics appeared to be the only hope of supplying the queen's want of money. The Bishop of Angoulême, ever faithful to the queen, again tried to relieve her monetary needs by applying to the French clergy for a loan of 500,000 crowns.[110] In a letter to his wife Charles authorized her to promise the pope freedom of conscience for Catholics in England in return for an immediate grant of money. Charles's concession was far less than the pope had demanded in the proposed treaty he had sent to Henrietta, and short of complying with all of the pope's wishes, Digby wrote from Rome, there was little help to be expected from there.[111]

During the winter months the passing of each week made the possibility of an army from Ireland more remote, until finally it was too late to profit from an Irish invasion of England. On learn-

---

107. *Letters of Charles I to Henrietta in 1646*, pp. 14–15; *MSS Clar. S. P. 2110*, fol. 33.

108. *Cal. S. P. Ven.*, XXVII, 243; *Cal. Clar. S. P.*, I, 299.

109. Clarendon, *History of the Rebellion*, IV, 181–182.

110. *Cal. S. P. Ven.*, XXVII, 240.

111. *Ibid.*, p. 242; *Letters of Charles I to Henrietta in 1646*, p. 24.

ing of Glamorgan's secret treaty with the Confederates, the king disavowed the agreement, contending that in acting without the approval of Ormonde, Glamorgan had exceeded his instructions.[112] Glamorgan's negotiations had been carried on simultaneously with the talks between the Supreme Council and Ormonde, whose parleys would not have been superseded until the king personally approved the provisions of Glamorgan's treaty.[113] So it was that conversations continued between Ormonde and the Supreme Council through the early months of 1646. Rinuccini opposed any agreement with Ormonde, saying that everything should await the outcome of the treaty pending between Henrietta and the pope.[114] Rinuccini's real purpose was to prevent any settlement between the Council and Ormonde, for he realized the Irish were inclined to compromise on religious matters, leaving the Church in a less advantageous position than the Bishop of Fermo desired. He had his ambition fixed on nothing less than the complete severance of Ireland from allegiance to the crown and the establishment of the Church's protection over the country, an ambition which he expressed in a letter to the pope:

> Therefore I am disposed to believe that in considering the subject of religion, which grows and is purified by opposition, the destruction of the King would be more useful to the Irish. In this case a union of the whole people to resist the forces of Parliament would immediately follow, and by choosing a Catholic Chief or Viceroy from among themselves, they would establish according to their own view all ecclesiastical affairs. . . . Nor am I daunted by the apprehension generally entertained of a sanguinary war waged against Ireland by the King and Parliament, inasmuch as if money be supplied from abroad, the kingdom is not so destitute of men but that it could defend itself against very large armies.[115]

112. Gardiner, "Charles I and Glamorgan," pp. 707–708; *Harl. MSS 6988,* fol. 117.
113. Carte, *Ormonde,* III, 229–230.
114. Rinuccini, *Embassy in Ireland,* p. 290; Bellesheim, *Papal Nuncio,* pp. 19–20.
115. Rinuccini, *Embassy in Ireland,* p. 146.

Rinuccini was trying to impose his will against the wishes of the majority of the Supreme Council, who, while desiring to practice their faith, did not want an endless struggle against England just to make Ireland a tributary of Rome. On March 28, 1646, or about four weeks after the Bishop of Fermo had declared his war policy, the Supreme Council and Ormonde reached agreement on a peace which, though not immediately published, deferred all final settlement on religious matters to the king's grace, with the understanding he would abolish the penal laws and probably grant such other allowances regarding religion as Ormonde felt unauthorized to concede.[116] Only two days before Ormonde's agreement with the Confederates, the king addressed a letter to his viceroy telling him to give up all thought of sending an army to England, for the city of Chester, where the Irish troops were to have landed, was lost some weeks since, and Royalist armies in England were too weak to fight another campaign.[117]

Indeed, the king had to think of his own safety. Since August he had repeatedly admonished Prince Charles to leave England and go to the queen, by whom he should be ruled in all things except religion.[118] As for himself, the king after some vacillation finally decided to find asylum with the Scottish army at Newark. Through the mediation of Montreuil, Charles had been promised he would be received in the Scottish army as sovereign, allowed any servants he wished to bring with him, and permitted freedom to move about as he desired. After having granted these privileges, the Scots then decided to retract them, giving no offer of guarantees in their place. Charles remained uninformed of this change in policy, for Montreuil's letter explaining the removal of the guarantees was intercepted in passage and never reached him.[119] Early on the morning of April 27, 1646, His Majesty, attended only by Dr. Hudson and John Ashburnham and traveling in disguise, rode

116. Carte, *Ormonde*, III, 229–230.
117. *Carte MSS*, XIV, 309; Carte, *Ormonde*, III, 231.
118. *Harl. MSS 6988*, fols. 113, 125; *Cal. Clar. S. P.*, I, 279, 303, 307, 311.
119. *Harl. MSS 6988*, fol. 142; *Cal. Clar. S. P.*, I, 309; Clarendon, *History of the Rebellion*, IV, 204–205; *Letters of Charles I to Henrietta in 1646*, pp. 31, 33.

out of Oxford in journey to Newark, where he submitted himself
to the command of the Scottish army.[120]

120. Henry Cary, *Memorials of the Great Civil War in England from 1646 to
1652* (2 vols., London, 1842), I, 12. Michael Hudson, D.D. (1605–48), was an
Oxford-educated clergyman who became chaplain to Charles I. Subsequent to
accompanying Charles to the Scottish army, he was released, was caught by
Parliamentary agents while trying to flee to France, was twice apprehended after
escaping from prison, and finally was killed in defending a fortified house where
he and some of his friends had taken refuge. *D.N.B.*, XXVIII, 152–153.

CHAPTER VIII

HOPE AND HEARTBREAK

1646-49 ON LEARNING that the king had surrendered himself to the Scottish army, Henrietta
became doubly concerned over the safety of Prince Charles, in
whom would rest hope of the restoration should her husband meet
with mishap. Her second son, the Duke of York, was still in be-
leaguered Oxford, and upon its surrender was to become a hostage
of Parliament along with Princess Elizabeth and the Duke of
Gloucester, who had been in Parliament's keeping since the beginning of the Civil War. Since the youngest child, Henrietta
Anne, had been left behind in Exeter when the queen fled to
France, Prince Charles was the only one of the royal children
outside the territorial area controlled by Parliament.

Prince Charles and his council had escaped from Cornwall to
Saint Mary's Island, one of the Scilly Islands situated southwest of
Lands End, on March 4, 1646. Henrietta did not believe her son
safe there, for the island was difficult to fortify and could hardly
be defended against attack. Accordingly, she sent Lord Colepeper
with orders that the prince be removed to the Channel island of
Jersey, and also remarked in her letter that should any necessity
drive her son to the coast of France, he would find comfortable
asylum there.[1]

1. *Calendar of Clarendon State Papers* (3 vols., ed. O. Ogle, W. Dunn Macray,

203

From Saint Mary's Prince Charles sent a request to George Digby in Ireland asking that he bring several hundred Irish soldiers for the defense of the castle on the island. Digby obeyed this request with alacrity, believing that he could thereby induce the prince to come to Ireland, where his presence would serve to reduce the troublesome opposition of Rinuccini and unite the Confederates in support of their king. By the time Digby reached the Scilly Islands, Charles had already gone to Jersey, and Digby proceeded to follow him to that place. After the council refused his plan to escort the prince to Ireland, Digby then went to Paris to win the queen's support for his design.[2]

But Henrietta was not to be denied her determination to have her son with her, as indeed the king had demanded in a letter of April 15.[3] As emphasis to Henrietta's wish, Lord Jermyn on May 4 addressed a letter to the prince's council imperiously ordering that their charge be brought to Paris. If members of the council protested that they had no means of livelihood in the French capital, at least they would be as solvent there as they were at Jersey; still, no more persons than were necessary should follow the prince, as the queen would have little to supply them.[4] On May 17 the queen dispatched Sir Dudley Wyatt as bearer of the king's letter that di-

---

and W. H. Bliss, Oxford, 1872–76), I, 310 (referred to hereafter as *Cal. Clar. S. P.*); Edward Hyde, Earl of Clarendon, *The History of the Rebellion and Civil Wars in England* (7 vols., Oxford, 1849), IV, 185–186. John (Lord) Colepeper (d. 1660) was until the 1640s a country man who remained in his estates and did not involve himself in national affairs. Elected to the Long Parliament, he spoke out against monopolies and supported proceedings against Strafford, but later as an upholder of episcopacy he broke with the popular party in Parliament. After serving the king during the war years, he was appointed to the Prince of Wales's council. Colepeper was caught up in a plan to place the prince at his mother's side in Paris. During the years of exile Colepeper was sent on secret missions—one of them to Russia—in effort to raise money for the Royalists. *D.N.B.*, XI, 293–296.

2. Thomas Carte, *The Life of James, Duke of Ormonde* (6 vols., Oxford, 1851), III, 234–235 (referred to hereafter as Carte, *Ormonde*); Clarendon, *History of the Rebellion*, IV, 190–194.

3. *Charles I in 1646. Letters of Charles I to Queen Henrietta Maria* (ed. J. Bruce [The Camden Society], Westminster, 1856), p. 36 (referred to hereafter as *Letters of Charles I to Henrietta in 1646*).

4. *MSS Clar. S. P. 2198*.

rected her to keep the prince in her company, and she also sent her own note imploring the prince to be a dutiful son.[5] Edward Hyde, Royalist Chancellor of the Exchequer and the prince's chief mentor, could see no advantage in the prince's going to France and thought it unwise to identify him with a foreign power in the eyes of the king's subjects, for if the English people were ever to restore kingship, it would be at their own behest rather than upon the promptings of another nation. Lord Colepeper, who had been dispatched with the queen's demand only a few weeks earlier, was now sent back to Paris along with Lord Capel to explain why Prince Charles's council thought he should remain on English soil so long as it was safe for him to do so.[6] Henrietta was of another opinion. The prince should be in Paris to lead an expedition which would be furnished by France. She said she was not to be moved by any reason that could be given for the prince's remaining at Jersey and that her resolution was "positive and unalterable."[7]

The queen had been strengthened in her resolution by the king's letter of May 28. Charles said it was increasingly apparent to him that the Scots intended to clip his power by settling upon England a Presbyterian government which would make the people judges over their monarch. He empowered his wife to promise the pope

---

5. *Cal. Clar. S. P.*, I, 317.

6. *Ibid.*, pp. 318, 347. Edward Hyde, Earl of Clarendon (1609–74), was a barrister who began his public career as a member of the Short and the Long Parliament. At first he opposed what he considered royal encroachments on Parliament's rights, but when the balance of power began to shift against the king, he abandoned the Puritan party and joined the king in York. He was Charles II's chief adviser during the years of exile, when he began writing his *History of the Rebellion and Civil Wars in England*. After the restoration he was made Earl of Clarendon and continued to be the leading minister until his overthrow in 1667. (*D.N.B.*, XXVIII, 389–393.) Arthur Capel, Lord Capel of Hadham (1610?–49), a country gentleman elected to the Long Parliament, joined the popular party under John Pym, but wishing no democratic revolution, he broke away from the king's opposition. During the ensuing struggle, the king had no adherent more faithful and devoted. In August, 1641, Capel was raised to the peerage. Later, as a member of the Prince of Wales's council, he opposed the prince's flight to France. Ultimately Capel was captured and beheaded by vote of Parliament only a few weeks following the execution of the king. (*D.N.B.*, IX, 10–12.)

7. Clarendon, *History of the Rebellion*, IV, 190.

toleration of Catholicism in England in return for Catholic help in restoring episcopacy, and continued: "I think not Pr. Charles safe in Jersey; therefore send for him to wait upon thee with all speed . . . and in God's name let him stay with thee til it be seen what ply my business will take, and for my sake let the world see the Queen seeks not to alter his conscience."[8]

Impatient over the obstinacy of the prince's council, Henrietta in June sent Lord Jermyn, Lord Colepeper, and Sir George Digby with instructions to accompany her son from his residence on the island of Jersey to her own court in Paris. Digby, wholly taken in by Mazarin's fair talk of assistance for the king, had given up his scheme of taking the prince to Ireland and now supported the queen's wishes. To Prince Charles the queen sent the king's letter of May 28, and tried to play upon the youth's manifest interest in the fair sex by including a miniature portrait of Mademoiselle, daughter of her brother Gaston.[9]

Heated debate arose between the queen's followers and Charles's councilors over the prince's removal from Jersey. The argument became so rancorous that the prince suspended the discussions. His councilors protested that Mazarin had sent the prince no invitation to come to France and that they could not be responsible for the prince's welfare in Paris. Regardless of the merits of the arguments on either side, the paternal admonition was too strong for the prince to resist, but Lord Capel, Lord Hopton, and Sir Edward Hyde refused to follow him to his mother's court.[10]

In Paris, meanwhile, Mazarin was preparing to send Pompone de Bellièvre as ambassador extraordinary to assist Jean de Montreuil, the French resident in London, in bringing about a treaty between the Scots and the king. Mazarin candidly admitted to George Digby that he had hoped to maintain a balance in the struggle between king and Parliament and regretted that the king

8. *Letters of Charles I to Henrietta in 1646*, pp. 41–42.

9. *Cal. Clar. S. P.*, I, 321; Clarendon, *History of the Rebellion*, IV, 200.

10. *Cal. Clar. S. P.*, I, 323; Clarendon, *History of the Rebellion*, IV, 217; *Calendar of State Papers, Venice* (38 vols., ed. Allen B. Hinds and others, London, 1864–1940), XXVII, 269–270 (referred to hereafter as *Cal. S. P. Ven.*).

had lost all military power. Now his design was to align the king and Scots against the Independents and possibly to throw in the assistance of an army from France to bolster Royalist fortunes.[11] The queen was almost wholly subservient to this plan of the French minister. While ostensibly she had been the one who named Bellièvre to go to England, she had done so on the suggestion of Mazarin.[12]

Since placing himself with the Scottish army, Charles, deprived of the servants he had brought with him and closely guarded by soldiers, had been treated as a prisoner of war. In letters to his wife he complained bitterly that the Scots tried to press him to sign the Covenant, and he could find no better epithet for them than "abominable relapsed rogues."[13] Around the middle of July he received the conditions, the so-called London Propositions, for a treaty between him and his opponents. These propositions were presented in the name of both houses of Parliament rather than by the Scots, although the commissioners representing Scotland in London had been consulted and satisfied about the terms. The propositions required Charles to sign the Covenant and impose Presbyterianism upon England and to assign the control of the army and navy to Parliament for a period of twenty years. The articles were to be accepted or rejected in their entirety and without discussion, since the persons who delivered them were not authorized to confer with the king in any way.[14]

Rather than consent to the propositions, Charles would see the monarchy go down in dust. To accept Presbyterianism would violate his conscience and belie his coronation oath to uphold the established church. Furthermore, monarchy could not stand, he argued, unless the king controlled the church. Control of the pulpit, the most powerful organ of public opinion, was essential to teach the people obedience to the royal will, whereas Presby-

---

11. Clarendon, *History of the Rebellion*, IV, 194–195.

12. *Ibid.*, pp. 219–220.

13. *Letters of Charles I to Henrietta in 1646*, p. 36.

14. John Rushworth, *Historical Collections* (8 vols., London, 1721–22), VI, 309–311.

terianism, as it upheld rebellion, undermined the very foundation of monarchy.[15]

Bellièvre did not arrive in England until after the propositions had been dispatched to the king.[16] Nevertheless, Charles was glad to receive the ambassador, for he believed consultation with the envoy would give excuse to delay an answer to the propositions as long as possible, although he was later to despise Bellièvre for trying to convince him to accept Presbyterianism.[17]

Charles still entertained the idea of going to London, where he planned to set Presbyterians and Independents against each other and seize power as a result of their division. In his answer to the propositions he said there were so many provisions requiring further elucidation and understanding that a definite reply was hardly to be expected unless he was allowed to proceed to London and there enter into discussions on particular terms. This response did not satisfy the conditions demanded by Parliament, and for a time Charles's fate remained in limbo.[18]

Henrietta was not displeased with Charles's reply to the propositions. While she thought he should agree to tolerate Presbyterianism, she was against his taking the Covenant and most definitely resisted granting Parliament any control over military forces.[19] If she could conceive of no agreement with Parliament, she thought Charles could persuade the Scots to fight for his restoration by conceding no more than Presbyterianism in England, as indeed Scottish agents sent to Paris had promised her.[20] Charles believed his wife to be mistaken in holding such sanguine hopes, for he was convinced the Scots would not support him unless he signed the

15. *Cal. Clar. S. P.*, I, 325; *MSS Clar. S. P. 2335*; *Letters of Charles I to Henrietta in 1646*, p. 71.

16. Rushworth, *Historical Collections*, VI, 318.

17. *Letters of Charles I to Henrietta in 1646*, pp. 51–52.

18. *The Diplomatic Correspondence of Jean de Montreuil and the Brothers de Bellièvre* (2 vols., ed. and tr. J. G. Fotheringham, vols. 29 and 30 in Publications of the Scottish Historical Society, Edinburgh, 1898–99), I, 229; Rushworth, *Historical Collections*, VI, 319–320.

19. *MSS Français 15994*, fol. 75; *Letters of Charles I to Henrietta in 1646*, pp. 56–57.

20. *Additional MSS 33569*, fol. 7.

Covenant. He begged her not to bother him any more on the subject of Presbyterianism and also to tell Mazarin that the issue was
closed. If she persisted in her entreaties, the king wrote, she would
break his heart.[21]

If Charles thought his request would end his wife's persuasions,
he greatly underestimated her tenacity. Upon Bellièvre's suggestion
that a person trusted by the king might be able to penetrate the
monarch's stubbornness, Henrietta sent the Cavalier poet William
Davenant. Davenant proved less discreet in trying to change the
king's mind than had Bellièvre. During an interview in which the
king seemed to have the better of the argument, Davenant at last
declared the established church to be an institution of little importance, whereupon Charles lost his royal composure and angrily
told Davenant he wished never again to see him.[22]

In the midst of debate over the London Propositions, the Prince
of Wales arrived in Paris without fanfare. The French court did
not even recognize his presence with the customary message of
congratulation on his safe arrival. To Parliament Mazarin represented the prince's visit as a matter of great embarrassment to the
French government, since the young man's coming was wholly
unexpected. In a note to Henrietta, Mazarin reflected another attitude by saying that despite the depleted state of French finances,
her monthly pension would be increased 10,000 livres in consideration of the prince's residence at her court.[23]

Prince Charles first received official recognition, although he
was still supposedly incognito, when he and his mother visited the

21. *Letters of Charles I to Henrietta in 1646*, p. 62.

22. *MSS Clar. S. P. 2325*; Clarendon, *History of the Rebellion*, IV, 224–225. Sir
William Davenant (1606–68) will be remembered as a Cavalier poet and play-
wright. In the latter capacity he attracted the attention of Henrietta Maria, and
though not necessarily through her influence, he was appointed poet laureate by
the king in 1638. During the Civil War he fought in Newcastle's army. With the
defeat of Royalist arms, he joined other exiles in Paris. After the restoration he
returned to his first love, the stage, as director of the Duke of York's theater.
D.N.B., XIV, 101–108.

23. Clarendon, *History of the Rebellion*, IV, 225, 227; Cardinal de Mazarin,
Lettres (9 vols., ed. P. A. Chéruel [*Collection de Documents Inédits*], Paris, 1872–
1906), II, 792; *Cal. Clar. S. P.*, I, 331.

queen regent and the boy king, Louis XIV, at Fontainebleau.[24] Before the visit could be arranged there was much fuss over formalities of etiquette and rank. Henrietta insisted her son be given precedence, since his father had been granted such privilege during his stay at the Spanish court in 1624, but the queen regent, Anne, replied that this honor had been given Charles's father in his capacity as King of Scotland, which title he had assumed during the trip to Spain. Too, there was the question of whether the prince was to be seated in the presence of Louis XIV. In the end it was agreed both of them would be seated in chairs of equal height and proportions. On only one occasion during their meetings at Fontainebleau did Charles remain standing in the presence of the French king, and then only because a scarcity of chairs forced him to give his own place to his mother, and only once did Louis XIV allow the prince to pass before him in leaving the room.[25]

Henrietta was much comforted to have another of her children with her when in August, 1646, Lady Morton escaped from England with the two-year-old Henrietta Anne. Coming into the queen's care at an early age, Henrietta Anne was instructed in the Catholic religion and was the only one of the royal children to be reared in her mother's faith. A little book of religious instruction which Henrietta had one of her Capuchins, Father Cyprien de Gamache, prepare for the youngest of her daughters was later to serve as a model for the religious education of other children.[26]

It was also in August that Ormonde proclaimed the Irish peace which had been drawn up between him and the Supreme Council during the preceding March.[27] The queen had a part, though by

24. Cal. S. P. Ven., XXVII, 275.

25. Ibid., p. 270; Françoise Bertaut, Madame de Motteville, Mémoires sur Anne d'Autriche et Sa Cour (4 vols., ed. M. F. Riaux, Paris, n.d.), I, 283–284.

26. Cal. S. P. Ven., XXVII, 276; Cyprien de Gamache, Memoirs of the Mission in England of the Capuchin Friars of the Province of Paris, from the Year 1630 to 1669 (in vol. II, 293–501, of Thomas Birch, The Court and Times of Charles I [2 vols., London, 1848]), pp. 409, 415 (referred to hereafter as Gamache, Memoirs); Cal. Clar. S. P., I, 327.

27. The Embassy in Ireland of Monsignor G. B. Rinuccini (tr. Anne Hutton, Dublin, 1873), p. 196 (referred to hereafter as Rinuccini, Embassy in Ireland); MSS Clar. S. P. 2425.

no means a prominent role, in this event. At the outset of the year the king had instructed Ormonde to follow the direction of the prince and the queen and to obey no command coming from England unless the nature of such a directive made its validity patent.[28] Early in June, Charles told Ormonde to enter into no peace with the Irish, but then in a letter of June 16 he explained to the queen that his admonition did not invalidate any treaty that might already have been concluded.[29] George Digby, who was in Paris at the time the king's instruction to Ormonde became known there, vigorously protested against the king's order, saying that it obviously had been made under duress or as a result of false information and that he would place his own life in surety for the king's concurrence in an agreement with the Irish.[30] Doubly supported by the king's letter and Digby's assurances, the queen told Ormonde he was to ignore the letter he had received from her captive husband and to proceed with the publishing of the treaty when the time was opportune.[31]

Because this treaty made no settlement for religion in Ireland but related only to civil affairs, Rinuccini used the strongest weapon he could wield in protest against it. Before an assembly of bishops he declared all persons who adhered to the peace with Ormonde excommunicate.[32] Since the king was now without power, the nuncio maintained, a treaty with him was meaningless anyway. Ireland must have a protector, he thought. The most natural choice for this office was the pope, but Rome was too far away to serve effectively as overlord for Ireland. The next choice was France, where Rinuccini thought he stood in high favor. But then, George Digby also believed himself especially in the good graces of Mazarin.[33]

For the moment, Irish affairs were subsidiary to the main ques-

28. *Diplomatic Correspondence of Montreuil and Bellièvre*, I, 226; *MSS Clar. S. P. 2425*.

29. *Letters of Charles I to Henrietta in 1646*, pp. 47–48; *Carte MSS*, XVII, 486.

30. Rinuccini, *Embassy in Ireland*, pp. 188–189.

31. *Ibid.*, p. 196; *Carte MSS*, XVIII, 721.

32. *Ibid.*, p. 468; Rushworth, *Historical Collections*, VI, 416, 417.

33. Rinuccini, *Embassy in Ireland*, pp. 182–184.

tion of whether the king and the Scots could be brought into a cooperative relationship. Upon further insistence of the French ambassadors, Charles decided to send a second answer to the London Propositions.[34] This time his communications were to be directed not to Parliament but to the Scottish commissioners in London.[35] The queen bore upon the king with all the influence she could command to obtain his consent to Presbyterian church government—she had Jermyn, Colepeper, and others write to him in support of her own pleadings, she communicated with the Earl of Lanark and the Duke of Hamilton soliciting their persuasion upon the king for the same effect, she tried to frighten the king by telling him he would be delivered into the hands of Parliament if he did not reach accord with the Scots, and she wrote hopefully of aid from France, since the wars of the Continent were soon to be concluded.[36] But Charles's fundamental position, despite the anguish the queen's letters caused him, remained unshaken. He told his wife he refused to discuss the religious issue with her any longer. On hearing from Davenant that the queen threatened to enter a monastery unless her husband came to agreement with the Scots, Charles replied in a letter to Jermyn and others, "I say no more of it; my heart is too big; the rest being fitter for your thoughts than my expression."[37] To be sure, Henrietta would not have him agree to the Covenant, for to do so might exclude forever the return of a Catholic queen to England; and above all, he was to make absolutely no concession regarding the militia.[38] Charles tried to explain to his wife that the militia was not so important in England, where there was no large standing army as in France, but that the

34. *Letters of Charles I to Henrietta in 1646*, p. 59; *The Hamilton Papers* (ed. Samuel Rawson Gardiner [The Camden Society], Westminster, 1880), p. 108.

35. *Letters of Charles I to Henrietta in 1646*, p. 65.

36. *Cal. Clar. S. P.*, I, 333; Mary Anne Everett Green, *Letters of Queen Henrietta Maria* (London, 1857), pp. 321–322; *MSS Clar. S. P.* 2327, 2368; *Hamilton Papers*, pp. 135, 139.

37. *MSS Clar. S. P.* 2325, fol. 351; *Letters of Charles I to Henrietta in 1646*, p. 62.

38. *Egerton MSS 2619*, fol. 24; *MSS Clar. S. P. 2362*, fol. 56; Green, *Letters of Henrietta Maria*, pp. 326, 333–334.

support of the pulpit was indispensable to monarchical power.[39]

After consultation with the bishops of London and Salisbury,[40] Charles in his second answer to the propositions agreed to Presbyterianism in England for a period of three years following his restoration, during which time an assembly of divines—one-third chosen by the Presbyterians, another third by the Independents, and a like proportion by himself—would decide the further settlement of church government. Charles knew a body so divided would never decide anything, and he planned by electing a parliament favorable to himself to reinstate episcopacy. Furthermore, he agreed to parliamentary control over the militia for a period of ten years.[41]

Will Murray carried Charles's second answer to the Scottish commissioners, arriving in London during the latter part of October. When Murray appeared before the commissioners, they immediately asked him whether Charles had granted the Covenant. Receiving no positive assurance from Murray's answer, the commissioners refused to consider Charles's offer or even to read the terms set forth in the document which Murray carried.[42]

On learning of the conditions Charles offered in his proposal to the commissioners, Henrietta's reaction was one of anger mixed with disappointment in the person whom she loved more than all the world. She was especially exasperated that Charles had granted Parliament power over the militia for a period of ten years. "Thus power is lost from your hands," she stormed:

> You are no more King. As for me, I will never set foot in England. Having given them this power, you can refuse them nothing, not even my own life if they demand it. But I will never place myself in their hands. I conjure you for the last time to concede no more. . . . Maybe it is yet possible to recover control of the militia, especially if Parliament rejects your offer. Again and again I have told you to

39. *Letters of Charles I to Henrietta in 1646,* pp. 79–80; *Cal. Clar. S. P.,* I, 337; *MSS Clar. S. P. 2335, 2381, 2360.*

40. Henry Ellis, *Original Letters* (12 vols. in 3 series, London, 1824–46), ser. 2, III, 326–327; *Cal. Clar. S. P.,* I, 335.

41. *Ibid.,* p. 351.

42. *Ibid.,* p. 337; *Letters of Charles I to Henrietta in 1646,* pp. 73, 75–76.

grant nothing more, but insensibly you go ahead and do so despite your stated resolutions. You stick at bishops and episcopacy, yet go ahead and betray your posterity. I tell you for the last time, if you concede anything more, you are lost, and I will never again return to England . . . I finish, praying that God will assist you.[43]

Her fury, if not her censure, seemed to have subsided somewhat when two weeks later, on December 14, she wrote: "In the first place you conclude correctly, that nothing but the abundance of my love could cause me to take up the unpleasant task of pressing things which are unacceptable to you, but where I find your interests so much concerned as in your present resolution, I should be faltier than you if I suffered you to rest in such an error as would prove fatal to you. . . ."[44]

Mazarin had given up any pretense of assisting Charles. The French minister could not understand why Charles refused to surrender episcopacy when he was willing to make more important concessions. As it became increasingly apparent that the Scots were preparing to turn the king over to Parliament, Charles thought of escape, but the queen told him not to come to France, for he could expect no support from there. Mazarin advised that he go to Scotland or Ireland or some other part of his kingdom. In truth, France did not want him.[45]

Many of Charles's followers who had sought refuge around the queen's court were experiencing lean living during the winter months of 1646–47. Sir Endymion Porter, who had rendered the king long and faithful service, and Secretary Nicholas commiserated with one another in their poverty. "I am a sad man to understand that your Honour is reduced to want," wrote Porter, "but it is all our cases; for I am in so much necessity, that were it not for an Irish barber, that was once my servant, I might have starved for want of bread. He hath lent me some monies, which will last for one fortnight longer, and then I shall be as much subject to misery

43. *MSS Clar. S. P. 2369*, fol. 216.
44. *Ibid.*, 2327.
45. *Ibid.*, 2379; Mazarin, *Lettres*, II, 334–335, 337.

as I was before. Here in our Court no man looks on me, and the Queen thinks I lost my estate for want of wit, rather than for my loyalty to my master."[46] The pension Her Majesty received from the French government, it was said, was not used as it might have been for the king's loyal followers now in need, but was squandered by her favorite, Henry Jermyn, who if not born to affluence had certainly acquired a taste for luxury. Edward Hyde complained that lack of financial support from the queen forced many of Prince Charles's advisers to live away from Paris in the less expensive provincial cities of France, much to the injury of the prince, who needed his advisers with him. For want of means elsewhere, some of the less prominent Royalist leaders sought such settlement with Parliament as they could obtain and returned to England.[47]

The sixteen-year-old prince was completely under the governance of his mother during these months, not even being permitted to cover his head in her presence. Henrietta had designs for the young man. While visiting Fontainebleau the summer before, she had urged Queen Anne to help her in promoting a match between the prince and the daughter of Gaston, the "great Mademoiselle" as she was called, the richest woman in France.[48] To be sure, the prince could use a large dowry. Henrietta was free to push her project to the utmost, for notice had been given Frederick Henry that negotiations for a marriage with the House of Orange were at an end, and the king had empowered his wife to treat for another match.[49]

Under the prompting eye of his mother, the prince became so open and persistent in his gallantries toward Mademoiselle that his attentions to her were the talk of the French court, but she remained cool to his suit. Mademoiselle, a young woman of in-

46. Ellis, *Original Letters*, ser. 2, III, 314.
47. *MSS Clar. S. P.* 2427, fol. 80; *Cal. Clar. S. P.*, I, 365; Clarendon, *History of the Rebellion*, IV, 343.
48. *Mémoires de Mlle. de Montpensier* (4 vols., ed. A. Chéruel, Paris, n.d.), I, 127–128 (referred to hereafter as Montpensier, *Mémoires*).
49. Guillaume Groen van Prinsterer, *Archives ou Correspondance Inédit de la Maison d'Orange Nassau* (4 vols., Utrecht, 1859), IV, 152–153; *Letters of Charles I to Henrietta in 1646*, p. 68.

sufferable vanity, looked upon the awkward youth three years her junior with contemptuous pity. Although he spoke hardly a word of French and understood the language but little better than he spoke it, he told one of his French cousins that he comprehended every word Mademoiselle said. Ridiculous, Mademoiselle thought.[50] Prince Charles was at great disadvantage in being unable to speak French. While Henrietta tried to point out her son's merits, Mademoiselle said any suitor who was to win her heart must talk for himself.[51] Anyway, as she would have us believe from her memoirs, she had admirers enough who made no end of compliment upon the brilliance of her hair, the beauty of her face, and the perfection of her figure. Whenever she appeared at court festivities, the prince was there with hat in hand to wait upon her, even holding the flambeau while she smoothed her coiffure or adjusted her dress before the mirror.[52] Late in the winter a *fête célèbre* was held at the Palais Royal. At this event Mademoiselle sat upon a throne intended for young Louis XIV but which he refused to occupy. She was bedecked from head to foot with jewels, some of which belonged to the crown of France. At her feet, on the stairs leading up to the dais, reclined Prince Charles and the boy Louis.[53] So adorned, so admired, so (as she thought) beautiful, and having a prince and a king to grace her footstool, could a lady know any greater glory? She looked down from the heights; her cup was full.

Perhaps a more fundamental reason for her hauteur toward the prince was her hope of a better alliance. She had her ambitions fixed on the Holy Roman Emperor. When her father objected that the emperor was older than himself, she answered that she cared not for a husband but for the elevation of her rank.[54]

The offers that Prince Charles could make in that respect were not promising. On January 30, 1647, the king had been given over

50. Montpensier, *Mémoires*, I, 138.
51. *Ibid.*
52. *Ibid.*, p. 128.
53. *Ibid.*, pp. 139–140.
54. *Ibid.*, pp. 142–143.

to the custody of Parliament in consideration of a payment of money, and the Scottish army retired across the Tweed.[55] The ensuing year was to be a period of widening rift between the Presbyterians and Independents in England, of attempts to reach agreement with the king on the part of the Scots and the army, and of Charles's lingering hopes to set one party against the other for his own advantage. The trends of the past year, therefore, merely continued their development, but after Charles left the Scottish army, the queen had increasingly less influence over affairs in England. True, she did send her agents to Ireland and England, but she had little to do with their instructions and did not enter directly into the negotiations conducted by them. There were several reasons for the decline in her influence. Mazarin had given up any intention of trying to balance the forces at strife in England, since the purpose of that policy was made less meaningful by France's nearness to victory in the Thirty Years' War, and elsewhere Henrietta's endeavors to obtain aid had already failed. There was no other power to which she could turn, for she had built her hope upon a foreign invasion to defeat her husband's enemies rather than upon appeal to any source of support indigenous to England. Nevertheless, she continued to stir the embers in blind hope that some force might yet be brought forth to save the king.

The best that Henrietta could have done at this point, short of the actual conquest of England by a foreign state intent upon restoring the monarch, would not have been enough to save Charles. Charles seems not to have recognized the political necessity of compromise unless he had sufficient power to impose his own will, and that power he certainly did not have.

Not yet fully aware of Charles's obduracy against any kind of lasting compromise, both Independents and Presbyterians, between whom distrust deepened, tried to reach accord with him. After the king was placed in the care of Parliament, the Presbyterians in the houses made overtures for his restoration on the basis

55. *MSS Français 15994*, fol. 92.

of the articles he had offered in reply to the propositions during the previous fall.[56] The officers of the army, becoming worried lest the king combine with the Presbyterians in Parliament, sent Cornet Joyce to seize him and bring him into their keeping.[57] Hearing that the king was well treated by his new keepers, the queen in July sent Sir John Berkeley to England for the purpose of mediating a settlement between her husband and his captors.[58] By this time the queen seems to have given up thought of her own concern in any treaty that might be concluded, for on June 6, 1647, she had advised Charles to make a treaty on any possible terms that would grant his own safety and well-being.[59] Although Berkeley spent every effort to bring about a treaty, the king was no less opposed to the Independents' wish for religious toleration than he had been to Presbyterian demands that he sign the Covenant, and he seemed to think it beneath his dignity to negotiate with people of such low position as the army officers. The leaders of the army, he thought, would have to accept him on his own terms, for they could

56. *Hamilton Papers*, p. 147; *Memoirs of Sir John Berkeley, Containing an Account of His Negotiation with Lieutenant-General Cromwell, Commissary-General Ireton and Other Officers of the Army* (in vol. I of Francis Maseres, *Select Tracts* [London, 1815]), p. 372 (referred to hereafter as Berkeley, *Memoirs*).

57. *The Clarke Papers* (4 vols., ed. C. H. Firth [The Camden Society], Westminster, 1891), intro. xxiv-xxv, xxvii-xxx. It is not to the purpose here to discuss the many and intricate dealings of Charles with the Scots and the army unless those negotiations related to the life of Henrietta.

Cornet George Joyce was said to have been a tailor in London before the outbreak of the Civil War, during which he apparently served in Cromwell's regiment. *D.N.B.*, XXX, 217–218.

58. Berkeley, *Memoirs*, pp. 355, 356; *The Memoirs of Edmund Ludlow* (2 vols., ed. C. H. Firth, Oxford, 1894), I, 151, 153 (referred to hereafter as Ludlow, *Memoirs*); Clarendon, *History of the Rebellion*, IV, 254. Sir John Berkeley, Baron Berkeley of Stratton (d. 1678), one of the king's generals in the southeastern sector of England, seems to have been of greatest assistance to the royal couple during time of flight. He was able to afford the queen a place of safety in Exeter for the birth of her youngest child when she was fleeing to France, and later he accompanied Charles from London to the Isle of Wight in attempted escape to France. After the defeat of Royalist arms he joined his kinsman Henry Jermyn at the queen's court in Paris. A great favorite of Henrietta Maria, he became mentor to the Duke of York and, though detested by Edward Hyde, was to enjoy favors and advancements in the court of Charles II following the restoration. *D.N.B.*, IV, 361–363.

59. *Cal. S. P. Ven.*, XXVII, 320.

not rule England without him.[60] After repeated attempts to come to some understanding with the king, the officers gave up the idea of reaching accord with him, and during the fall murmurs demanding that the king be brought to trial were heard among the ranks. Also, an intercepted letter in which the king informed his wife that he had no intention of abiding by any agreement with the army apparently destroyed the confidence the higher officers had in their king. It was pointless to deal with Charles if he refused to act in good faith.[61]

The Scots, believing Presbyterianism unsafe in Scotland unless it were also implanted in England, had another turn in dealing with the king.[62] The clergy and the party led by the Earl of Argyll would make no agreement to restore Charles unless he guaranteed the Covenant.[63] But another faction, led by the Duke of Hamilton, who on the destruction of the king's military forces had been released from prison,[64] was ready to bargain with the monarch on less exacting terms. Lords Loudon, Hamilton, and Lanark were in London to treat with him when on October 10 he escaped his captors and got as far as Carisbrooke Castle on the Isle of Wight in his effort to flee from England.[65] It was at Carisbrooke, on December 26, that Charles at last signed an agreement, or Engagement as it was called, with Hamilton and the other lords. If the Engagement did not grant as much as the Scottish lords wished, it

60. Ludlow, *Memoirs*, I, 154, 156, 158; Berkeley, *Memoirs*, pp. 367–368, 390–393; *Harl. MSS 6988*, fol. 210.

61. Berkeley, *Memoirs*, pp. 373, 394; Carte, *Ormonde*, III, 334–335.

62. *MSS Français 15994*, fol. 156.

63. *Ibid.*, fols. 148, 151, 165, 166. Archibald Campbell, Marquis and Earl of Argyll (1598–1661), was a leader of one of the most powerful Highland clans in Scotland. Feeling no strong personal commitment to either episcopacy or Presbyterianism, he became a defender of the Covenant when he saw such a course offered the greater possibility for wielding leadership. He advocated Scottish assistance for Parliamentary forces because he thought the autonomy of Scotland could not be permanent without the victory of Parliament in England. *D.N.B.*, VIII, 319–329.

64. Gilbert Burnet, *The Memoirs of the Lives and Actions of James and William, Dukes of Hamilton and Castleherald* (London, 1677), p. 291; Clarendon, *History of the Rebellion*, IV, 320–321.

65. Berkeley, *Memoirs*, pp. 375, 377, 380–382; Burnet, *Memoirs of Hamilton and Castleherald*, pp. 313, 318–319, 323–324.

was thought to be a sufficient concession to justify a Scottish invasion of England in the king's behalf. Charles agreed to confirm the Covenant for a period of three years and to satisfy Scottish sensibilities on religious matters insofar as his conscience would allow. The Prince of Wales was to be permitted to go to Scotland to participate in the invasion of England, and the queen was to be enjoined to assist the Scots to the limit of her ability.[66]

Montreuil, who was in Scotland to raise mercenary levies for the French army, perceived that the Engagement was no basis for a lasting peace. The Scots, he knew, were concerned not so much over the restoration of the king as over the preservation of Presbyterianism. Even if the Scottish army were to overrun England, the war would not be over nor the king reinstated, for then they would try to enforce the Covenant permanently on Charles, who would never agree to such an exaction. With no great exercise of foresight, Montreuil advised Mazarin to have nothing to do with the Scottish invasion of England.[67]

In no part of Charles's kingdom were political affairs more complex or unsettled than in Ireland. First of all, the Irish were at war among themselves. The population was divided into two parts, the Old Irish and the Anglo-Irish. The Old Irish, strongest in the western parts of Ireland and in Ulster, were those whose ancestors had inhabited Ireland for time out of memory. Little concerned in commercial enterprise, they were looked upon as a slow, backward people. The Anglo-Irish, though no less Catholic in religion than the Old Irish, stemmed from English families who had been established in Ireland. There had, of course, been intermarriage with the Irish, but the distinguishing stamp was still maintained. Having profited from confiscations of church property and the despoiling of the Old Irish, they were the great landowners and the commercial classes. The more aggressive and enterprising people of the nation, they could appreciate the role of the crown in

66. *MSS Français 15994*, fols. 211, 212, 266; Berkeley, *Memoirs*, pp. 392–393; Burnet, *Memoirs of Hamilton and Castleherald*, p. 334; *Cal. Clar. S. P.*, I, 405; Clarendon, *History of the Rebellion*, IV, 322, 326.

67. *MSS Français 15994*, fols. 158, 159, 195, 196.

maintaining law and order for the safety of private property.[68] Rinuccini introduced a disturbing element into this civil division. He thought the Catholic Church could still lord it over nations and peoples, although the papacy had provided but scant resources to bring Ireland under its protectorship. Aligning himself with the Old Irish, the nuncio served only to aggravate the faction that already existed and to prevent any sort of settlement in the bleeding country. He was determined that the king's authority in Ireland be destroyed, and under Rinuccini's leadership the Confederate Assembly revoked the treaty the Supreme Council had concluded with Ormonde.

In March, 1647, Henrietta sent Dr. George Leyburn to seek another treaty between the Supreme Council and Ormonde.[69] Having little awareness of political realities, Rinuccini professed not to trust the queen, though in fact she was ready to concede to the Irish as much as the power entrusted to her would permit.[70] On dispatching Leyburn to Ireland, she instructed him to go to the nuncio in the event Ormonde had already surrendered Dublin to Parliament, with whom the viceroy had been dealing since the beginning of the year, and to indicate the goodwill she felt toward the religious aspirations of the Confederates. For her own part, she was willing to surrender the churches and church lands in Ireland to the Confederates.[71]

While Parliamentary ships burdened with troops and horses waited in the harbor at Dublin, Confederate troops conducted a desultory siege from the landward side of the city. Leyburn passed back and forth between the Council and Ormonde in futile effort

---

68. Rinuccini, *Embassy in Ireland*, pp. 485–486.

69. *The Memoirs of George Leyburn* (London, 1722), p. 29. George Leyburn, D.D. (1593–1677), stemmed from an English Catholic family that had been much reduced in wealth by fines against their religion. Educated at the Catholic school of Douay across the Channel and ordained a priest in 1625, Leyburn was sent as a missionary to England in 1630. There he was imprisoned but then released on intercession of Henrietta Maria, who made him one of her chaplains. *D.N.B.*, XXXIII, 212.

70. Rinuccini, *Embassy in Ireland*, p. 261.

71. Leyburn, *Memoirs*, p. 42.

to bring about agreement.[72] Fearing the retributions of the Old Irish under the military leadership of Owen O'Neill, and believing himself unable to hold Dublin any longer against Irish forces, Ormonde surrendered the city to Parliament on June 28, 1647, and in so doing terminated Henrietta's efforts to bring about peace with the Confederates.[73]

After a temporary eclipse of political power, the Anglo-Irish again gained control of the Assembly when it met in November, largely because the seventy delegates from Ulster failed to appear at the session.[74] Rinuccini was determined that Ireland be placed under a protector, preferably the pope,[75] and in deference to his demand delegates were sent to Rome, Paris, and Madrid. Only after Rome had been consulted was Ireland to be offered to France or Spain, the agents to those places being meanwhile occupied in attempts to secure money and arms.[76] Of the emissaries sent to Paris, two, Lord Muskerry and Geoffrey Brown, were partisans of the Anglo-Irish, and the third, Lord Antrim, adhered to Rinuccini's faction. The Anglo-Irish, or Ormondists, intended their representatives in France to reach an agreement for restoring the treaty previously made with Ormonde and to bring Prince Charles back to Ireland regardless of the content of official instructions.[77]

The day was too far spent and the hazards were too great for Rome to undertake anything in behalf of the Confederates. Having failed to receive a satisfactory reply to the terms submitted to Henrietta or to obtain Charles's conversion to Catholicism, Rome had already decided to leave the king to his fate. Sir Kenelm Digby had returned to Paris early in 1646 for a conference with the queen, but was back in Rome by the fall of the following year.[78] The most

72. *Ibid.*, pp. 50–81 *passim.*
73. Carte, *Ormonde*, III, 305.
74. Rinuccini, *Embassy in Ireland*, p. 343; Alphonsus Bellesheim, *The Papal Nuncio among the Irish Confederates* (tr. W. McLoughlin, Dublin, 1908), p. 45 (referred to hereafter as Bellesheim, *Papal Nuncio*).
75. Rinuccini, *Embassy in Ireland*, p. 146.
76. *Ibid.*, pp. 344–355.
77. Carte, *Ormonde*, III, 347–348.
78. *Calendar of State Papers, Domestic Series, of the Reign of Charles I, 1625–*

the queen could promise His Holiness in return for aid was toleration of Catholicism in England once her husband was restored.
Negotiations with Rome were brought to an end when in November, 1647, Digby read to the pope a paper charging him with bad
faith in sending Rinuccini to Ireland to deprive His Majesty of
that part of his kingdom.[79]

Having written off Rome as a source of aid, the queen turned
to the business of furnishing what supplies she could muster for
the Scottish invasion of England. Early in January, 1648, she sent
Sir William Fleming to sell the last of her jewels still held in pawn
in Holland and to carry to Scotland the military equipment pur-
chased with the proceeds of the sale.[80] The Venetian ambassador
in Paris wrote of having seen Henrietta, her eyes full of tears,
waiting in one of the chambers of Mazarin's offices, where she
had gone to confer with the minister.[81]

In Scotland during the spring months of 1648, the Duke of
Hamilton and the Earl of Lanark were trying to raise an army
in accordance with the treaty made with Charles on the Isle of
Wight. The clergy of the Kirk and the nobility led by the Earl of
Argyll, dissatisfied with the halfhearted promises the king had
made regarding the Covenant, resisted the levying of an army.[82]
After promising that further assurances safeguarding the Covenant
would be obtained from the king, Lanark in April succeeded in
getting the Scottish parliament to ignore the protests of the clergy
and vote for the raising of an army.[83] Montreuil again warned the
queen that even with a Scottish victory, the king would be no

---

1649 (23 vols., ed. John Bruce and others, London, 1858–97), 1645–47, p. 209
(referred to hereafter as *Cal. S. P. Dom.*); *Cal. S. P. Ven.*, XXVII, 222; Rinuccini,
Embassy in Ireland, pp. 576, 578.

79. *Cal. S. P. Dom.*, 1645–47, p. 571; *Cal. S. P. Ven.*, XXVIII, 30.

80. "The Hamilton Papers Addenda," *The Camden Miscellany*, IX (ed. Samuel
Rawson Gardiner [The Camden Society], Westminster, 1895), 1–2, 26, 35 (referred
to hereafter as *The Camden Miscellany*, IX).

81. *Cal. S. P. Ven.*, XXVIII, 39.

82. *MSS Français 15994*, fols. 288, 291, 292, 299.

83. *Ibid.*, fols. 315, 322; Burnet, *Memoirs of Hamilton and Castleherald*, pp.
338–339, 341, 343.

less a prisoner than he then was.[84] In May recruitment of the army was begun, although resisted in some places by riots of the populace.[85]

At the queen's court in Paris there was much dissatisfaction over the slowness of her most trusted officials in gathering supplies for the Scots.[86] The queen's days, melancholy as they were, were somewhat brightened when in May she learned that her second son, James, Duke of York, had escaped from the hands of Parliament and fled to the Netherlands.[87] But in general, discord prevailed because of complaints against Jermyn's influence, who was accused of squandering more than half of the queen's French pension for his personal expenses.[88]

Attention to developments in Scotland was momentarily diverted by the arrival of the three commissioners sent by the Council of the Confederates in Ireland. In the attempt to form another treaty with the Irish rebels, the queen was advised by Ormonde, who after surrendering Dublin to Parliamentary forces had spent several months in England before escaping to France.[89] Though Dublin was held by Parliament, the possibility of again establishing Royalist support in Ireland appeared most promising. In that turbulent country the division between the Old Irish and the Anglo-Irish had deepened. During the previous spring the pope had sent the sword of Tyrone as a gift to Owen O'Neill, the military champion of the Old Irish.[90] To the Anglo-Irish this act appeared to symbolize the conferment of sovereignty upon O'Neill under the aegis of Rome. Lord Inchiquin, who had military control over Munster and who long had opposed the Old Irish faction, signed a

84. *MSS Français 15994*, fols. 241, 281, 301.

85. *Ibid.*, fols. 344, 351, 352.

86. *The Camden Miscellany*, IX, 25, 35.

87. *Cal. S. P. Ven.*, XXVIII, 57, 59; Clarendon, *History of the Rebellion*, IV, 360–361.

88. *The Correspondence of Sir Edward Nicholas* (3 vols., ed. George F. Warner [The Camden Society], London, 1886–97), I, 97.

89. Rinuccini, *Embassy in Ireland*, p. 299; Clarendon, *History of the Rebellion*, IV, 316–317, 340; Carte, *Ormonde*, III, 341.

90. Bellesheim, *Papal Nuncio*, pp. 47–48.

truce with the pro-Royalist Council, and General Preston, largely out of jealousy toward O'Neill, also brought his forces over to the side of the Anglo-Irish.[91] Perceiving that the papal representatives aligned with the Old Irish had lost control of the rebellion in Ireland, Rinuccini excommunicated Preston, together with all other persons who backed the truce with the Council, and retired to the safety offered by O'Neill's army.[92]

Before any great strides could be made toward the restoration of royal authority in Ireland, the Scottish invasion of England had taken place.[93] On June 1, 1648, the queen held a meeting of the lords at her court to announce that the prince would depart to join the Scottish army.[94] The Royalists received a great windfall when toward the end of the month eleven ships under the leadership of Captain Batten deserted Parliament and went to Holland to be taken under command of the Prince of Wales. Prince Charles, accompanied by Jermyn and Prince Rupert, went to Calais. Other than a small amount of expense money, Mazarin contributed nothing to the prince's campaign.[95]

At the time the prince left Paris, toward the beginning of July, the queen went into temporary retreat at the convent of the Carmelites in Paris. Here she was visited by Madame de Motteville. When the visitor arrived, Henrietta had to defer the meeting for a short time until she had finished writing some letters which she said were of great political importance. In the course of the visit Henrietta showed Madame de Motteville a small gold drinking cup, which was the only gold that she, the Queen of England, possessed, for she had had to sell all of her valuable possessions to furnish money for the officers accompanying the prince.[96]

From Calais the prince and those with him sailed to the Neth-

91. Rinuccini, *Embassy in Ireland*, pp. 381, 385.
92. *Ibid.*, pp. 383, 392, 393.
93. *Cal. Clar. S. P.*, I, 378; *MSS Français 15994*, fol. 364.
94. *MSS Clar. S. P. 2798*, fol. 106; *Hamilton Papers*, p. 207; *Cal. S. P. Ven.*, XXVIII, 61.
95. Clarendon, *History of the Rebellion*, IV, 364–365, 371; *Cal. S. P. Ven.*, XXVIII, 65; *The Camden Miscellany*, IX, 39.
96. Motteville, *Mémoires*, II, 104.

erlands, where they joined the newly acquired fleet. Much to the disappointment of Jermyn, Rupert was made admiral, with Batten as his second in command. In the interest of the morale of the crews aboard the ships, the prince wished to put to sea as soon as possible. About the middle of August the fleet sailed from Brill and finally anchored in the Downs.[97] Here, on August 26, Marmeduke Landale informed the prince that the Scottish army had been destroyed by Oliver Cromwell's forces, making the intended journey to Scotland no longer of any purpose.[98]

Mazarin permitted the Duke of Ormonde to leave Paris even more empty-handed than had Prince Charles, for indeed the French treasury after the strain of long years of war was no longer plentifully supplied.[99] Ormonde arrived at Cork, where he was received as the king's viceroy on September 29, 1648. The Assembly had already been in session since the beginning of the month, and negotiations for a peace after so long and disturbed an interlude were again to be resumed. Rinuccini, who in the previous July had gone to Galway, a place of easy escape from Ireland, announced his intention of leaving the country. As a farewell message, the Assembly declared him a traitor against the crown of England.[100]

With the waning of the year various plans to aid the king were entertained, none of which came to fruition. The queen came out of another period of retreat at the convent to announce that the Duke of York would go to Ireland with the fleet. Also, there were

97. *Carte MSS*, XXII, 360; Clarendon, *History of the Rebellion*, IV, 371, 375, 376.

98. *Hamilton Papers*, p. 236; *Cal. Clar. S. P.*, I, 435. Sir William Batten (d. 1667) had had extensive administrative experience in the king's navy before becoming second in command of the Parliamentary fleet. He was largely responsible for delivering the navy over to Parliament when the conflict started. Batten commanded the ships that fired on Henrietta when she landed at Bridlington Bay, though he did not know she was present at the scene of action. However, his loyalty to Parliament was equivocal, for in 1648 he took eleven ships and placed them at the disposal of Prince Charles. After the restoration he regained his old office of surveyor of the fleet. *D.N.B.*, III, 418–420.

99. Clarendon, *History of the Rebellion*, IV, 371; Carte, *Ormonde*, III, 382.

100. Rinuccini, *Embassy in Ireland*, pp. 422–423; Bellesheim, *Papal Nuncio*, pp. 58–59; *Carte MSS*, XX, 298; Carte, *Ormonde*, III, 382.

various schemes allowing the occupation of the Channel Islands by foreign armies to prevent their seizure by Parliament. The Duke of Lorraine was to have Guernsey, and French forces under command of Jermyn were to hold Jersey.[101] Too much an Englishman to permit any of his country's soil to be occupied by soldiers of a foreign state, Edward Hyde declared that rather than permit French troops to land on Jersey, he would call upon the Earl of Northumberland, a moderate Independent, to help him hold the island.[102]

All of these considerations were soon overshadowed by the onrush of events in London. During most of December officers of the army debated what treatment should be meted out to the king. On January 3, 1649, the House of Commons passed an act creating a court of high justice to try the king on a charge of treason.[103] On the sixth, Henrietta wrote the speakers of both houses asking that she be granted a safe conduct to visit her husband in England. Probably guessing the content of the writing contained in the packet received from the queen, the House of Commons voted to lay aside the letters, which were not opened until thirty-five years later.[104] Charles appeared for his trial in historic Westminster Hall on January 20. His sentence was read on the twenty-seventh, and three days later he was led to the scaffold.[105]

During the month of Charles's trial, the wars of the Fronde, which began shortly after the signing of the Peace of Westphalia during the preceding October, raged in and around Paris. The Frondeurs had seized the city, and the French court had retreated to St. Germains. While under no threat from the rebels, Henrietta was barricaded in the Louvre, where she suffered want, since she had not been paid her pension for almost six months. On going to visit her, Cardinal de Retz found little Princess Henrietta Anne

101. *Carte MSS*, XXII, 438; *Cal. Clar. S. P.*, I, 449.

102. *MSS Clar. S. P.* 2339, fols. 265, 266.

103. *Journals of the House of Commons*, VI, 92, 93, 102–103, 104, 105, 109–110.

104. Green, *Letters of Henrietta Maria*, pp. 348, 349–350; *Cal. Clar. S. P.*, I, 467.

105. *State Trials* (34 vols., ed. Thomas Howell, London, 1816–28)‚ IV, cols. 1068–1070, 1115–1121, 1135–1141.

confined to bed because there was no fuel to heat the room, and merchants refused to extend the queen any more credit. Through the influence of the cardinal, the Parlement of Paris was prevailed upon to grant the queen 40,000 livres to supply the needs of her household.[106]

Henrietta did not hear of her husband's death until more than a week after the event, partially because the news was for a time withheld from her and also because information was slow in leaking through to the besieged city of Paris. On the ninth of February the guards allowed her courier to pass from Paris to St. Germains, where he was to obtain news of the latest dispatches from London. At dinner that evening the queen wondered why the messenger was so late in returning. By way of preparing her for the terrible truth, Jermyn answered that if the news had been good, surely the courier would have returned sooner. The queen immediately sensed that something was amiss and demanded that Jermyn tell what was being withheld from her. On being told of Charles's execution, she was so deeply shocked that for an hour or two she seemed to be oblivious to her surroundings, as if in a trance. When finally the tearful Duchesse de Vendôme approached Her Majesty and kissed her hand, Henrietta's grief burst forth in uncontrolled weeping.[107]

Overwhelmed by her loss, the queen remained abed for several days. On the second day of her sorrow she was visited by Madame de Motteville, who, having taken refuge in the queen's palace to escape the violence of the discordant elements of Paris, had obtained a pass to go to St. Germains and was about to depart. Learning that her visitor was going to the queen regent of France, Henrietta

106. Jean François Paul de Gondi, Cardinal de Retz, *Memoirs* (London, 1723), p. 142; Motteville, *Mémoires*, II, 300–301, 342–343. Briefly, the Fronde (1648–53) was a civil war, or rather a series of three civil uprisings, growing out of middle-class and aristocratic resentment against the power of the central government in France. During the Thirty Years' War and under the direction of Cardinal Richelieu, the power of the monarch had been considerably augmented. To some extent, also, the conflict was a national protest directed at the hated foreigner, Cardinal Mazarin, who was the queen dowager's favorite and the chief minister in the state.

107. Gamache, *Memoirs*, pp. 381–382.

wished to send some advice.[108] She admonished the French queen not to irritate her subjects unless she had power to suppress them, for the people were a beast which, once excited, was uncontrollable, as Charles's tragic death bore witness. Above all, Queen Anne was to listen to those who would tell her the truth, to strive to discover the truth, and to believe that only indifference to truth could destroy her kingdom. If only Charles had realized the truth!

The truth, indeed! But had Henrietta through her experience arrived any closer to an understanding of reality? In a letter to her oldest son she expressed regret that she had not been with her husband during his last hours. Perhaps she felt remorse that she had ever left him. Belatedly she realized, she said, that Mazarin had never intended to help, but only to deceive her. She perceived that the Venetian ambassador's avowal of desire to avenge the beheaded king (were it not for the threat of the Turk) was just empty talk. Her son would have to look to Ireland or Scotland for his restoration, although she was dubious of the fidelity of the Scots, who had sold their king for "a few pieces of money." And then, to cap all other advice, she told Charles that if he would declare himself a Catholic, as he had promised her, he would find loyal subjects in the Irish, for people who feared God could not be faithless to their prince.[109]

108. Motteville, *Mémoires*, II, 352–353.
109. Green, *Letters of Henrietta Maria*, pp. 352–357.

TROUBLED TWILIGHT

1649-69   DURING the last twenty years of her life— 1649 to 1669—Henrietta did not exercise significant control over the political interests of her son, who in the Royalist view was the rightful King of England after his father's execution. Ready as she was to give him advice and to counsel him, she found Charles II an unwilling listener. Her husband, if by no means following all of her admonitions, had usually been willing to give an ear to her opinions, but her son never took his mother entirely into his confidence. On occasion Henrietta was almost exasperated that Charles II did not reveal his thoughts to her, although in that respect she was not especially disfavored, for Charles early acquired the habit of withholding his opinions from other people. The eagerness of the mother to serve her son and his resentment toward what he considered overbearing counsels sometimes led to quarrels and distant relations between them. Although not wholly indifferent to his mother's guidance at first, Charles ultimately withheld all knowledge of his affairs from her and her court, leaving her pretty much in the dark concerning his business.

Henrietta attributed her inability to direct her son not so much to the stubbornness of the young man himself as to the conflicting jealousy of other advisers around him. There were two groups or councils competing for control over the king's mind: one, the queen's party, counted Lord Jermyn as the principal member under her leadership and also included Sir George Digby, Sir John Colepeper, and Lords Henry Percy and Henry Wilmot; the other group, which ultimately was to gain ascendancy over Charles, was headed by Sir Edward Hyde and supported by Secretary Edward Nicholas, the Duke of Ormonde, and Lords Francis Cottington and Christopher Hatton.[1] About a month after the execution of Charles I, Secretary Nicholas wrote to Lord Hatton, "I hold Jermins counsells as pernitious and destructive as ever and his power as vast and exorbitant."[2] Jermyn was purported to have said that if the king, Charles II, kept Hyde, Cottington, and others in his council, the monarch would be ruined. Hyde spoke as much truth as prejudice in saying that Charles did not like Jermyn.[3] Certainly Jermyn did not have enough mental ballast to direct Charles's business, however willing he might have been in the attempt. Even Madame de Motteville was quick to recognize Jermyn's limitations: he had a pleasant and affable manner in company and was a loyal factotum for the queen mother, but he had not the ability to form policy and to follow it to completion.[4]

So long as Henrietta could have Charles at her court and away from Hyde and her other rivals for the king's ear—for certainly Henrietta's opponents would find small entertainment at her court —there was some chance that she would acquire control over him. Whenever the king remained with his mother for any length of

1. *The Correspondence of Sir Edward Nicholas* (3 vols., ed. George F. Warner [The Camden Society], London, 1886–97), I, 117, 128–129 (referred to hereafter as *Nicholas Papers*).

2. *Ibid.*, p. 117.

3. *Calendar of Clarendon State Papers* (3 vols., ed. O. Ogle, W. Dunn Macray, and W. H. Bliss, Oxford, 1872–76), II, 37 (referred to hereafter as *Cal. Clar. S. P.*).

4. Françoise Bertaut, Madame de Motteville, *Mémoires sur Anne d'Autriche et Sa Cour* (4 vols., ed. M. F. Riaux, Paris, n.d.), I, 223. The reader is reminded that on the death of Charles I, Henrietta was no longer in the strict sense Queen of England, but rather the queen mother. From the Royalist viewpoint her son immediately inherited his father's title.

time, Hyde and his coterie became anxious lest they lose their own influence and standing with the king. Thus, when, following an abortive attempt to subjugate England by invasion from Scotland, Charles sojourned at his mother's court (in 1652), Edward Nicholas wrote Lord Hatton that the king consulted Henrietta and Jermyn on important business without letting Hyde and Ormonde know what he was doing.[5] Even so, the mother's momentary triumph was not absolute, for she and her son quarreled so bitterly that he went to Chantilly to escape her company.[6] When in June, 1654, political conditions in France required Charles to leave that country, the future role of the queen mother in her son's counsel seemed precarious indeed. Evidently her quarrels with him had been periodic during the whole time he was with her. Shortly after leaving France, he answered her most recent complaints in a letter to Jermyn. He said that he could not in fairness accuse himself of having treated his mother badly, as she charged. His keeping knowledge of business from the queen mother was no ill usage of her, for to reveal all would sometimes break faith with others; and to promise to follow any advice whatever it might be would ascribe too much trust to any one person. In closing his letter he asked Jermyn to name the enemies to whom his mother so often referred.[7]

After Charles left France to begin his wanderings from one place to another, with a somewhat longer stay at Cologne than elsewhere, his mother's part in his business was almost nil. He seems never to have written her of his political affairs; in fact, he seems to have written too seldom to show a proper regard for his filial duty. The aging queen sometimes wrote in an almost plaintive manner. In a letter of June 11, 1655, she expressed impatience to know more of Charles's affairs. "All that I can now contribute," she said, "is my prayers, which are never lacking."[8] Though far

5. *Nicholas Papers*, I, 298.
6. *Ibid.*, II, 25.
7. *Cal. Clar. S. P.*, II, 348.
8. *A Collection of the State Papers of John Thurloe* (7 vols., ed. Thomas Birch, London, 1742), I, 676 (referred to hereafter as Thurloe, *Collection*).

apart and seldom seeing one another, they still quarreled. In 1656 Charles protested when his sister Mary, Princess of Orange, planned an extended visit with her mother in Paris, because, he said, his family had been too much insulted to accept the hospitality of a government that had expelled him and his brothers. Henrietta answered that someone put foolish notions into his head, and that his interest would be in no way prejudiced by his sister Mary's coming to France.[9] To the end, however, Henrietta never gave up trying to control her son. Almost upon the eve of his restoration to the English throne, she asked him to come to Paris to consult with her council and Mazarin, believing that even with his return to England, French assistance might be necessary for him to maintain his position.[10]

Unsuccessful as she was generally in her attempt to domineer Charles, there was a considerable period following the death of her husband when her counsels prevailed against those of Hyde and other contenders for the king's confidence. At first, during the spring and summer of 1649, Henrietta proposed that Charles go to Ireland, where Ormonde had concluded a treaty with the Confederates in January.[11] She favored this course as opposed to his going to Scotland, for she did not believe the Scots were to be trusted. No purpose would be served were he to take up residence in the Netherlands as a place of departure for England, because she did not anticipate an uprising among his English subjects for the recall of their king; and if later conditions for his journey to Scotland did appear propitious, Ireland would afford convenient access to his northern kingdom of Scotland.[12] In May, 1649, she sent Sir John Denham with written instructions directing Charles to go to Ireland. If the king agreed to comply with her wish, she

9. *Ibid.*, p. 678; *Nicholas Papers*, III, 244; *MSS Lambeth Palace Library 645,* fol. 101.

10. Thurloe, *Collection*, I, 737; Cardinal de Mazarin, *Lettres* (9 vols., ed. P. A. Chéruel [*Collection de Documents Inédits*], Paris, 1872–1906), IX, 608–609.

11. Godfrey Davies, *England under the Early Stuarts* (Oxford, 1938), p. 160; *Nicholas Papers*, I, 161–162.

12. *Ibid.*, pp. 120–121, 122.

would send Jermyn before him to prepare the way for his arrival, while Denham would proceed to Scotland to learn what succor might be expected from there. Her son-in-law, the Prince of Orange, would be asked to furnish money for Charles's journey, and Denmark also would be solicited for assistance.[13]

Charles and his mother soon fell into differences. After returning from The Hague to Paris, where he remained but a short time, he was on the island of Jersey in September, 1649, awaiting the turn of events in Ireland. The Venetian ambassador in Paris said that Charles had taken his brother James with him more to spite the queen mother than for any other reason. Between Charles and his mother, the ambassador added, there was little love lost.[14]

Henrietta's policy regarding her son's going to Ireland changed abruptly when toward the end of the year the Scottish parliament sent agents to invite Charles to their country. Probably realizing that Ormonde and the Confederates would not be able to stand against the army that the parliament in Westminster had sent to Ireland under the leadership of Cromwell, Charles left Jersey to meet with Scottish commissioners at Breda. On the way he was met by his mother at Beauvais.[15] It was she and her party who advocated cooperation with the Scots, although Henrietta apparently thought little would result from the negotiations. Hyde and his faction were opposed to the king's trusting his fortunes in Scottish hands.

13. Mary Anne Everett Green, *Letters of Queen Henrietta Maria* (London, 1857), pp. 362–364. Sir John Denham (1615–69) held a minor if by no means a negligible place among seventeenth-century English poets. More to the interest of this book, he composed satirical verses on the Presbyterians and Parliament. During the period of Royalist exile, he was entrusted with various missions, among them escorting the Duke of York from London to Holland in 1648. Following the restoration he was awarded several grants of land and leases, including that on Scotland Yard. In 1660 he became the surveyor of general works, though he knew little about architecture. The reputation of his office was greatly enhanced when he acquired Sir Christopher Wren as his deputy. *D.N.B.*, XIV, 346–349.

14. Hermann Ferrero, *Lettres de Henriette-Marie à Sa Soeur Christine* (Rome, 1881), p. 74; *Calendar of State Papers, Venice* (38 vols., ed. Allen B. Hinds and others, London, 1864–1940), XXXIII, 119, 136 (referred to hereafter as *Cal. S. P. Ven.*).

15. Ferrero, *Lettres à Christine*, p. 81; *Cal. Clar. S. P.*, II, 4, 7, 9–10, 45, 46, 49; *Nicholas Papers*, I, 156.

It was probably to get rid of this opposition that Hyde and Cottington were sent on embassy to Spain in a quest for money.[16]

Henrietta never guessed how far her son, only a youth of nineteen who was inexperienced in diplomacy, would go in satisfying Scottish demands. Charles agreed to the Covenant, to impose it on all members of his family, to extirpate popery once he had regained his kingdoms, and to renounce any treaties with the Irish rebels, although somewhat in mitigation of his responsibility these exactions were not wrung from him until he was already en route to Scotland. Once there, he was hardly less a prisoner than his father had been under the Scots. In further humiliation, he was constrained to sign a paper deploring his father's opposition to the Covenant and his mother's idolatry. After bowing to this last measure of insult, Charles said he would never again be able to look his mother in the face. Back in France, Henrietta was in tears over what appeared to be her son's cowardice in conceding terms that would forever separate her from him.[17]

Meanwhile, her second son brought her no more comfort, for James soon was at odds with his mother. Henrietta's desire to rule her children probably made it difficult for them to live in harmony with her, although James's contentious spirit would have tried even the most indulgent of parents. After a bitter quarrel, during which James accused his mother of loving Henry Jermyn more than her own children, the disobedient son ran off to Brussels. Henrietta was embarrassed by this rash act because Spain, to whose territory he fled, was then at war with France. Her refusal to send money for his sustenance in Brussels ultimately forced him to return to his mother's house.[18]

For many months Henrietta did not know what had happened

16. *Ibid.*, pp. 173–174; Thurloe, *Collection*, I, 147–148; Samuel Rawson Gardiner, *History of the Commonwealth and Protectorate* (3 vols., London, 1894–1901), I, 264–265.

17. Thurloe, *Collection*, I, 147–148; *Nicholas Papers*, I, 173–174; *Calendar of State Papers, Domestic Series, 1649–1660* (13 vols., ed. M. A. E. Green, London, 1875–86), 1650, p. 324 (referred to hereafter as *Cal. S. P. Dom.*).

18. *Nicholas Papers*, I, 196, 198, 207, 218, 254; Green, *Letters of Henrietta Maria*, pp. 367–368.

to Charles in Scotland. By November, 1650, she heard that he had been crowned there, but she was dubious of Scottish support of him in any military enterprise.[19] During the following weeks she waited anxiously. Such news as she received in the following year was far from favorable, and finally in August, 1651, she learned of the defeat of Charles's Scottish forces that invaded England at the battle of Worcester. The fate of the king, whether dead or alive, was for a time unknown. While the queen mother in Paris attempted to circulate a story telling of her son's victory over Cromwell, the king in England was being hunted like a fleeing animal. He succeeded in making his escape from England late in October and arrived in Paris a few days later.[20]

Henrietta was overjoyed to have her son safely with her again. He did look a little unusual for a king, since to effect his disguise following his escape from the battle at Worcester, it had been necessary for him to crop his hair. He had had a wearisome experience in Scotland: no women, no music, no gaiety—nothing but long sermons and severe scoldings.[21] A true grandson of Henry IV, he was soon to make amends for lost pleasures, but during the early days of his stay in Paris he was sullen and morose. On being told that Jersey had been taken by the Parliamentary fleet, he said not a word, while the Duke of York, who often spoke childishly, gloried that the island had held out for two days against attack.[22]

Charles remained with his mother until July, 1654, when his departure from France was necessitated by Mazarin's recognition of Cromwell's government in England. Immediately Charles went to Spa to visit his sister Mary, who already had journeyed there.[23] The affront given to the Stuart family by French recognition of Parliament was ignored insofar as the Duke of York was concerned.

19. Ferrero, *Lettres à Christine*, p. 93; *Cal. S. P. Ven.*, XXVIII, 195, 202–203.
20. *Cal. S. P. Dom.*, 1651, p. 311; Green, *Letters of Henrietta Maria*, pp. 372–373.
21. *Mémoires de Mlle. de Montpensier* (4 vols., ed. A. Chéruel, Paris, n.d.), I, 321.
22. *Cal. S. P. Dom.*, 1651–52, p. 3.
23. Ferrero, *Lettres à Christine*, pp. 103, 109–110, 111–112; Thurloe, *Collection*, I, 311–312; *Cal. S. P. Ven.*, XXIX, 235; Mazarin, *Lettres*, V, 409, 625.

After serving for a time as captain of a group of Scottish body-guards to Louis XIV, he went off to fight as a volunteer in Tu-renne's army.[24]

After spending a few months at Spa, where Charles complained there was not a fiddler who could tell a "hymn from a coranto," the king went to Cologne, which was to be his home for several years. Here he was joined by the Duke of York in 1655 when an agreement with Cromwell required that France harbor none of the sons of Charles I.[25]

So disappointing were political prospects during the years of exile that these worries alone were enough to break the ordinary spirit, but the queen mother had other heartbreaks, anxieties, and sufferings. No years of calm followed the crushing blow of her husband's execution; rather, each year that followed seemed to multiply her sufferings. In the remove of time, her grief is likely to be overlooked, although any personal or humane consideration for her causes one to wonder how she bore all her troubles. Quite apart from the tragedy of Charles I and the dispossession of her children, she was to lose most of her family before her own death. Her second daughter, Elizabeth, a girl of fourteen years, died at Carisbrooke Castle in 1650.[26] A year later her son-in-law, Prince William of Orange, also met an untimely end but a few days before the birth of his son and heir.[27] Besides these deaths, and more were to follow, there were incessant quarreling with her children, the

---

24. Thurloe, *Collection*, I, 312; Green, *Letters of Henrietta Maria*, pp. 374–375.

25. *The Writings and Speeches of Oliver Cromwell* (4 vols., ed. Wilbur Cortez Abbott, Cambridge, Mass., 1937–47), III, 274–275, 876; Henry Ellis, *Original Letters* (12 vols. in 3 series, London, 1824–46), ser. 2, III, 376–377; Thurloe, *Collection*, I, 645–646, 666, 690; Ferrero, *Lettres à Christine*, pp. 113–114; Green, *Letters of Henrietta Maria*, p. 379.

26. D.N.B., VI, 650–651; *Nicholas Papers*, I, 190–191; Ferrero, *Lettres à Christine*, p. 93. In the brief glimpses we get of this second daughter through short and sporadic references to her, she appears to have been a precocious girl of angelic soul. She had been a prisoner of Parliament since her seventh year, and we are indebted to her for the account of the last interview that the king, Charles I, had with his two children (Gloucester being the other) who were still held by Parliament in 1649. See *The Works of Charles I* (2 vols., Aberdeen, Scotland, 1766), II, 348.

27. *Nicholas Papers*, I, 200; Ferrero, *Lettres à Christine*, p. 94.

contumely of her enemies, and the stark poverty of her court. After the uprising of the Fronde, Henrietta's French pension was paid irregularly if at all, and all that she could possibly spare was contributed to Charles's needs. There were times when she thought of permanent retirement to a convent, largely because of her inability to meet the financial demands of her court.[28] To all of these burdens must be added the continuing physical infirmities which troubled her. She told Madame de Motteville that she knew hardly a day free from physical pain since her coming to France, and in attempt to mitigate her sufferings she made yearly visits to the baths at Bourbon.[29]

Confronted by overwhelming tribulations, Henrietta, always devoted to the faith in which she was educated, increasingly found comfort in religion. To her the universe appeared God-centered, and all events were by His allowance. She believed that the Civil War in England derived ultimately from the infidelity of the people to the Church, because a nation not religiously ordered would never remain faithful to its sovereign. Obedience to God and obedience to a prince were complementary.[30]

During her remaining years the queen mother sought spiritual comfort by periodic retreats into monastic life, which with time became more frequent and of longer duration. Following the death of Charles I, she retired to the convent of the Carmelites located in the faubourg St. Jacques.[31] Repeatedly she expressed a weariness with the mundane cares of this life and a desire to quit the world. The world could hold no more joy for her, she wrote her sister in May, 1649, and in comment on the death of the Prince of Orange, she said she believed God wished to detach her from the world by removing all people with whom she felt a close bond.[32] Disappoint-

28. *Ibid.*, p. 82; *Nicholas Papers*, I, 274; Frances Verney, *Memoirs of the Verney Family* (4 vols., New York, 1892–99), II, 403.

29. *Cal. Clar. S. P.*, III, 308, 353; Ferrero, *Lettres à Christine*, p. 116.

30. Motteville, *Mémoires*, I, 187–190.

31. Cyprien de Gamache, *Memoirs of the Mission in England of the Capuchin Friars of the Province of Paris, from the Year 1630 to 1669* (in vol. II, 293–501, of Thomas Birch, *The Court and Times of Charles I* [2 vols., London, 1848]), p. 382.

32. Ferrero, *Lettres à Christine*, pp. 71, 79, 93.

ment and mischance in her son's political concerns also turned her mind to the solitude of the cloister, where her sorrow might be healed. "Reasons of state are terrible," she wrote her sister in 1654, "and I avow that I do not understand them at all, possibly because they are always against me. At this time it is necessary to resign all into the hands of God, for I have little other consolation in this world. . . ."[33]

In June, 1651, Henrietta fulfilled an ambition which had been forming in her mind for some time: she established a foundation of her own at Chaillot, which stood approximately where the Palais de Chaillot is today but which was then in a suburban area of Paris.[34] Chaillot, situated on rising ground on the north bank of the Seine, was a grand country mansion surrounded by lovely gardens. The mansion had been built by Henrietta's old friend Marshal de Bassompierre, and after his death it had been notorious as a house of sin. Henrietta selected the estate as a place suitable for the establishment of a nunnery. At first there was trouble with Bassompierre's heirs in acquiring possession of the property, but having the assistance of the French dowager queen in raising contributions of money, Henrietta at last won out against all other claimants. The nuns established there—originally only eleven including the superior and her assistant—belonged to the Order of the Visitation, an order founded by St. Francis de Sales for ladies of gentle birth and upbringing. Since it was assumed the members had never been accustomed to physical rigors, the rules of the order were not so austere as in most other monastic establishments.[35] Even so, the nuns transferred to Chaillot at first refused to live in any part of the house but the attic until the luxurious fixtures and furniture had been removed. The front part of the house was reserved for the queen mother's apartments. While at Chaillot, where she always went for the observance of special religious seasons and where she stayed for as long as three months at a time,

33. *Ibid.*, p. 107.

34. The story of the founding of Chaillot is taken from *MSS Mazarine 2436*, fols. 525, 529, 531, 532, 537–539, 540–547.

35. Ann Fanshawe, *Memoirs* (London, 1907), p. 573.

Henrietta subjected herself to the rules of the establishment, considering herself subservient to the mother superior and talking to her visitors through a grill as did the others.

Her religious zeal grew almost to the point of fanaticism. A few months before the establishment of her convent at Chaillot, she informed her servants that those who were not Catholics or who refused to become converts would have to look for employment elsewhere. When Charles returned from his trip into Scotland and England, she asked him not to attend the Anglican services at the home of Sir Richard Brown, since to do so would violate the oath he had taken to uphold the Covenant! In 1656 she prohibited the use of any space in her palace for the holding of Protestant services by persons of the Anglican religion at her court, and when later she learned that Dr. Cosin gathered communicants in his own room, she also disallowed that practice.[36]

But the most glaring example of her bigotry was her attempt to force the conversion of her youngest son, Henry, Duke of Gloucester. Gloucester had been released by Parliament early in 1652 and sent to join other members of his family on the Continent. Subsequent to his landing at Dunkirk, he went to the court of his sister Mary. Mary was very fond of her little brother, a handsome and bright lad of twelve years. A year later Charles gave in to his mother's entreaties that young Gloucester be placed in her care. Princess Mary was reluctant to let her brother leave and expressed a fear that her mother would try to make him a Catholic, although Henrietta had promised Charles that she would not infringe upon the boy's conscience. In June, 1653, Henrietta wrote her sister

36. *Cal. S. P. Dom.*, 1651–52, p. 3; *Cal. Clar. S. P.*, III, 207, 333; *Nicholas Papers*, I, 233. Dr. John Cosin (1594–1672) had been vice-chancellor of Cambridge University and a close supporter of Laud's reforms in the Church of England. Among the earliest churchmen to fall into dispute with the Puritans, he retired to Paris, where by order of Charles I he officiated as chaplain to those of Henrietta's household who belonged to the Church of England. Following the restoration he became Bishop of Durham. (*D.N.B.*, XII, 264–271.) Sir Richard Brown (1605–83) had been the king's resident at the court in Paris for well over a decade before Henrietta found refuge in that city. He provided at his capacious residence a chapel to which English Protestants in exile went for religious services. (*D.N.B.*, VII, 55–57.)

Christine of the arrival of "the little cavalier" at her court. Gloucester must have been an attractive lad, for his presence was favorably
reported among the nobility of Paris, and his mother's court was
frequented by visitors who came to have a look at the boy.[37]

In the fall of 1654, Charles, then living at Cologne, received
disturbing news regarding the treatment of his brother. Henrietta
wrote the king that she was sending Gloucester to the abbey of
Pointoise, where he would be removed from the evil company of
other boys his age and where he could better apply himself to his
studies. It was untrue, she protested, that she was attempting to
force him in matters of religion, but out of motherly duty she was
having him instructed in her own faith.[38] He was to be under the
tutelage of Henrietta's longtime associate Walter Montagu, Abbot
of Pointoise, who after going over to the Catholic Church in 1631
had taken the vows of priesthood twenty years later.[39]

Henrietta promised Gloucester that she would not deprive him
of his Protestant tutor, Richard Lovell, and that after a few weeks
at Pointoise, where the lad was sent much against his will, she
would allow him to rejoin his tutor. In Gloucester's absence, she
told Lovell that he had to leave Paris. When Lovell reminded her
of the promise she had made to the king, she said that her promise
had been exacted under duress. While Henrietta could hardly be
excused for breaking faith with the king and Gloucester, she was
probably guided in her action by the advice of Montagu, who informed Lovell that the queen mother was to be obeyed in her own
house regardless of what attitude the king might take.[40]

Jermyn seems to have been indifferent to the whole controversy.
He was not shrewd enough to see the repercussions of this attempt
against Gloucester's religion, and was quite willing to comply with
Henrietta's wish merely to please her. Overpowered by the counsel
of Montagu, he even suggested that the duke be naturalized in

37. *Nicholas Papers*, II, 5–6; Ferrero, *Lettres à Christine*, pp. 104–105.
38. *Cal. Clar. S. P.*, II, 414.
39. *Nicholas Papers*, I, 220.
40. *Cal. Clar. S. P.*, II, 416; *Nicholas Papers*, II, 121.

France so that he might hold preferment there after becoming a priest.[41]

In Cologne, Charles, though lethargic and given to pleasures, was shocked into action when he learned of what was being done to his brother. He immediately dispatched Ormonde, who had been with him for some time past, to Paris with orders to bring Gloucester to Cologne despite any resistance the queen mother might show.[42] Ormonde took with him Charles's letters to his mother, Gloucester, the Duke of York, Jermyn, and Lovell. To Jermyn the king sent a stinging rebuke, which seemed to knock some sense into the courtier's head. In his letter to his mother, he reminded her of the promise she had made to him regarding Gloucester's conscience, and pointed out that if the boy became a Catholic, the Stuarts would never again rule in England, because the people there would not excuse the heir to the throne for his brother's conversion but would assume his complicity in the act.

On arriving in Paris, Ormonde found the queen mother in retreat at Chaillot and the Duke of Gloucester taken away to Pointoise. After waiting a day or two, Ormonde had his first meeting with Henrietta. She told him that there was an obligation upon her conscience to have her son reformed of his errors, and that the promise made to Charles applied only to forcing the Catholic religion on Gloucester. When Ormonde began to question her claim that Lovell had been dismissed upon his own consent, she was at last forced to withdraw her statement. Without giving any notice or asking permission, Ormonde on the day following his interview with the queen mother went to Pointoise, where his talk with the duke was less restricted than it would have been had his coming been advertised. Encouraged by Ormonde's vigorous action and learning of the king's determination in the matter, Jermyn, John Berkeley, and even Lord Percy joined in support of Gloucester. In subsequent talks with Ormonde, Henrietta referred to the right

41. *Ibid.*, p. 122; *Cal. Clar. S. P.*, II, 415.
42. The letters relating to the attempt to bring about the conversion of Gloucester to Catholicism are found in *Cal. Clar. S. P.*, II, 414–438.

given her to raise her children in her religion by the treaty made at the time of her marriage, but this allowance extended only to the thirteenth year of her offspring.

Gloucester was taken back to Paris. One morning after his return, Henrietta called him into her presence and asked him to obey her command to enter a Jesuit college. He was given the remainder of the day to consider her demand and was called back the same evening to give his reply. Gloucester, even against the entreaties of the French dowager queen, Anne, to whom Henrietta had applied for support in this controversy, unhesitatingly refused his mother's wish. Thereupon Henrietta behaved in a way that is difficult to understand. She told her son that she wished never again to see his face, ordered him and his belongings immediately removed from her house, and forbade all English persons in Paris to offer him asylum. When upon leaving her presence the boy asked his mother's blessing, she turned away from him in scorn. A few days later Gloucester left Paris in the escort of Ormonde to go to the king in Cologne.

Following the removal of Gloucester from Paris and the expulsion of York from France a year later, Henrietta was estranged for a time from all her sons. The later years of exile were a period of frustration and hopelessness for her. Her worries were doubled when upon the outbreak of war between the Protectorate and Spain in 1655, Charles and his brothers went to Flanders to fight with Spanish armies against France. In an attack upon Mardyke, Charles narrowly escaped with his life. Henrietta cautioned him to be careful. Somewhat later York and Gloucester were almost captured as a result of foolhardy chances they took in the siege of Dunkirk.[43]

Charles's character, perhaps none too strong even under the best circumstances, seemed to be deteriorating from the enervating effects of idleness occasioned by his exile. He seemed to have given himself over entirely to sensuality. One of Cromwell's spies, reporting on the activities of the king while he was at Brussels late

---

43. Green, *Letters of Henrietta Maria*, pp. 384, 387, 388; *MSS Lambeth Palace Library 645*, fol. 105; Thurloe, *Collection*, I, 679.

in 1656, commented: "I think I may truly say, that greater abominations were never practiced among people, than at this day at Charles Stuart's court. Fornication, drunkenness, and adultery, are esteemed no sins amongst them; so that I persuade myself God will never prosper any of their attempts."[44] If this report exaggerated the truth, there were nevertheless many of Charles's more serious followers who expected little favor from the Almighty as long as their king continued to live scandalously. Young Louis XIV was reported to have said that were he in Charles's position, he would be on his knees praying to God for the restoration of his kingdoms rather than pursuing amours as did the English king.[45]

In 1658 Henrietta was ill more than usual. After returning from her yearly visit to Bourbon, she wrote Charles that she longed for the day when her family could be together again and prayed daily for the fulfillment of her wish.[46] The day of Charles's restoration was nearer than Henrietta could from all appearances hope for—certainly nearer than Mazarin guessed. Toward the end of summer, 1658, Cromwell died. "I thought you would hear with joy of the death of that wretch,"[47] Henrietta wrote to her sister Christine. Yet the queen mother's heart was too full of sadness for her to take much delight in the death of the person whom she hated and whom she held responsible for much of her suffering.

Following the death of Cromwell, England passed through a troubled year and a half. During part of this time Cromwell's elder son, Richard, held nominal authority as Lord Protector; but "Tumble-down-Dick" soon dropped from view, leaving the army commanders to maneuver for power. At last General Monk, who had commanded the army of occupation in Scotland, marched southward with his soldiers to back the civilian population against further continuance of army rule. The surviving members of the Long Parliament reconvened and issued a summons for a new election, which resulted in the Convention Parliament.

44. *Ibid.*, V, 645; *Nicholas Papers*, III, 92.
45. Thurloe, *Collection*, VII, 325–326.
46. *MSS Lambeth Palace Library 645*, fol. 106.
47. Green, *Letters of Henrietta Maria*, pp. 388–389; Mazarin, *Lettres*, IX, 535.

The king was called back to England amid the acclamations of his people, and after many a season he entered London on his thirtieth birthday, May 29, 1660.[48] Henrietta was overjoyed by the unexpectedness of the event. She had a *Te Deum* sung in thanksgiving at Chaillot and celebrated with a ball at the Palais Royal, where she had moved to after the marriage of Louis XIV to the Infanta Marie Thérèse.[49]

Parliament voted the restoration of Henrietta's dower lands and revenues a few weeks after Charles's return to England, and repairs on Somerset House, her former residence, were soon to be undertaken in preparation for her arrival. The king urged his mother's speedy departure from France. After long lean years of wandering in the wilderness, the Stuarts were again to return home and live off the fat of the land. Princess Mary was planning to go to England, so Henrietta's wish to have all the family together would finally be fulfilled.[50]

But the joy of homecoming was not to be complete. A month before the queen mother and her youngest daughter, Henrietta Anne, sailed for Dover, the Duke of Gloucester died of smallpox. His doctors, believing his infection to be slight and of a kind that seldom had fatal results, had prescribed no medicine and had predicted his rapid recovery. To no one had the duke appeared very sick.[51] This shock was followed by another blow to Henrietta. For some time past the Duke of York had been carrying on an amour with Anne Hyde, the chancellor's daughter, who, the queen mother now learned, was heavy with a child begotten by her lover, lately made her husband by secret marriage. "God grant that it belongs to him," Henrietta wrote to Christine. "A woman who gives herself to a prince will just as readily give herself to another." The

48. "England's Joy," *Stuart Tracts* (ed. C. H. Firth, New York, n.d.), pp. 427–430; Motteville, *Mémoires*, IV, 193.

49. *MSS Lambeth Palace Library 645*, fol. 120; Green, *Letters of Henrietta Maria*, p. 398; John Reresby, *Memoirs* (ed. James J. Cartwright, London, 1875), p. 45. Louis was married by proxy to the Spanish infanta on June 3, 1660.

50. *Cal. S. P. Ven.*, XXXII, 159; Ferrero, *Lettres à Christine*, p. 121.

51. *Fifth Report of the Royal Commission on Historical Manuscripts* (London, 1876), p. 156; *Cal. S. P. Ven.*, XXXII, 196, 198.

queen mother loathed Edward Hyde and all his kind, and the chancellor's daughter was about the last woman in the world to whom she would have a son of hers joined in wedlock. She ended her letter to Christine by saying, "God does not wish that I should be entirely content."[52]

Henrietta did not leave France until shortly before All Souls' Day. Well disposed as the people of England seemed that year to welcome royal arrivals and drink toasts, the dowager's presence in London was by comparison almost unheralded. The bells of the city were dutifully rung, but Samuel Pepys wrote in his diary that he observed no more than three bonfires in the streets of London on the night of her arrival.[53] A few days later Pepys saw her in the presence chamber at Whitehall, where she impressed him as "a very little, plain old woman, and nothing more in her presence in any respect nor garbe than any ordinary woman."[54] Thus had the years of suffering and exile outraged her beauty.

Henrietta refused to acknowledge any relationship with Anne Hyde or even to receive the girl's father unless the chancellor promised not to mention his daughter. Though disappointed by the marriage, the king said his brother would have to make the best of a bad situation, and himself accepted conditions so far as to act as godfather to York's child. Mazarin advised the queen to follow Charles's example, because it was obvious that Anne's position was going to be recognized at court regardless of Henrietta's obstinacy, which if overruled by general opinion would result in the humiliation of Henrietta rather than her daughter-in-law. Sound as Mazarin's advice was, he had a secondary reason in giving it, for he hoped to profit by doing a good turn for Edward Hyde, who, he knew, guided Charles's counsels. However bitter the surrender,

---

52. Ferrero, *Lettres à Christine*, p. 124; *Fifth Report of the Royal Commission on Historical Manuscripts*, p. 157; *Cal. Clar. S. P.*, III, 45; Motteville, *Mémoires*, IV, 227.

53. *Ibid.*, p. 226; Samuel Pepys, *Diary and Correspondence* (4 vols., ed. Richard Braybrooke, Philadelphia, n.d.), I, 119–120; *Fifth Report of the Royal Commission on Historical Manuscripts*, p. 175.

54. Pepys, *Diary*, I, 125.

Henrietta at last bowed to the inevitable and received Anne into her company. Soon thereafter York's wife began to be addressed in the manner befitting a duchess.[55]

As the year of the restoration drew to a close, Henrietta prepared to return to France. She had intended her first visit to be a short one, for before leaving France her daughter Henrietta Anne had been affianced to the Duke of Orleans, brother of Louis XIV, and it was now necessary to go back to France for the wedding.[56] The queen was ready to depart from London about the middle of December when her daughter Mary fell ill of a "malignant fever" and died before the year was out.[57] Henrietta did not plan to remain long in England following her daughter's death, since she could take her bereavement with her. At Portsmouth, from where she proposed to sail, she was again delayed. On first putting out of harbor, her ship ran onto a sandbar and was blown back into port after being freed by the rising tide. While still on shipboard in the harbor, Princess Henrietta Anne broke out with measles. The queen must have wondered what further affliction could possibly befall her. For several days the princess was extremely ill and her survival was in doubt, but slowly she recovered and by the beginning of February landed in France with her mother.[58]

Henrietta Anne was married to the Duke of Orleans on the last day of March as then reckoned by the French calendar.[59] Not long after the event the queen mother, who no longer felt the necessity of being in society for her daughter's sake, moved from the Palais Royal into semiretirement at the château of Colombes, located on the outskirts of Paris.

During the summer months of 1661 the court of Louis XIV frolicked at Fontainebleau. The dowager queen began to hear

55. Mazarin, *Lettres*, IX, 668–669, 679–680; *Cal. S. P. Ven.*, XXXII, 228, 237.

56. *Ibid.*, p. 242; Motteville, *Mémoires*, IV, 226.

57. *Cal. S. P. Ven.*, XXXII, 231, 235.

58. Pepys, *Diary*, I, 141; *Fifth Report of the Royal Commission on Historical Manuscripts*, p. 202; *Cal. S. P. Ven.*, XXXII, 242, 244, 246.

59. Motteville, *Mémoires*, IV, 256; *Cal. S. P. Ven.*, XXXII, 274. The date of Henrietta Anne's marriage was March 21 by the Julian or Old Style calendar used for fixing dates throughout this work.

disconcerting news from there concerning the behavior of her youngest daughter, a lovely young woman who had attracted the amorous attentions of Louis XIV. To be sure, she was married to Louis's brother, but the Duke of Orleans, a man of weak emotions, seemed indifferent to his wife's escapades. If Louis's brother did not mind his wife's indiscretion, there was another person who did, and that was Louis's Spanish queen. Her jealousy finally enflamed the dull passions of Orleans, so that it required the utmost tact of Anne of Austria, Henrietta Maria, and Madame de Motteville, all of them long experienced in settling court quarrels, to quiet jealousies and restore harmonious relations.[60]

By the end of the year Henrietta was planning to return to England, possibly to live there the remainder of her days, but she delayed her departure until her daughter, who was pregnant, had been delivered of her firstborn.[61] She looked forward to her return to England, where she landed about the beginning of August, 1662, because Charles's bride, Princess Catherine of Portugal, had arrived not long before. Henrietta was delighted with her daughter-in-law. She wrote to Christine that the new queen was a saint.[62] A saint, to be sure, was hardly to Charles's taste. Only a few weeks after coming to England, Catherine was objecting to the brazen presence at the court of Charles's favorite mistress, Madame Castelmaine, but the little queen was to learn to endure a lifetime of such insult.[63] Henrietta was soon hopeful that her daughter-in-law would become pregnant, although Catherine's frail body and immature physical characteristics showed small promise of robust motherhood. If without much personal charm, the new queen, according to Pepys, had a "good, modest, innocent look,"[64] which probably supplied a refreshing bit of variety in the circle of Charles II.

60. *Cal. S. P. Ven.*, XXXII, 268–275, 278–279.
61. *Ibid.*, XXXIII, 68, 77, 84.
62. *Ibid.*, pp. 131, 146, 168, 169, 171; Ferrero, *Lettres à Christine*, p. 128; *Lansdowne MSS 1236*, fol. 123.
63. *Cal. S. P. Ven.*, XXXIII, 171–172.
64. Pepys, *Diary*, I, 324.

During the following winter Henrietta's court far outshone that of the sober little queen, who was better suited for the convent than the gay life of Restoration England.[65] Though buffeted by much ill fortune, the queen mother had retained a natural levity of spirit; she could still laugh, and from a long and varied life, including acquaintance with most of the important people of her time, could relate many an interesting story, some sad and some humorous. Indeed, for a few years she experienced the greatest happiness and contentment she had known since the beginning of the Civil War. The king her son was married, she had hopes of being made a grandmother by the new queen, there were indications that Chancellor Hyde was losing his power over Charles, and the kingdom was restored to her children. She described herself as "the most contented person in the world" in a letter to her sister. "The King my son shows me so much love and confidence," she continued, "that I have never hoped for better."[66] Sad memories probably welled up in her heart at times, but the prospect of better days ahead quieted the grief of the past.

Happy as were her personal relations, England was still unkind to her. This time it was the climate that caused her to leave the country. In the spring of 1663 she suffered from a serious catarrh that was aggravated by bad weather. At length she decided to take a change of air, and set sail in June, 1665, just as the plague was beginning to rage in London. At the time she left she probably intended only a short stay of six months or so in France, but as it happened she was departing England for the last time.[67]

The tranquillity of her last years was disturbed by war between the two countries she counted her own. In a sense it had always been the national animosities of England and France that had upset the tenor of her life and caused her so much heartache. In her personal relationships she began to experience the sorry prelude to rupture between the two states. At the French court Henrietta

65. *Ibid.*, p. 385.

66. Ferrero, *Lettres à Christine*, p. 126; *Cal. S. P. Ven.*, XXXIII, 217; Motteville, *Mémoires*, I, 214, 223.

67. *Cal. S. P. Ven.*, XXXIII, 126; XXXIV, 125, 161.

Anne became the object of unfriendly glances and bitter words, and was finally brought to bed at least in part over worry resulting from such unpleasantness. Throughout these troubles the French king, Louis XIV, remained kind and respectful toward Henrietta Maria, loving her, it was said, as if she had been his own mother. Henrietta attempted to mediate between the two kings, but Charles spurned her efforts. Chancellor Hyde objected to the queen mother's having any hand in the diplomatic relations of the two countries.[68] The King of England demanded that his mother return to London, on the excuse that her residence in France prejudiced him in the opinion of his subjects. Since the queen mother showed no indication of complying with her son's request, the income from her dower lands was reduced twenty-five per cent in 1668.[69]

While Henrietta protested vigorously against this measure of retaliation, she did not have long to concern herself with the contumely of the world. Already many of her friends had gone on before her, her sister Christine having died in 1663 and Anne of Austria in 1666.[70] In March, 1669, Henrietta had another of her many recurrent spells of sickness but seemed to recover, only to suffer a relapse the following June. Her recovery from the setback was slow, and throughout the summer she was ailing.[71] Upon the insistence of her daughter, the most prominent physicians in Paris held a conference at her home in Colombes on the condition of her health. Present at this meeting were the first physician to the Queen of France, the first physician to the Duke of Orleans, and the first physician to Henrietta Anne. They approved of the prescriptions that Henrietta's physician-in-ordinary had been giving her, except that M. Vallot, the French queen's physician, prescribed three

68. *Ibid.*, pp. 239, 280, 281; XXXV, 63, 74, 101.

69. Green, *Letters of Henrietta Maria*, pp. 412–413.

70. *Historical Manuscripts Commission, Report on the Manuscripts of the Duke of Buccleuch and Queensberry* (3 vols., London, 1899–1926), I, 432 (referred to hereafter as *Rept. MSS Buccleuch*); Motteville, *Mémoires*, IV, 444; *La Grande Encyclopédie* (31 vols., Paris, n.d.), VI, 280.

71. Green, *Letters of Henrietta Maria*, pp. 415, 416; *Cal. S. P. Ven.*, XXXVI, 42.

grains of laudanum to be taken on going to bed as a preventative against the insomnia which had distressed her. Overhearing his statement, Henrietta objected that her former physician, Dr. Mayerne, had warned her never to take opiates in any form. Vallot replied that had his knowledge of medicine advised him against giving her the grains, he would never have prescribed them.[72]

That evening she dined with her customary company at Colombes, showing as much appetite as was usual with her and conversing merrily at the table. At ten o'clock she retired, but remaining sleepless for about an hour, she called her doctor and asked that the opiate be administered. After taking the medicine mixed in the white of an egg, she appeared to fall into a deep sleep. Somewhat later one of the ladies attending her went into her room to waken her for some reason not clearly explained. Unable to rouse her mistress, the servant became alarmed and sent for the doctor and the priests residing in Henrietta's household. The doctor tried to evoke some signs of life from the queen, while the priests exhorted her to contrition for her sins. The physician believed her unconsciousness to be caused by "vapors rising to the head," a condition which was only temporary, but in preparation for the worst the vicar of Colombes was sent for to administer extreme unction. Finally, between three and four o'clock on the morning of August 21, 1669, the queen expired without having regained consciousness.[73] By her contemporaries, the immediate cause of her death was attributed to an overdose of opiate.[74]

72. Gamache, *Memoirs*, pp. 465–466.
73. *Ibid.*, pp. 466, 467–469; *Rept. MSS Buccleuch*, I, 440.
74. *The Memoirs of Edmund Ludlow* (2 vols., ed. C. H. Firth, Oxford, 1894), II, 420. Commenting on the queen's death, Mademoiselle de Montpensier, the "great Mademoiselle," wrote in her *Mémoires*, IV, 138: "She was a very delicate woman, almost always sick; she took some pills on going to bed which caused her to sleep so soundly that she never woke up at all." Mademoiselle had never really liked Henrietta. An epigrammatist of the time, referring to the deaths of Henry IV, Charles I, and Henrietta, is said to have written:

Tous tois sont morts par assassin,
Ravaillac, Cromwell, et medecin.

Fanshawe, *Memoirs*, p. 383.

Upon learning of the queen mother's death, Lord Arlington, the English ambassador in Paris, asked the King of France to have all of Henrietta's household goods placed under seal to prevent Jermyn from carrying away what possessions of value she had left.[75] As she had requested, her heart was sent in a small silver box for burial at Chaillot.[76] Louis XIV decreed a state funeral at the abbey of St. Denis, where the body was to be interred near the tomb of her father, Henry IV, in the choir of the abbey church.[77]

The most notable memorial to Henrietta, however, was not the obsequies ordered by Louis XIV, but a funeral sermon preached by Jacques Bossuet, Bishop of Condon, some weeks later in the chapel at Chaillot upon the request of Madame, her youngest daughter.[78] Bossuet spoke with an oratorical flourish suited to the taste of that age. "Christian people," he perorated,

> whom the memory of a great queen, daughter, wife, mother of kings so powerful, and sovereign of three realms calls from all sides to this sad ceremony, this discourse will reveal to you one of the terrible examples which unfolds to the eyes of the world all the extremes of its vanity. You will see in a single life all the extremities of things human; happiness without bound as well as misery; the long and peaceful enjoyment of one of the most noble crowns in the universe; all that which can render birth and position most glorious heaped upon one head, and then exposed to the outrages of fortune; the good cause at first followed by good success, and then sudden reverses and changes unprecedented; rebellion long held in abeyance finally gaining complete mastery. . . . There is the lesson which God gives to kings; thus does He show to the world the worthlessness of its pomp and grandeur.[79]

75. *Rept. MSS Buccleuch*, I, 440.
76. *MSS Mazarine 2436*, fol. 571.
77. *MSS Archives Nationale*, K 119, no 7, "Obsequies de Tres Auguste Princesse."
78. Gamache, *Memoirs*, p. 471; Jacques Bossuet, *Oraisons Funèbres* (ed. P. Jacquinet, Paris, n.d.), pp. 8–9.
79. *Ibid.*, pp. 15–17.

BIBLIOGRAPHICAL ESSAY

MATERIALS USED FROM MANUSCRIPT COLLECTIONS

MUCH of the source material on the life of Henrietta Maria is to be found in manuscript form in the libraries and archives of England and France. The principal depositories in England are the British Museum and the Lambeth Palace Library in London, and the Bodleian Library in Oxford; and in France, the Bibliothèque Nationale, the Bibliothèque Mazarine, and the Bibliothèque St. Geneviève in Paris. The manuscript sources cited in this work, except for those in the British Museum, were read from microfilm copies prepared at the places mentioned.

A. Manuscripts in the British Museum and the Lambeth Palace Library, London.

One of the most extensive collections relating to the life of Henrietta is the *Harleian Manuscripts* (British Museum), containing information on the Spanish marriage negotiations, the French marriage, the first five parliaments of Charles I's reign, and the Scottish rebellion. Especially valuable are manuscripts *6988* and *7379*. The former consists of letters written by Charles I, the Duke of Buckingham, Henrietta Maria, the Elector Frederick, and the elector's wife, Elizabeth, sister of Charles I. The latter designates forty letters exchanged between Charles and Henrietta.

The *Additional Manuscripts* (British Museum) supply scattered folios pertaining to the queen, but few if any manuscript numbers dealing exclusively with affairs touching upon her life. Here again there are manuscripts pertaining to the Spanish and French marriage negotiations; and there is information on the Tyburn incident, George Digby's negotiations, and government policy toward recusants in England.

Other manuscript collections in the British Museum yield little material not to be found in published sources, but occasionally they contain a few folios that are essential in the study of some particular incident in the queen's life. In the *Lansdowne Manuscripts* are the *Burghley Papers*, which contain a copy of the marriage treaty between Charles and Henrietta (vol. XCIII, part 1, fol. 37). The *Stowe Manuscripts* help clarify the negotiations in 1612 for a marriage between Henry, Prince of Wales, and Christine, second daughter of Henry IV. Also there are the letters of the Earl of Bristol concerning the Spanish marriage negotiations and Buckingham's speech to Parliament on his return from Spain. The *Egerton Manuscripts* have some of the letters sent by Henrietta to Charles between 1642 and 1645 (no. *2619*).

In the *Lambeth Palace Library Manuscripts* (no. *645*) are ten or so letters written by Henrietta during the later part of her life.

B. Manuscripts in the Bodleian Library, Oxford, and the Public Record Office, London.

The papers gathered by Edward Hyde and by Thomas Carte for the writing of their histories are deposited in the Bodleian Library at Oxford. Approximately thirty of the letters from the *Clarendon State Papers* were used in the preparation of the present work. These letters, extending from 1639 to 1649, are so varied in content that it is difficult to generalize upon them except to say that they relate to topics of the Civil War years. Among the letters are five addressed from the queen to her husband. Sixty folios drawn from the *Carte Manuscripts* concern Irish affairs during and after the Civil War.

A few of the letters written by the pope's personal representatives to the queen were used in the preparation of this biography. Such letters are contained in the *Roman Transcripts*, which are deposited at the Public Record Office. The dispatches of the pope's envoys to Henrietta, while reflecting the peculiar views of Catholic priests on mission to a Protestant country, do reveal something of the state of the Catholic religion in England during the years immediately preceding the civil upheaval and also tell of the queen's early attempts to secure aid from the pope.

C. Manuscripts in the Bibliothèque Nationale, Bibliothèque Mazarine, and Bibliothèque St. Geneviève, Paris.

The French collections are much easier to describe than those in England because they are more systematically classified, having all materials relating to a particular topic arranged under a given manuscript number. This more precise ordering of materials is possible in large part because many of the French manuscripts consist of transcriptions rather than the original documents.

The *Manuscrits Français* reveal the diplomatic negotiations between England and France before and after the marriage of Charles and Henrietta. *3692* contains a complete copy of the marriage articles, diplomatic papers on the expulsion of the French attendants, and the papers relating to Bassompierre's mission to England. *3818* has a few of the early letters of Henrietta and the instructions of Marie de Medici to the royal governess, Madame de Montglat. *15992* gives additional information on Bassompierre's negotiations. *15993* tells of Santerre's embassy to England from 1635 to 1637, and *15994–15995* contain the dispatches of French ambassadors in England and Scotland during the Civil War.

The manuscripts in the *Archives Nationale,* also deposited at the Bibliothèque Nationale, give full information on the obsequies for Henrietta as ordered by the king, Louis XIV. The manuscripts of the *Bibliothèque Mazarine* include a long and detailed account of the founding and history of the convent at Chaillot, which was established by Henrietta. Manuscript *820* of the *Bibliothèque St. Geneviève* consists of the dispatches of Leveneur de Tillières, French ambassador to England during the early phases of the marriage negotiations between England and France.

CALENDARS OF MANUSCRIPT COLLECTIONS

There are several excellent calendars of manuscript collections pertaining to the Stuart period of English history. The most useful of these is the *Calendar of State Papers and Manuscripts Relating to English Affairs Existing in the Archives and Collections of Venice and in Other*

Libraries of Northern Italy (38 vols., ed. Allen B. Hinds and others, London, 1864–1940). The entries in this calendar are full and complete, many letters being fully translated, and extend through the whole period of Henrietta's life. It would require too much space to convey an idea of the wealth of material contained in the dispatches of the Venetian ambassadors, men who were trained to observe public affairs closely in the countries to which they were accredited and to report their findings to their home government. The dispatches give information on nearly every phase of public life in England during the reign of Charles I. So rich a deposit of historical material must often be consulted in a detailed study of the Stuart period. Of course the volumes in this calendar are not limited to the seventeenth century, but range far beyond, both before and after.

Descriptions of state papers in the Public Record Office in London are published in the *Calendar of State Papers, Domestic Series, of the Reign of James I, 1603–1625* (5 vols., ed. Mary Anne Everett Green, London, 1857–59), and in the *Calendar of State Papers, Domestic Series, of the Reign of Charles I, 1625–1649* (23 vols., ed. John Bruce and others, London, 1858–97). Although yielding some indispensable information, the state papers on domestic affairs are not as rich in resources on the life of Henrietta as might be expected.

The *Calendar of the Clarendon State Papers Preserved in the Bodleian Library* (3 vols., ed. O. Ogle, W. Dunn Macray, and W. H. Bliss, Clarendon Press, Oxford, 1872–76) is based on the resource materials collected by the Earl of Clarendon, Edward Hyde, for the writing of his great history. Most of the papers are described in considerable detail.

PUBLISHED DOCUMENTARY MATERIALS AND LETTERS

There are a number of published collections of papers, documents, speeches, court trials, and letters drawn from the reign of Charles I. Foremost among such works is John Rushworth, *Historical Collections* (8 vols., printed for D. Brown, London, 1721–22). The compiler of these volumes was an avid collector of all papers that related to state affairs, and attended court sessions and state occasions to take down shorthand notes of the proceedings. In 1640 he was appointed an assistant clerk to the House of Commons, but was prohibited from taking notes while in attendance unless ordered to do so by the house. After the organization of the New Model army, he became secretary to General Fairfax and later served Cromwell in the same capacity. Being thus employed, he had unusual access to information, but insofar as the life of Henrietta is concerned, Rushworth's collections are more useful for the earlier than the later years of Charles I's reign.

Second most valuable of the published collections is *A Collection of the State Papers of John Thurloe* (7 vols., ed. Thomas Birch, London, 1742). John Thurloe served in various secretarial and administrative capacities during the time of the Commonwealth and Protectorate, and was one of Cromwell's most trusted assistants. Having served at the head of the offices of post and intelligence as well as in Cromwell's council, Thurloe came into possession of important papers. Not published until after his death, the papers were found stuffed between double ceilings of rooms which their owner had once occupied.

Sir Bulstrode Whitelocke, *Memorials of English Affairs during the Reign of Charles I* (printed for J. Tonson, London, 1732), is difficult to classify. Consisting of one large folio volume, it is neither a compilation nor a narrative account, but a combination of both. Although the work has inaccuracies, it is valuable where the author describes events in which he had a part, a not inconsiderable merit since Whitelocke was a distinguished lawyer who lived close to public affairs.

Thomas Frankland, *The Annals of King James and King Charles the First* (London, 1681), and Philip Yorke, Earl of Hardwicke, *Miscellaneous State Papers* (2 vols., printed for W. Strahan & T. Cadell, London, 1778), were compiled by men who had no part in the political upheaval of Charles I's reign. Frankland gathered his material from private papers presented to him by his friends and from published letters, speeches, and pamphlets of the Civil War period, which were found in considerable abundance in the author's day. Hardwicke's two volumes consist of state letters drawn mostly from the *Harleian Manuscripts* and the State Paper Office.

The Works of Charles I (2 vols., printed by J. Chalmers for William Coke, Aberdeen, Scotland, 1766) contains within two small volumes a potpourri of Charles's letters, his purported autobiography, his trial proceedings, the treaty proceedings at Uxbridge, and other papers relating to the martyr king. For the purpose of the present work, only the king's letters are important. A convenient though by no means complete reference for documents on the Stuart period is Samuel Rawson Gardiner, *The Constitutional Documents of the Puritan Revolution* (Clarendon Press, Oxford, 1906).

There are two published collections of Henrietta's letters. One, Charles, Comte de Baillon, *Lettres de Henriette-Marie, Reine d'Angleterre* (Didier et Cie., Paris, 1877), is prefaced with a sketch of Henrietta's life; the other, Mary Anne Everett Green, *Letters of Queen Henrietta Maria* (Richard Bentley, London, 1857), is interspersed with notes in explanation of the letters. Neither volume includes all the letters Henrietta wrote, and there is much duplication of content in the two books. Both editors take their material from manuscript collections. Perhaps Baillon is slightly preferable, since the letters are published in the language that Henrietta wrote, but Green's translations faithfully represent the contents of the original letters. Henrietta's correspondence with her sister Christine, Duchess of Savoy, is published in Hermann Ferrero, *Lettres de Henriette-Marie à Sa Soeur Christine* (Bocca Freres, Rome, 1881). Henrietta's letters to Christine are rather scant until about 1638. Henry Ellis, *Original Letters* (3 series of 4 vols. each, Richard Bentley, London, 1824–46), contains some letters written by Henrietta and many more which pertain to her life. Ellis's volumes consist of letters extending from the Tudor to the Hanoverian periods of English history and garnered from manuscript collections in the British Museum. Of more limited use for the life of Henrietta is George Bromley, *A Collection of Original Royal Letters* (J. Stockdale, London, 1787), consisting for the most part of letters written by the Elector and Electress of the Palatinate and their children.

Most illuminating for the marriage negotiations and Buckingham's diplomacy are the letters of state found in *Cabala, Mysteries of State* (printed for Bedell & E. Collins, London, 1654). Revealing the Spanish side of the abortive attempt to arrange a marriage between Prince Charles and the Infanta Dona Maria is Francesco de Jesus, *Narrative of the Spanish Marriage Treaty* (tr. and ed. Samuel Rawson Gardiner [The Camden Society], Westminster, 1869). Gardiner finds de Jesus honest in presenting the facts of his narrative, albeit his inferences from those facts do not represent an unbiased view. The *Debates in the House of Commons in 1625* (ed. Samuel Rawson Gardiner [The Camden Society], Westminster, 1873) shows the attitude of the English people as represented in Parliament toward a Catholic marriage for the Prince of Wales and their distrust of Buckingham's foreign policy. "The Earl of

Bristol's Defense" (in vol. VI of *The Camden Miscellany* [The Camden Society], Westminster, 1871) also sheds light upon the Spanish marriage fiasco. Bristol was the English ambassador in Madrid when Buckingham and Prince Charles went there to woo the infanta. It was Bristol on whom was cast the odium resulting from the defeat of Buckingham's policy toward Spain. Although the *Salvetti Correspondence* (*Manuscripts of Henry Duncan Skrine, Historical Manuscripts Commission, Eleventh Report,* Appendix, part I, Her Majesty's Stationery Office, London, 1887) might more logically be mentioned along with other reports of the Historical Manuscripts Commission, it is so valuable for the domestic and foreign concerns of the first five years of Charles's reign that it is not out of place at this point. Salvetti, a Florentine correspondent living in London, made detailed and penetrating reports on the court of Charles I. Unfortunately, his dispatches were available for the Manuscripts Commission only to the year 1631.

Richelieu's published letters are almost indispensable in determining the purpose for which the cardinal arranged an English marriage and his real attitude toward England in years following the marriage: Armand J. du Plessis, Duke of Richelieu, Cardinal, *Lettres, Instructions Diplomatiques et Papiers d'État* (8 vols., ed. Denis M. L. Avenel [*Collection de Documents Inédits sur l'Histoire de France*], Paris, 1853–77). Of similar value for later years is Cardinal de Mazarin, *Lettres* (9 vols., ed. P. A. Chéruel [*Collection de Documents Inédits sur l'Histoire de France*], Paris, 1872–1906). These volumes of letters are part of a plan of great scope first projected by François Guizot in 1834 when he was minister of public instruction. Guizot aimed at no less than editing all of the outstanding source materials on the history of France. Within the same series is the *Recueil des Lettres Missives de Henry IV* (7 vols., ed. M. Gerger de Xivrey [*Collection de Documents Inédits sur l'Histoire de France*], Paris, 1853–76), which has significance for Henrietta's early life.

Two sources that can be used together in studying the influence and activity of Henrietta at the court during the 1630s are Thomas Wentworth, Earl of Strafford, *The Earl of Strafford's Letters* (2 vols., ed. William Knowler, printed by William Bowyer, London, 1734), and William Laud, Archbishop of Canterbury, *Works* (7 vols., ed. James Bliss, John Henry Parker, Oxford, 1854–60). During the years Wentworth was Lord Deputy in Ireland, Laud enjoyed the confidence of the king at the court. These two trusted ministers regularly corresponded, and Laud in his letters often described the opposition he met from the queen.

The *Journals of the House of Commons* (vols. I–VI) and the *Journals of the House of Lords* (vols. III–X) reveal Parliament's opposition to the Catholic marriage and to Catholicism in general, and show the animus of the Long Parliament toward the queen. The Commons *Journals* contain little more than an outline of the proceedings of that body, whereas the Lords *Journals* contain, in addition, copies of bills, letters, and petitions. To supplement the brevity of the former journals during the first important months of the Long Parliament, we have *The Journal of Sir Simonds D'Ewes* (ed. Wallace Notestein, Yale University Press, New Haven, 1923). The editor completed his work only to the trial of Strafford, leaving much yet to be done in editing the full text of D'Ewes's notes on the proceedings of Commons. Fortunately, however, the best part of D'Ewes's journals is given to the public in this work, since the Long Parliament's most constructive period was during the beginning months of its meetings and D'Ewes later became less exact and full in recording his notes. Complementary to the *Journal* is the *Autobiography and Correspondence of Sir Simonds D'Ewes* (2 vols., ed. James Orchard Halliwell, London, 1845).

The Letters and Journals of Robert Baillie (3 vols., printed by the Bannatyne Club, Edinburgh, 1842) is informative for the Scottish view of the king's attempt to enforce the prayer book on Scotland. Baillie was a theologian of formidable erudition, a member of the General Assembly which heralded the Scottish rebellion, and later a representative in the Westminster Assembly. *The Correspondence of Sir Edward Nicholas, Secretary of State* (3 vols., ed. George F. Warner [The Camden Society], London, 1886–97), and *The Private Correspondence between Charles I and His Secretary of State, Sir Edward Nicholas* (in vol. II, part 2, of *Memoirs Illustrative of the Life and Writings of Sir John Evelyn* [2 vols., ed. William Bray, London, 1819]), help uncover what was going on at the court during the troubled months preceding the outbreak of civil war, and what the queen did during the time Charles was in Scotland, from August to December, 1641. *The Hamilton Papers* (ed. S. R. Gardiner [The Camden Society], Westminster, 1880) and "The Hamilton Papers Addenda" (in vol. IX of *The Camden Miscellany*, ed. S. R.

Gardiner, Westminster, 1895) relate to campaigns for the subjugation of the Scots.

Indispensable for understanding the marriage treaty between England and the Prince of Orange and for studying the later attempts of Henrietta to obtain assistance from the Netherlands is *Archives ou Correspondence Inédit de la Maison d'Orange Nassau* (4 vols., ed. Guillaume Groen van Prinsterer, Kemink et Fils, Utrecht, 1859). As the title implies, these volumes include the correspondence between Orange and his ambassadors in England. *The Clarke Papers* (4 vols., ed. C. H. Firth [The Camden Society], Westminster, 1891), while invaluable in the study of the Parliamentary army, are of only incidental use in writing of the life of Henrietta. Henry Cary, *Memorials of the Great Civil War in England from 1646 to 1652* (2 vols., Henry Colburn, London, 1842), contains letters drawn from the Tanner collection of manuscripts in the British Museum, and is most useful for information on the later years of the Civil War. *Charles I in 1646. Letters of Charles I to Queen Henrietta Maria* (ed. John Bruce [The Camden Society], Westminster, 1856) is an important source, since it indicates Charles's response to the queen's insistence that he accept Presbyterianism.

Henrietta's attempts to procure foreign armies for the restoration of her husband are exposed in "The King's Cabinet Opened," *The Harleian Miscellany* (12 vols., printed for Robert Dutton, London, 1808–11). This title is one of the many pamphlets drawn from the *Harleian Manuscripts* and published in the *Miscellany*. The pamphlet here cited was first published in 1645, and consisted of letters, among them many written by Henrietta, found in the king's cabinet seized at the battle of Naseby. Digby's letters, captured at a skirmish near Sherburn, were likewise given to the public in pamphlet form, under the title *The Lord George Digby's Cabinet* (London, 1646), and served to supplement the information contained in the king's cabinet. Both pamphlets contain valuable material for untangling the queen's intrigues to bring about an invasion of England in her husband's cause.

The Embassy in Ireland of Monsignor G. B. Rinuccini (tr. Anne Hutton, Alexander Thom, Dublin, 1873) does not convey by its title any notion of the importance of its contents. The volume consists of the correspondence of Rinuccini, who was sent to Ireland as the pope's nuncio in 1644. The letters are most significant in studying the queen's relations with the Irish rebels. Richard Polwhele, *Traditions and Recollections* (2 vols., London, 1826), consists of the papers of a Cornish family and contains some material on the Civil War in western England.

Mazarin's later efforts to bring about a settlement between the king and the Independent army are revealed in *The Diplomatic Correspondence of Jean de Montreuil and the Brothers de Bellièvre* (2 vols., ed. and tr. J. G. Fotheringham, vols. 29 and 30 in Publications of the Scottish Historical Society, University Press, Edinburgh, 1898–99). *The Writings and Speeches of Oliver Cromwell* (4 vols., ed. Wilbur Cortez Abbott, Harvard University Press, Cambridge, 1937–47) represents an outstanding job of editing and replaces the similar work of Thomas Carlyle. Far from being an ordering of documents of a dry-bones sort, it constitutes a biography of most excellent scholarship.

A considerable amount of valuable information concerning the life of Henrietta can be derived from the reports of the Historical Manuscripts Commission. Established in 1869, the commission has published many volumes of manuscripts held in private collections throughout England. Often the reports consist of no more than a brief description of the content of a collection; again, a catalogue of the manuscripts is published; and sometimes a collection or a portion of it is printed. Reference has already been made to the *Salvetti Correspondence*, which was edited by the commission. Other of the reports yield varying amounts of material relating to the life of Henrietta: *Fourth Report on Historical Manuscripts* (Royal Commission on Historical Manuscripts, Her Majesty's Stationery Office, London, 1874) contributes information on the queen's first visit to England following the restoration; *Manuscripts of J. Eliot Hodgkin, Historical Manuscripts Commission, Fifteenth Report* (Appendix, part 2, Her Majesty's Stationery Office, London, 1897), relates to the queen's financial negotiations in Holland; *Manuscripts of Lord Montagu of Beaulieu, Historical Manuscripts Commission Report* (Her Majesty's Stationery Office, London, 1900), concerns numerous events from 1640 to 1648; *Historical Manuscripts Commission, Report on the Manuscripts of the Duke of Buccleuch and Queensberry Preserved at Montagu House, Whitehall* (3 vols., Her Majesty's Stationery Office, London, 1899–1926), yields a few facts on the later years of Henrietta's life; *Manuscripts of Earl Cowper, Historical Manuscripts Commission, Twelfth Report* (parts I and II, Her

Majesty's Stationery Office, London, 1888), has some material on George Digby's defense of Wentworth and the queen's first request to go to the Continent; *Appendix to the Third Report of the Royal Commission on Historical Manuscripts* (Her Majesty's Stationery Office, London, 1872) touches upon Kenelm Digby's mission to Rome.

MEMOIRS

Memoirs supply so important a part of the information relating to the life of Henrietta that they deserve separate consideration. Persons of Henrietta's day, whether to portray to the world their part in public life or to preserve their memory for the private edification of their own families, wrote numerous memoirs. These works were of varying merit, and sometimes contained as much information on public events as biographical material.

Of these works, the one pertaining to the earliest part of Henrietta's life is Jean Héroard, *Journal sur l'Enfance et la Jeunesse de Louis XIII* (2 vols., ed. Eudoxie Soulié and Edouard de Barthélemy, F. Didot Frères, Fils et Cie., Paris, 1868). Héroard, the benevolent physician to the children of Henry IV, must have taken great delight in recording the day-to-day incidents in the play and training of his charges. Although his book mentions Henrietta only incidentally, it does describe the environment in which she spent her nursery years. Relating to the wider events and concerns of the French court during Henrietta's early years are Maximilien de Bethune, Duke of Sully, *Mémoires* (5 vols., Stirling and Slade, Edinburgh, 1819), and François de Bassompierre, *Journal de Ma Vie: Mémoires* (4 vols., ed. Marie J. A. LaCropte, Librairie Renouard, Paris, 1870–77). The Duke of Sully was Henry IV's chief minister and head of the national treasury. He was a great admirer of Henry, in whose service he grew rich, and tried to show how scurvily the queen treated him following Henry's death. Bassompierre, a most candid narrator, not only described his experience as a young man at the court of Henry IV, with whom he was a great favorite, but also told of his embassy to England in 1626 to settle differences over the queen's household. Pierre de L'Étoile, *Mémoires-Journaux* (12 vols., ed. G. Brunet, A. Champollion, E. Halphen, Paul Lacroix, Charles Read, and Tamisey de Larrogue, Librairie des Bibliophiles, Paris, 1875–96), is interesting in that it indicates what people were discussing, reading, and thinking at the French capital during the early years of the seventeenth century.

For the study of the French side of the marriage negotiations and later troubles between Charles and Henrietta, there is Armand J. du Plessis, Duke of Richelieu, Cardinal, *Mémoires* (10 vols., ed. P. M. Charles, François Bruel, and Robert Lavallée [Société de l'Histoire de France], Paris, 1907–31). Richelieu's story must be used with caution and reservation, but the basic facts he relates concerning the marriage dealings, when checked against his letters and other accounts of the subject, are found to be essentially correct. Also concerning the marriage treaty and early differences between Charles and Henrietta is Leveneur de Tillières, *Mémoires* (ed. M. C. Hippeau, Paulet-Malassis, Paris, 1862). Tillières seems to have been opposed to the marriage mainly because, as French ambassador in England, he felt himself slighted by his own government in the conduct of the negotiations. After being recalled to France, he returned to England as Henrietta's chamberlain.

A rather curious collection, George Ballard, *Memoirs of Several Ladies of Britain* (printed by W. Jackson, Oxford, 1752), contains the narration of the prognosticator Eleanor Davies, whom Henrietta consulted on at least one occasion. Reflecting the attitude of an English Protestant during the early years of Charles's reign is the *Diary of Thomas Rouse* (ed. Mary Anne Everett Green [The Camden Society], Westminster, 1856). Rouse was a country parson who possessed considerable intelligence.

The story of the negotiations leading to the exchange of personal representatives between Henrietta and the pope is told in Gregorio Panzani, *Memoirs* (in *The History of the Decline and Fall of the Roman Catholic Religion in England* [tr. the Rev. Joseph Berington, printed by H. Tempe for G. Offer, London, 1813]). Not understanding the strength of Protestantism in England, Panzani tries to make the reader believe that it was the opposition of the Jesuits and their party in Rome which obstructed his endeavors to bring England back to Catholicism. Father Cyprien de Gamache, *Memoirs of the Mission in England of the Capuchin Friars of the Province of Paris, from the Year 1630 to 1669* (in vol. II of Thomas Birch, *The Court and Times of Charles I* [2 vols., Henry Colburn, London, 1848]), tells of Catholic activity in England under the auspices of the queen. We are indebted to Gamache not only for the relation of the experiences of her little colony of priests, but also for many incidents relating to the life of Henrietta, since the author lived near the queen during the greater part of her life. Following the death of Father Philip, Gamache became the queen's confessor.

A description of the English court during the 1630s is given in François de Val, Marquis of Fontenay-Mareuil, *Mémoires* (vols. 40 and 41 of *Collection Complète des Mémoires Relatifs à l'Histoire de France*, ed. M. Petitot, Foucault Librairie, Paris, 1826). Mareuil was the French ambassador to England during part of the decade.

One of the most interesting personal accounts of the Civil War period is *The Memoirs of Edmund Ludlow* (2 vols., ed. C. H. Firth, Clarendon Press, Oxford, 1894). Ludlow was of republican political sentiments, and hence was opposed to the queen. Lucy Hutchinson, *Memoirs of the Life of Colonel Hutchinson* (Henry G. Bohn, London, 1848), gives the attitude of a Puritan woman toward the "daughter of Heth." The war years from the Royalist point of view are told in Lady Ann Fanshawe, *Memoirs* (John Lane Co., London, 1907). Lady Fanshawe's husband, Sir Richard Fanshawe, was variously employed in the service of Charles I, sometimes in a diplomatic capacity. Driven into exile along with other Royalists, Lady Fanshawe vividly described the years of wandering and penury. Alongside the memoirs of Ludlow and Fanshawe might be placed the *Memoirs Illustrative of the Life and Writings of Sir John Evelyn* (2 vols., ed. William Bray, London, 1819). While not holding high office himself, Evelyn was well acquainted with many of the leading personalities of the reigns of James I, Charles I, and Charles II, and recorded every event or experience he thought important. His observations are the more valued because be was free from religious bigotry or malice.

Several persons whom the queen employed in her service during the war years have left records of their experiences. *The Memoirs of George Leyburn* (printed for W. Lewis, London, 1722) tells of Leyburn's mission to Ireland to mediate a peace between the Confederate Irish and Ormonde, and the *Memoirs of Sir John Berkeley* (in vol. I of Francis Maseres, *Select Tracts* [London, 1815]) narrates the author's attempt to bring about a settlement between Charles I and the army. Both works indicate the declining power of Henrietta in political affairs after 1646. The *Private Memoirs of Sir Kenelm Digby* (Sanders and Otley, London, 1827) unfolds almost nothing of the writer's missions to Rome to solicit money for the Royalist cause from the pope, and is otherwise not very dependable.

Memoirs are no less revealing in describing the queen's life during the years of exile after Charles's death. Françoise Bertaut, Madame de Motteville, *Mémoires sur Anne d'Autriche et Sa Cour* (4 vols., ed. M. F. Riaux, Paris, n.d.), might have been mentioned earlier. Madame de Motteville's *Mémoires* reveal more of the experiences and trials of Henrietta than any other published work, and pertain not only to the queen's exile but to the whole of her life. Madame de Motteville was one of Queen Anne's closest friends and also became a confidante to Henrietta Maria. Since the *Mémoires* were not intended for publication during the author's life, Madame de Motteville was surprisingly frank at times in telling of events at the French court. In the course of long conversation and close friendship, Henrietta related her experiences as Queen of England to Madame de Motteville, who wrote down what she was told. Because Henrietta was always direct and honest unless she had some immediate purpose in giving a false impression, there is no reason to disbelieve her stories, although Madame de Motteville does seem to overdramatize them at times. The *Mémoires de Mlle. de Montpensier* (4 vols., ed. A. Chéruel, Paris, n.d.) relates to the period following Henrietta's flight to France. Mademoiselle de Montpensier was the "great Mademoiselle," niece to Henrietta, and the rich young woman with whom the English queen tried to match her son Charles. To Mademoiselle the Stuarts were just so many burdensome relatives, who, having run into hard times, had come to France to impose themselves on their kinfolk. Something of the hard times the queen suffered during her exile is told by the clerical worldling Jean François Paul de Gondi, Cardinal de Retz, *Memoirs* (J. Brotherton, London, 1723). The *Memoirs of John Reresby* (ed. James J. Cartwright, Longmans, Green, & Co., London, 1875) describes the court of Henrietta in Paris not long before the restoration. And of course there is Samuel Pepys, *Diary and Correspondence* (4 vols., ed. Richard, Lord Braybrooke, deciphered the Rev. J. Smith, David McKay, Philadelphia, n.d.), to furnish eyewitness accounts of the queen in London following the restoration. Pepys, who in his smug selfishness liked to think his own wife the most prized possession in the world, was deprecatory of Henrietta and her daughters.

HISTORIES, ARTICLES, AND PAMPHLETS

As for more general works giving the historical background to Henrietta's life, there stand above all others the contributions of the magisterial doctor, Samuel Rawson Gardiner: *History of England from the Accession of James I to the Outbreak of the Civil War, 1603–1642* (10 vols., Longmans, Green, & Co., London, 1896–99); *History of the Great Civil War, 1642–1649* (4 vols., Longmans, Green, & Co., London, 1894); *History of the Commonwealth and Protectorate* (3 vols., Longmans, Green, & Co., London, 1894–1901). Whether or not the reader agrees with Gardiner's conclusions, which do not necessarily follow from the facts he presents, the facts are nevertheless there to serve as reference. Charles Harding Firth rounded out Gardiner's projected work in *The Last Years of the Protectorate* (2 vols., Longmans, Green, & Co., London, 1909). Within the scope of one volume, the most judicious evaluation of the Stuart period up to the restoration is Godfrey Davies, *England under the Early Stuarts* (in the Oxford Series, ed. G. N. Clark, Clarendon Press, Oxford, 1938). More readable is George Macaulay Trevelyan, *England under the Stuarts* (vol. V of A History of England series, ed. Sir Charles Oman, Methuen & Co., London, 1926). Trevelyan's literary style is colorful and vivid without being ornate, but in striving for metaphors the author sometimes becomes obscure in his meaning. This book is weighted in favor of Charles's opponents, and although offered as an introductory work on the period, it really requires some prior knowledge to be fully appreciated. More limited temporally, but possibly offering the most direct comprehension of men's motives in the years immediately preceding and during the Civil Wars, are C. V. Wedgwood's two skillfully written volumes, *The King's Peace, 1637–1641* (Macmillan Co., New York, 1955), and *The King's War, 1641–1647* (Collins, London, 1958).

Of historical works written by contemporaries of the Stuarts, there is Edward Hyde, Earl of Clarendon, *The History of the Rebellion and Civil Wars in England* (7 vols., Oxford, 1849). It is preferable to use C. H. Firth's edition of this history if it is available. So much has been written in criticism and evaluation of Clarendon's contribution as a historian that extended comment is omitted here. The most penetrating analysis of Clarendon's work is found in C. H. Firth, "Clarendon's 'History of the Rebellion,'" *English Historical Review* (vol. XIX, ed. Reginald L. Poole, Longmans, Green, & Co., London, 1904).

Mention should be made of an old work, Isaac Disraeli, *Commentaries on the Life and Reign of Charles I* (2 vols., ed. and rev. Benjamin Disraeli, Henry Colburn, London, 1851). The editor was the author's son, later famous as leader of the Conservative party. In its bias against the Whig tradition, Disraeli's book might be considered a party tract pertaining to the author's own day. Rather than chronologically order the events of Charles's reign, Disraeli lifted certain episodes out of the context of time and wrote on those particular matters which interested him.

In Agnes Strickland, *Lives of the Queens of England* (8 vols., Brown & Taggard, Boston, 1860), is a section devoted to the life of Henrietta. Miss Strickland was uncritical of her sources. She often made careless mistakes of fact, and in her prejudice against Henrietta's enemies, she distorted the real picture. Interesting as an early attempt to narrate the life of Henrietta is a forty-one-page pamphlet, *The Life and Death of Henrietta Maria de Bourbon* (printed for Dorman Newman, London, 1685, reprint 1820). It is a piece of political writing which attempts to cast odium on the Parliamentary party.

Hardouin de Beaumont de Péréfixe, *The History of Henry IV* (printed by James Cottrell for John Martin, London, 1663), is an early work glorifying the reign of Henry IV, but containing many pertinent facts. The author was Archbishop of Paris and later confessor to Louis XIV. "The Trial of Ravaillac," *Bibliotheca Curiosa* (40 vols. in 9, ed. Edmund Goldsmid, Edinburgh, 1885), consists of the court record of Ravaillac's trial for the murder of Henry IV. Lucy Crump in her *Nursery Life 300 Years Ago* (G. Routledge & Sons, London, 1929) leans heavily upon Héroard for her material in telling of the upbringing of Henry IV's children. Rodolphe Pfnor, *Monographie du Palais de Fontainebleau* (3 vols., A. Morel, Paris, 1863), describes one of the palaces where Henrietta spent a part of her childhood. The story of Henrietta's mother is given by Louis Batiffol, *La Vie Intime d'une Reine de France* (Calmann-Levy, Paris, 1911). The women of the French court during the first half of the seventeenth century seemed to be a favorite topic of Batiffol, who also wrote *The Duchesse de Chevreuse* (Dodd, Mead & Co., New York, n.d.). An older, but somewhat better, biography of the fair adventuress is Victor Cousin, *Madame de Chevreuse* (5th ed., Didier et Cie., Paris, 1869). Cousin's book is valuable chiefly for the documents printed in the appendix, which includes the brief of the evidence for Richelieu's treason case against the Marquis of Chateauneuf.

Much useful material on political happenings and court life in France is found in *Le Mercure François* (25 vols. in 27, ed. J. and E. Richter, Paris, 1611–44). This publication, contemporaneous with the events it describes, is a sort of yearly almanac or survey of the news of that day, and is especially rich in details on matters of public interest. It is believed that Richelieu contributed information to the editors. Other works offering background material on the political history of France during the early seventeenth century are: Henri Hauser, *La Prépondérance Espagnole* (vol. IX in the Peuples et Civilizations series, ed. Louis Halphen and Philippe Sagnac, Librairie Felix Alcan, Paris, 1933), which is useful for international relations of the period; Pierre Aldol de Chéruel, *Histoire de France pendant la Minorité de Louis XIV* (4 vols., Hachette et Cie., Paris, 1879–80); Cicely Veronica Wedgwood, *Richelieu and the French Monarchy* (English University Press, London, 1949), a little book giving a good analysis of the character of Louis XIII; and Katherine Alexandra Patmore, *The Court of Louis XIII* (Methuen & Co., London, 1909), about the only work in English relating exclusively to the subject of which the author writes.

Proceeding to the period of Henrietta's early years in England, there is Thomas Birch, *The Court and Times of Charles I* (2 vols., Henry Colburn, London, 1848), which might have been included in another category, since it consists largely of letters as well as of the *Memoirs* of Gamache cited above. For the most part it relates to the years up to 1630, being somewhat brief on the period following that date. On Henrietta's journey to England and the first impression she made upon the country, there is Arnold Harris Mathew and Anette Calthorp, *The Life of Sir Tobie Matthew* (Elkin Mathews, London, 1907). Sir Tobie Matthew, who was secretly a Jesuit, acted as Henrietta's interpreter in England for a brief time. The book is based largely on firsthand material. L'Abbé M. Houssaye in his article "L'Ambassade de M. de Blainville," *Revue des Questions Historiques* (vol. XXIII, 1878), applauds the envoy's aggressiveness in behalf of English Catholics at a time when the government in France followed a policy of precaution in its relations with England.

Quite complete for the international relations of England during the 1630s is Leopold von Ranke, *A History of England in the Seventeenth Century* (4 vols., tr. C. W. Boase and others, Clarendon Press, Oxford, 1875), wherein the author explains the connection between Chateauneuf's plotting against Richelieu in France and the attempts of the queen's party to deprive Weston of office in England. An article by Arnold Oscar Meyer, "Charles I and Rome," *American Historical Review* (vol. XIX, Oct., 1913), shows that Charles I's clemency toward Catholics during the decade preceding the outbreak of the Civil Wars arose not only from the promptings of the queen, whom the writer does not even mention, but also from the king's own objection to persecution of the religious minority. The religious question is also considered in Peter Heylin, *Cyprianus Anglicus: The History of the Life and Death of William Laud* (printed for J. M. by A. Seile, London, 1671). Having been a friend of Laud, the author makes him a heroic martyr, but in credit to his work, Heylin had access to the best sources.

Besides comprehensive histories of the period, such as Clarendon's *History of the Rebellion*, there are other works relating especially to the war years. Sir Philip Warwick, *Memoirs of the Reign of Charles I* (Richard Chiswell, London, 1702), contains nothing that cannot be found elsewhere, but the author is fair and honest and does relate some anecdotes illustrative of the character of some of the outstanding personalities. Bartholomew Warburton used the original papers of his subject in writing the *Memoirs of Prince Rupert and the Cavaliers* (3 vols., Eliot Warburton, London, 1849). Warburton was severely critical of Henrietta Maria. Another biography dealing with a leading Royalist general is Mark Napier, *The Life and Times of Montrose* (Oliver Boyd, Edinburgh, 1840), which is also written from original materials. Gilbert Burnet, *The Memoirs of the Lives and Actions of James and William, Dukes of Hamilton and Castleherald* (printed by J. Grover for R. Royston, London, 1677), tries to explain why the Duke of Hamilton was misunderstood and to exculpate him from charges of shifty and treasonable acts. The last three works are copiously supplied with letters and are all commendatory of the persons written about. A work of much labor and research, Thomas Carte, *The Life of James, Duke of Ormonde* (6 vols., Oxford University Press, Oxford, 1851), takes a favorable attitude toward Ormonde and Charles I. The sixth volume consists of letters taken from the huge collection of papers and correspondence that the author used in gathering material for the biography. With meticulous consideration, Samuel Rawson Gardiner in his article "Charles I and the Earl of Glamorgan," *English Historical Review* (vol. II, London, 1887), contends that Charles was not guilty of betraying a power he had given his servant to deal with the Irish. Supplementary to Rinuccini's papers and correspondence is Dr. Alphonsus Bellesheim, *The Papal Nuncio among the Irish Confederates* (tr. the Rev. W. McLoughlin [Catholic Truth Society of Ireland], Dublin, 1908). To be sure, the author is biased in favor of the nuncio, but he is faithful to the facts as he found them in Rinuccini's letters. One of the most interesting works on the Civil War period is Frances Parthenope Verney, *Memoirs of the Verney Family* (4 vols., Longmans, Green, & Co., New York, 1892–99). The material for this book was compiled from volumes of papers preserved at the Verney family home, Claydon House. The story reveals how families were divided by the civil conflict: Sir Edmund Verney, the father, acting as the king's standard bearer, was killed at the battle of Edgehill, while his son, Ralph, fought with the Parliamentary army.

The war years saw a great outpouring of polemical pamphlet material. In addition to those titles found in *The Harleian Miscellany*, there were other printings in some way illustrative of the life of Henrietta Maria: the ubiquitous William Prynne kept his pen busy turning out such products as "The Popish Royall Favourite" (by Authority of Parliament, London, 1643) and "Romes Masterpiece" (London, 1644); John Pym, "The Reasons of the House of Commons to Stay the Queenes Going into Holland" (London, 1641); and, most descriptive in title, J. Goodwin, "The Butcher's Blessing or the Bloody Intentions of the Romanish Cavaliers against the City of London" (London, 1642).

James B. Perkins, *France under Mazarin* (2 vols., G. P. Putnam's Sons, New York, 1902), is somewhat useful in studying Mazarin's policy toward England during the revolution and after. "England's Joy or a Relation of His Majesty's Arrival at Dover to His Entrance at Whitehall," *Stuart Tracts* (ed. C. H. Firth, E. P. Dutton & Co., New York, n.d.), is a pamphlet reflecting the general rejoicing at the time of the restoration. In Jacques Bossuet, *Oraisons Funèbres* (ed. P. Jacquinet, Belin Frères, Paris, n.d.), will be found the funeral sermon for Henrietta Maria, the oration that established Bossuet's homiletical reputation.

271

INDEX

Abingdon, England, 170
Adolphus, Gustavus, 94
Albert, Louis d', Duke of Luynes, 14; seeks closer relations with England, 15
Amiens, France, 35
Anglicanism, 100
Anglo-Irish (Ormondists), 222, 224
Angoulême, Bishop of, almoner to Henrietta, 102, 152; collects money for Henrietta, 183–184, 199
Anne of Austria, Queen of France, regent, 50, 167, 177, 179, 210, 248; visited by Charles and Buckingham, 18; at Henrietta's wedding, 32; with Buckingham at Amiens, 36; sends aid to Henrietta, 171; assures Henrietta a pension, 173; greets Henrietta outside Paris, 174; death in 1666, 250
Antrim, Earl of, Randal Macdonell, 222
Apprentices of London: clamor against bishops in House of Lords, 135
Argyll, Earl of, Archibald Campbell, 219
Arlington, Lord, English ambassador in Paris, 223, 252
Arundel, Earl of, Thomas Howard, 141, 191, 192n

Ashburnham, John, 201; and officers' plot, 124
Ashby-de-la-Zouch, England, 165
Aubert, Marie: seized by pursuivants, 75

Baltimore, Lord. See Calvert, Sir George
Barberini, Cardinal: reprimands Panzani, 90; sends artistic works to Henrietta, 90–91; states conditions for papal aid, 112
Bassompierre, François de, Marshal, 4; instructed on embassy to England, 60; quarrels with Henrietta, 61; obtains concessions for queen's household, 62
Batten, William, Captain, 225, 226n
Bautre, Nicholas de: sent as special envoy to England, 51
Beal, Thomas, 133
Bedlam, asylum at: visited by Their Majesties, 97
Bellièvre, Pompone de, 206, 208
Berkeley, Sir John, 218n
Bernini, Giovanni: commissioned to sculpt busts of Their Majesties, 91
Berulle, Father: writes letter of admonition for Henrietta, 36; recalled from England, 48

Berwick, Scotland, 86, 144; treaty of, 111

Blainville, Sieur de: receives first instructions for mission to England, 47; receives second instructions, 48; arrives on embassy to England, 49; prevails on Henrietta to join company of Buckingham's womenfolk, 53; out of touch with policy in France, 54; receives recall to France, 55

Bohemia, 16

Bordeaux, France, 63, 81

Bossuet, Jacques, Bishop of Condon, 252

Boulogne, France, 37

Bourbon, France, watering place, 173, 238

Bourbon, ruling family of France, 162

Bradford, England, 162

Breda, The United Netherlands, 144, 234

Brett, Walter: chosen as Henrietta's first envoy to pope, 92

Breves, François Savary de: tutor to Henrietta, 11

Bridlington Bay, England, 158

Brill, The United Netherlands, 142, 226

Bristol, England, 170, 196

Brittany, 173

Brown, Geoffrey, 222

Brown, Sir Richard, 240

Brussels, Spanish Netherlands, 80

Buckingham, Countess of, 53; comments on Henrietta's melancholy, 39; member of queen's bedchamber, 56

Buckingham, Marquis and Duke of, George Villiers, 38, 44; proposes journey to Spain, 17; reports to Parliament on journey to Spain, 20; soundings for French marriage treaty, 21; intervenes in French marriage negotiations, 26; detained in England by obsequies for James I, 31; arrives in Paris to escort Henrietta to England, 32; seeks French military alliance against Spain, 33; chagrin over Richelieu's refusal of military alliance, 34; and French queen, 35; French say he is cause of marital discord, 45; wants his womenfolk placed in queen's bedchamber, 46; prepares fleet to sail against Spain, 49; tries to form alliance against Spain, 50; involvement in personal dispute between king and queen, 53; asks queen not to see Blainville, 54; tries to instruct queen on various topics, 56; entertains Bassompierre, 61; wishes to return Bassompierre's visit, 62–63; prepares fleet to attack France, 64; expedition against French, 65; assassinated, 66

Bullion, Duke of: offers army to Charles, 195

Cadenet, Marshal de: sent to England to negotiate marriage contract, 15

Cadiz, Spain, 50

Calais, France, 225

Calvert, Sir George, Lord Baltimore, 28, 29n

Canterbury, England, 141; Charles awaits bride's arrival at, 39; Henrietta and Charles spend first night at, 42

Capel, Arthur, Lord, 205n, 206

Capuchins, queen's, 103, 104, 113; brought to serve Henrietta's chapel, 74; forbidden to christen prince, 76; open living quarters for public visit, 101; transported to France, 160

Carisbrooke Castle, 219, 237

Carleton, Sir Dudley: sent to explain reason for expulsion of Henrietta's French household, 54, 57, 59

Carlisle, Countess of: member of Henrietta's bedchamber, 56; queen informs her of Charles's resolve to arrest several members of Commons, 137

Carlisle, Earl of, James Hay, 65; sent to Paris to further treaty negotiations, 25; attends Henrietta's wedding, 32; escorts the queen from Paris, 34

Carmelites, convent of, Paris, 225

Carr, Robert, 98

Castelmaine, Madame, 248
Catherine of Portugal, wife of Charles
    II, 248
Catholic Church in England, 37; con-
    dition about 1630, 88–89
Catholics in England, 44, 47, 60, 88,
    101, 110, 112, 117, 118, 120, 183;
    recusancy laws relaxed in 1624, 30;
    attend mass in queen's chapel, 74;
    persecution relaxed after birth of
    prince, 77; flock to queen's chapel,
    100; proselytize with new vigor, 102;
    decree against conversions, 104–105;
    contributions to king's war chest, 109;
    public clamor against, 116, 133–134
Catholics in Ireland, 133, 176
Chaillot, convent of, 239–240, 252
Chapel, queen's, at Somerset House:
    opened in December of 1636, 100;
    destroyed by Parliamentary soldiers,
    160
Charles I, King of England, 64, 112,
    113, 126, 134, 135, 161, 166, 167, 190,
    193, 201, 218, 220; determines not
    to fulfill Spanish marriage treaty on
    return from Spain, 19; first meeting
    with Henrietta, 40; meets first
    parliament, 43; expects wife to be
    obedient, 45–46; dissolves first
    parliament and invokes religious
    laws, 47; unfriendly toward Blain-
    ville, 49–50, 54, 55; quarrels with
    wife over her household, 51; corona-
    tion in England, 52; wishes wife to
    obey Buckingham's request, 53;
    finds excuse to dismiss queen's
    household, 56–57; tells queen her
    French friends to be sent away, 57–
    58; urges Buckingham to expedite
    return of queen's French servants,
    59; forbids speech by Blainville, 60;
    meets Buckingham on latter's return
    from Rhé, 65; ends queen's interview
    with prophetess, 65; comforted by
    queen, 67; refuses restoration of
    French household, 68; decides to rule
    without Parliament, 69; letter to

queen mother of France, 70; refuses
    Catholic baptism for prince, 76;
    expresses affection for wife, 77; re-
    fuses to take measures against
    Fontenay-Mareuil and supports
    Richard Weston, 80; ill of smallpox,
    82; forbids dueling at court, 85; goes
    to Scotland for coronation, 86;
    allows queen to exchange representa-
    tives with pope, 90, 91; hopes for
    restoration of Palatinate, 94–95;
    pleased by pope's gift to wife, 99;
    enchanted by queen's new chapel,
    101; against Catholic proselytizing
    at court, 104; prepares to invade
    Scotland, 107; and arrival of mother-
    in-law, 108; first Scottish invasion,
    109; calls election of Short Par-
    liament, 111; calls council of peers,
    112; convenes Long Parliament, 113;
    enforces laws against Catholics, 116;
    and marriage treaty with Nether-
    lands, 119; retracts reprieve of
    Goodman, 121; signs attainder of
    Strafford, 127, 128; goes to Scotland,
    130; attempts to arrest five members
    of House of Commons, 136, 137; bids
    wife farewell at Dover, 139, 141; to
    let Parliament commit first act of
    hostility, 144; raises battle standard
    at Nottingham, 152; assures wife
    he will sign no treaty with Parlia-
    ment, 153; makes headquarters at
    Oxford, 155; follows Hamilton's
    advice on Scotland, 159; will feign
    attempt to negotiate, 160; demands
    wife come to Oxford, 164; meets wife
    at Edgehill, 165; wants Newcastle to
    engage Cromwell in eastern counties,
    166; tries to bring division between
    Parliament and London, 167; con-
    venes Royalist parliament at Oxford,
    168; begs Dr. Mayerne go to the
    queen, 170; treats with Parliament,
    177; explains negotiations with
    Parliament to Henrietta, 178;
    expects no results from negotiations

at Uxbridge, 179; promises one year's suspension of penal laws, 182; warns queen against Hertogan, 183; promises Catholic toleration in return for aid, 184; sends Glamorgan to Ireland, 192; returns to Oxford after defeat at Naseby, 196; thinks he is indispensable, 196–197; will not surrender episcopacy, 197; proposes to raise new army, 198–199; makes promises to Catholics, 199; renounces Glamorgan's treaty, 200; goes to Scottish army, 201; wants Prince Charles to go to mother, 205–206; cannot accept Presbyterianism, 207; answer to London Propositions, 208, 212; angered by Davenant, 209; places Irish affairs under queen's direction, 211; refuses to discuss religion, 212; concessions to Presbyterianism, 213; in custody of Parliament, 216–217; signs Engagement, 219; trial and execution, 227

Charles II, King of England, 77, 126, 131, 199, 203, 204, 225, 232, 234, 236, 243; birth, 73; enters London with father, 135; father tells him to escape from England, 201; arrives in Paris, 209; courts Mademoiselle, 216; in Royalist view, becomes King of England in 1649, 230; dislikes Jermyn, 231; quarrels with mother, 232; meets Scottish commissioners at Breda, 234; agrees to Covenant, 235; with Scottish forces, defeated at Worcester, 236; goes to Cologne, 237; receives disturbing news about Gloucester, 241; sends Ormonde to rescue Gloucester, 242; scandalous living while in exile, 243; restoration, enters London, 245; demands mother return to England, 250

Charles Louis, Elector of the Palatinate, 155; confers degrees at Oxford, 98

Chateauneuf, Marquis of: negotiates details of peace treaty, 70; leads opposition to Richelieu, 79; imprisoned, 82

Chester, England, 196, 201

Chevreuse, Duchess of: visited by Lord Kensington, 22; promotes friendship between Queen Anne and Buckingham, 33; escorts Henrietta from Paris, 34; letter to Buckingham, 50n; enlists Chateauneuf against Richelieu, 80; exile in England, 109

Chevreuse, Duke of: proxy for Charles at wedding, 31; escorts Henrietta from Paris, 34; recalled from England, 48

Cholmley, Sir Hugh, 159

Christchurch College, Oxford, 98

Christine, Duchess of Savoy, sister of Henrietta, 8, 130, 150, 238; marriage to Duke of Savoy, 13; death in 1663, 250

Civil Wars, English, 112

Clarendon, Earl of. See Hyde, Edward

Cleves, duchy of, 4, 5, 13

Clink, prison, 117

Cochrane, Sir John, 186

Coke, John, 89n; informs king of Panzani's arrival, 89

Coke, Sir Edward: criticizes Buckingham in Parliament, 66

Colepeper, Sir John, Lord, 203, 204n, 205, 206, 212, 231

Cologne, Germanies, 237

Colombes, château of, near Paris, 247, 250

Con, George, 103, 120; as papal representative, arrives at court, 99; directs Catholic contributions to king, 109–110; returns to Rome, 111

Concini, Concino, 13

Condé, Prince of: flees with wife to Spanish Netherlands, 4

Condé, Princess of, 13; favorite of Henry IV, 4

Confederate Assembly, Irish, 222, 226; renounces treaty with Ormonde, 221

Confederate Irish, 183

Contarini, Alvise: uses offices of queen to further peace, 68; comments on conciliatory attitude of queen, 69

Cork, Ireland, 226

Cornwall, county of, England, 199
Cosin, Dr. John, 240
Cottington, Francis, Lord, 231, 235;
   refuses to join cabal against Weston,
   79; contends for office of Lord
   Treasurer, 96
Council of peers: at York, signs truce
   with Scots, 112
Council of Trent, 187
Courland, Duke of, 186
Covenant, National, in Scotland, 105,
   158, 167, 207, 220
Crisp, Sir Nicholas, 189
Cromwell, Oliver, 166, 226, 236;
   death, 244
Crosby, Sir Piers, 106

Davenant, William, 209, 212
Davies, Eleanor: consulted by queen, 65
Denbigh, Countess of, 141; holds
   Protestant service at Titchfield, 49;
   made member of queen's bedcham-
   ber, 56
Denham, Sir John, 233, 234n
Denmark, 50, 155, 163, 186, 196, 234
Derby, Earl of, James Stanley, 162
D'Ewes, Sir Simonds, 100n, 120, 122
Dieussart, François, artist, 101
Digby, George, Lord, 123, 149, 183,
   204, 206, 211, 223, 231; flees to
   Holland, 139; declared traitor by
   Parliament after interception of
   letter, 140; cabinet captured, contents
   published, 195
Digby, Sir Kenelm, 121n, 188, 196,
   222; testifies before Commons, 120;
   sent to Rome, 184; in Rome, 191;
   reports no help to be expected from
   Rome, 199
Dona Maria, Infanta, 16; papal dis-
   pensation for marriage to Charles,
   17; frightened by Charles's visit, 18
Dover, England, 141; arrival of
   Henrietta in, 39
Downs, 226
Dublin, Ireland, 224
Dunkirk, siege of, 243
Durham, England, 155

Edgehill, England, 165
Effiat, Marquis d': recalled from
   England, 48
Elizabeth, daughter of Henry IV, 8;
   betrothed to Philip IV, 13
Elizabeth, Princess, daughter of
   Henrietta, 119, 203; death in 1650, 237
Elizabeth I, Queen, 43, 138
Engagement (treaty), 219–220, 223
Epernon, Duke of: seizes English wine
   fleet, 63
Essex, Earl of, Robert Devereaux, 161,
   164, 171
Exeter, England, 170

Fairfax, Thomas, Lord, General, 162,
   169, 199
Falmouth, England, 171
Felton, John: assassinates Buckingham,
   66
Ferdinand, Archduke of Austria, 16
Finch, Sir John, 150, 151n
Fitzwilliams, Oliver, Colonel, 189, 192;
   plans to enlist Irish soldiers for king,
   184
Fleming, Sir William, 223
Fontainebleau, palace of, 210, 247
Fontenay-Mareuil, Marquis of, 79, 93;
   brings queen's Capuchin monks to
   England, 74; and theft of de Jars's
   correspondence, 80
France, 50, 163; foreign policy in 1624,
   24; stipulations for marriage treaty,
   25; importance of Valtelline to, 25;
   terms of marriage treaty with
   England, 26; modification of treaty
   on queen's household, 62; shipping,
   English raids on, 63; leaders want
   no military alliance with England,
   63; abatement of war against England, 68; treaty terms with England
   in 1629, 70, 71; results of marriage
   alliance with England, 71–72
Frederick, Elector of the Palatinate,
   73; driven out of Bohemia, 16
Fronde, wars of the, 227
Frondeurs, 227

Galway, Ireland, 226

Gamache, Father Cyprien de, 210

Gaston, Duke of Orleans, brother of Henrietta, 8, 174, 198; attends Henrietta's wedding, 31

Germany, 50

Glamorgan, Earl of, Edward Somerset, 200; sent by Charles to form alliance with Confederate Irish, 192; signs treaty, 193

Gloucester, Duke of, Henry, son of Henrietta, 203; mother attempts to force conversion to Catholicism, 240–243 *passim*; goes with Ormonde to Cologne, 243; death, 245

Gloucester, England, 166

Goffe, Dr. Stephen, 175n; and negotiations with Prince of Orange, 174, 180, 185

Goodman, John, a Jesuit, 120, 121

Goring, George, Earl of Norwich, 127, 132, 141, 168; and officers' plot, 124; sent on embassy to Paris, 175

Graham, Sir Richard, 59

Grand Remonstrance, 135

Gravesend, England, 42

Greenwich, England, 70, 141

Guernsey, Channel island, 227

Guildhall, London, 135, 136

Haesdonck, John van, Captain, 185, 189

Hague, The, The United Netherlands, 143

Hamilton, Duke of, James Hamilton, 113, 158, 168n, 212, 219, 223; as king's commissioner in Scotland, dissolves Assembly of the Kirk, 107

Hampden, John, 129

Hampton Court, 45, 52, 135, 139

Hapsburgs, 5

Harcourt, Count of: sent by Mazarin to mediate between king and Parliament, 167

Hastings, England, 199

Hatton, Christopher, Lord, 231

Heenvliet, Baron de, 147

Heidelberg, University of, 98

Henrietta Anne, Princess, Duchess of Orleans, youngest child of Henrietta, 203, 227–228, 247, 249–250, 252; birth, 171; brought to France, 210; marries Duke of Orleans, 247

Henrietta Maria

—from 1609 to 1625: birth, 3; attends rites for father, 7; first letter, 10; instructed in arts, 11; childhood play, 12; publicly ignored in childhood, 12; as princess, attends public functions, 13; does not accompany mother into exile, 14; consider marriage for, 15; Charles's first sight of, 18; views portrait of Charles, 22; terms of marriage treaty, 26; receives papal letter on marriage, 29; description of wedding, 30–32; itinerary from Paris to England in 1625, 34; at Channel coast en route to England, 38; arrival in Dover, 39; poor accommodations on arrival in England, 39–40; first meeting with Charles, 40–41; first impressions of Charles's court, 41

—from 1625 to 1638: reprimanded by Buckingham, 45; interrupts Protestant services, 49; dispute with Charles over household appointments, 51; refuses to attend husband's coronation, 52; theatrical activities in 1625, 52; differences with husband at opening of his second parliament, 52–53; refuses to scorn Blainville, 54; spurns Buckingham's advice, 56; prays for Catholics executed at Tyburn, 57; protests expulsion of French household, 58; letter to mother on expulsion of French household, 58n; emotional state on Blainville's arrival, 60; entertained at Buckingham's home, 61, 64; tries to promote peace with France, 64; asks Lord Treasurer for money, 64–65; consults prophetess, 65; receives English prisoners seized on Rhé, 66; reaction to Buckingham's death, 67;

awakens affection of king, 67; asks husband for money, 67–68; promotes peace between France and England, 68; conciliatory attitude on household, 69; first pregnancy, 70; dislikes Weston's parsimony, 75–76, 78; receives linens from mother, 76; extent of influence over husband in 1630, 77; and plot to overthrow Richelieu, 79; letters found in de Jars's cabinet, 82; defeated in opposition to Weston, 82; presents a play, 83; accusation of scandal, 85; moral innocence, 86; no longer wishes protection of French court, 88; disappointment over Barberini's gift, 91; political standing in 1636, 92; urges alliance with France against Hapsburgs, 95–96; inquires about de Jars's release, 96; supports Cottington for Lord Treasurer, 96; frightened by rumor, 98; concerned about Catholic conversions at court, 104–105; shown new prayer book for Scotland, 106; intercedes for friends against Wentworth, 107; welcomes mother, 108; solicits money from Catholics, 109, 110

—from 1638 to 1642: advises king to stand firm against Scots, 112; charges of Parliament against her, 115; advises Rossetti to leave England, 118; saddened by death of daughter Anne, 118; apologizes for assessment of Catholics, 121; thinks of leaving England, 122, 128–129; views wedding of daughter Mary, 126; defiant toward Parliament, 128; spirits depressed, 130; lets Prince Charles go to Richmond, 131; and incident at Oatlands, 131–132; appeals to Secretary Nicholas, 134; accused of conspiracy with Irish, 136; informs Countess of Carlisle of king's intention to arrest several members of Commons, 137; retracts accusation of threats made against, 138

—from 1642 to 1645: plans to escort Mary to Holland, 139; sails for Holland, 141; not welcomed by Dutch burghers, 143; pawns jewels in Netherlands, 144; advises king to seize Hull, 144; suffers from toothache, 145; advises Charles not to give Parliament control of army, 145–146; advises Charles on conditions for mediation, 146; considers going from Holland to France, 146; buys military supplies in Netherlands, 147; ships military supplies from Netherlands, 147–149 passim; estimate of money raised in Netherlands, 149; unhappy in Netherlands, 150; professes love for husband, 151; tells Charles to make no peace without her consent, 152; thinks of going to France, 153; hears rumors from England, 154; negotiates for aid from Denmark, 155; Dutch are glad to see her depart, 156; survives storm at sea, 156–157; second departure from Netherlands, 157; escapes Parliamentary fleet at Bridlington Bay, 157–158; gives arms to Earl of Newcastle, 158, 162; warns against compromise with Parliament, 160; dissembles in interceding for Parliament, 161; impeached in Commons, 162; suggests marriage between Prince Charles and daughter of Orange, 164; travels from Newark to meet husband, 165; scolds Newcastle for not writing oftener, 166; must leave Oxford, 169; bids final farewell to Charles, 170; goes to Falmouth, 171; writes Charles of suffering, 171–172; declaration of love for Charles, 172; escapes Parliamentary fleet off Falmouth, 173

—from 1645 to 1649: lands in Brittany, travels to Bourbon, 173; ravages of ill health, arrival in Paris, 174; no letters from Charles, 177; admonishes Charles concerning talks at Uxbridge, 179; attempts to hire

Lorraine's army, 179–180; and Irish rebellion, 182; loses confidence in Hertogan, 183; endorses plan of Fitzwilliams, 184; sells tin mined in Cornwall, 185; health still precarious, 186; does not meet Rinuccini, 188; schemes to detain Rinuccini in Paris, 189; tries to send supplies to Montrose in Scotland, 195; does not understand Charles's stand on episcopacy, 198; appeals to her brother Gaston for military assistance, 198; concerned over safety of children, 203; demands Prince Charles come to Paris, 205; tells Ormonde to publicize treaty with Supreme Council, 211; scolds Charles, 213; promotes match between Prince Charles and Mademoiselle, 215–216; influence declines, 217; fears for Charles's safety, 218; attempts another treaty with Confederate Irish, 221; negotiations with Rome, 223; sacrifices personal possessions, 223, 225; wishes to visit imprisoned husband, 227; suffers want during wars of the Fronde, 228; despair on hearing of Charles's execution, 228–229
—from 1649 to 1669: wields little influence over affairs of Charles II, 230; in opposition to members of Charles II's council, 231; disputes with son Charles, 232; continues attempts to guide son's affairs, 233; approves son's going to Scotland, 234; does not know what happened to son Charles in Scotland, 235–236; deprivation and sorrow as an exile, 238; establishes convent at Chaillot, 239; allows only Catholics in household, 240; attempts to force conversion of Duke of Gloucester, 240–243 passim; writes Christine of Cromwell's death, 244; opposes James's marriage to Anne Hyde, 245; overjoyed by restoration of son to throne of England, 245; returns to England, 246; returns to France for daughter's wedding, 247; last visit to England, 248; final return to France, 249; death in 1669, 251

Henry IV, King of France, 4, 173, 252; prepares for war, 5; assassination, 6; romps with children, 11

Hertford, Marquis and Earl of, 131

Hertogan, Father: promotes plan for Irish aid to Royalists, 177

Histoire Universelle de 1550 jusqu'a l'An 1601, 196

Histrio-mastix, 83, 92

Holland, Earl of, Viscount Kensington, Henry Rich, 22n, 103, 113, 131; emissary for French alliance, 21; describes Henrietta to Charles, 22; first interview with Henrietta, 23; at Henrietta's wedding, 32; escorts Henrietta from Paris, 34; dispatched to French court on invitation of Richelieu, 54; conveys Contarini's request to queen, 68; leader of opposition to Weston, 78; in support of Marie de Medici, 81; challenges Jerome Weston and suffers king's displeasure, 84, 85; retreats from Scotland, 111

Holland, province of The United Netherlands, 50, 139, 144

Hopton, Sir Ralph, 206

Hospital of Lovers, The, drama, 98

Hotham, Sir John, Captain, 165; seizes Hull for Parliament, 139–140

Hudson, Dr. Michael, 201

Hudson, Geoffrey, 126

Huguenots, 49, 55

Hull, England, 139, 144, 162; held by Parliament, 165

Humber River, England, 149

Hussey, Mrs. Anne, 120

Hyde, Anne, Duchess of York, 245

Hyde, Sir Edward, Earl of Clarendon, 148, 205n, 206, 215, 227, 246, 250; leader of Charles II's council in exile, 231; opposes Charles II's going to Scotland, 234

Inchiquin, Earl of, Murrough O'Brien, 224

Independents, 179, 194; rift with Presbyterians, 217

Innocent X, Pope, 190, 191, 193; sends Rinuccini to Ireland, 187; instructions to Rinuccini, 188; stipulates conditions for aid to Charles I, 191–192

Inns of Court: present a masque, 92–93

Ireland, 145, 167, 177, 178, 179, 187, 189, 190, 192, 196, 199, 204, 211, 222; outbreak of rebellion in, 133; rebellion in Ulster, 136; year's cessation of arms, 182; conditions in 1647, 220

Irish, Old, 224

James I, King of England, 15; seeks treaty with Spain to restore Palatinate to son-in-law, 16; opposes son's journey to Spain, 17; convenes last parliament, 19; sees necessity of land warfare, 21; and marriage treaty with France, 27; postpones meeting of Parliament, 28; relaxes enforcement of recusancy laws, 30; death, 30; Richelieu promises arms for Mansfeld, 34

Jars, Chevalier de, 94, 96; agent of Chateauneuf in England, 80; sentenced and reprieved, 82

Jermyn, Henry, 84n, 106, 150, 163, 165, 173, 175, 181, 204, 206, 212, 224, 225, 241, 252; quarrels with Jerome Weston, 84; refuses to marry Eleanor Villiers, banished from court, 85; and officers' plot, 124; flees from England, 127; supporter of Confederate Irish, 183; squanders Henrietta's French pension, 215; leader of Henrietta's council in Paris, 231

Jersey, Channel island, 203, 204, 227, 236

Jesuits in England, 140; oppose sending bishop to England, 89

Jones, Inigo, 98

Joyce, George, Cornet, 218

Juxon, William, Bishop of London: supported by Laud, 96; appointed Lord Treasurer, 97

Kensington, England, 85

Kensington, Viscount. See Holland, Earl of

Kent, county of, 199

Kirk, in Scotland. See Presbyterians in Scotland

Lambe, Dr.: consulted by Buckingham, assassinated, 66

Lambeth Palace: attacked by mobs, 113

Lanark, Earl of, William Hamilton, 212, 223

Lancashire, 162

Landale, Marmeduke, 226

Lands End, Cornwall, 203

La Rochelle, France, 64, 65, 74, 81

Laud, William, Archbishop of Canterbury, 97, 100, 102; supports Juxon for Lord Treasurer, 96; not inclined to Catholicism, 99; ignores Con's presence at court, 100; disavows Catholicism, 103; and conversion of Countess of Newport, 104; queen is again friendly toward, 105; and Scottish prayer book, 105; moves to Somerset House, 113

Leeds, England, 162; besieged by Newcastle, 163

L'Étoile, Pierre de, 3

Leyburn, Dr. George, 221

London, England, 86, 112, 120, 167, 227, 245; plague in 1625, 42–43; welcome to new queen, 43; plague worsens in 1625, 44; plague subsides in 1626, 52; public hails victory of Scots, 113; prepares to regale king, 134; king's return from Scotland, 135; protects proscribed members of Parliament, 138

London Propositions, 207

Long Parliament. See Parliament of 1640

Lorkin, Thomas, 48

Lorraine, Duke of, 176, 227
Loudon, Lord, John Campbell, 219
Louis XIII, King of France, 8, 49, 50,
    55, 59, 62, 127; marriage to Infanta
    Anne, 13; overthrows regency, 14;
    attends Henrietta's wedding, 31; and
    subjugation of La Rochelle, 64; sets
    up standards captured at Rhé, 70;
    supports Richelieu against enemies,
    79, 82; cannot refuse sister asylum,
    146
Louis XIV, King of France, 210, 244,
    248, 250; marriage, 245; decrees state
    funeral for Henrietta, 252
Louvre, palace, 3, 174, 227
Lovell, Richard, 241

Majesties, Their, Charles I and
    Henrietta: visit Oxford University,
    97-98; visit habitation of queen's
    Capuchins, 102; resolve to leave
    London, 139; at Woodstock, 165
Manchester, England, 162
Mansfeld, Ernst von, Count, 44;
    employed by James I to invade
    Palatinate, 28
Mardyke, Spanish Netherlands, 243
Marie de Medici, Queen of France,
    regent, 3, 117, 119; coronation, 5;
    keeps children away from Paris, 8;
    observes formal decorum in presence
    of children, 10; neglects education of
    children, 11; regency, 13; banished
    to Blois, 14; reconciled to son, 15;
    responds favorably to suggestions of
    English marriage for Henrietta,
    21; allows Kensington interview
    with Henrietta, 23; at Henrietta's
    wedding, 31; gives letter of advice
    to Henrietta, 36; reacts to expulsion
    of Henrietta's French household,
    59-60; escapes to Flanders, 79; tries
    to gain admission to England, 80;
    hopes of overthrowing Richelieu, 81;
    arrives in England, 107; general
    reaction to visit, 108; leaves England,
    130; death, 150
Marie Thérèse, Infanta, 245

Marriage treaty with France: terms of,
    26-27; assessment of terms, 27-28;
    results on English domestic politics,
    28; papal dispensation for, 29
Marston Moor, battle of, 177
Mary, Princess of Orange, daughter of
    Henrietta, 119, 122, 126, 128, 139,
    142, 236; marriage to William of
    Orange, 125; plans to visit mother in
    Paris, 233; plans for return to
    England, 245; death, 247
Mary, Queen of Scots, 110
Matthew, Sir Tobie, 103; as Henrietta's
    interpreter, 39
Mayerne, Dr. Theodore, 129, 251; goes
    to Exeter to attend queen, 170
Mazarin, Cardinal, 155, 167, 189,
    190, 195, 206, 225, 246; not inclined
    to extend aid to Royalists, 175; will
    do nothing to transport Lorraine's
    army, 181; attempts treaty between
    Charles I and Scots, 194; reaction to
    Prince of Wales's arrival in Paris,
    209; gives up pretense of assisting
    Charles I, 214; policy toward
    England in 1646, 217; recognizes
    Cromwell's government, 236
Mende, Bishop of, 35, 51; objects to
    Protestant women in queen's
    household, 46; sent to France by
    Blainville, 54
Monk, George, General, 244
Montagu, Sir Walter, 57n, 103, 155,
    241; sent to French court, 57; writes
    pastoral, 83; seeks de Jars's release,
    95; testifies on Catholic assessment,
    120; imprisoned by Parliament, 167
Montglat, Madame de, 14; confidante
    of royal family in France, 9
Montpensier, Mademoiselle de,
    daughter of Gaston, 206; courtship
    with Prince Charles, 215-216
Montreuil, Jean de, 197, 201, 206, 223;
    sent to Scotland, 194; gives advice to
    Mazarin, 220
Montrose, Marquis and Earl of, James
    Graham, 158, 163, 185, 186; sent to
    fight for king in Scotland, 168; leads

only undefeated Royalist army, 194–195; defeated at Philipbaugh, 196

Moray, Sir Robert, 194, 197*n*

Morton, Lady, 210

Motteville, Madame de, Françoise Bertaut, 45, 106, 149, 225, 248; recognizes Jermyn's limitations, 231

Munster, province of Ireland, 224

Murray, William, 134*n*, 213

Muskerry, Earl of, Donough MacCarthy, 222

Naseby, battle of, 187

Netherlands, Spanish, 4

Netherlands, The United, 50, 153, 180, 181; and marriage treaty with England, 119; policy in dealing with English parliament, 146

Nevers, France, 174

Newark, England, 164, 201

Newcastle, Earl and Duke of, William Cavendish, 140*n*, 150, 155, 156, 158, 162, 163, 166, 177; directed to seize Hull, 139; besieges Leeds, 163; between armies of Scots and Parliament, 169

Newcastle-upon-Tyne, England, 112, 144, 149, 162

New Forest, Hampshire, 49

Newgate, prison, 117

New Model army, 194

Newport, Countess of: conversion to Catholicism, 103

Newport, Earl of, Mountjoy Blount: protests wife's conversion, 103

Nicholas, Sir Edward, 130, 132*n*, 134, 178, 214, 231

Noel, Jacques de, Abbot of Peron, 89

Northumberland, Earl of. *See* Percy, Algernon

Notre Dame, Cathedral of, Paris, 70

Nottingham, England, 152

Nottinghamshire, 165

Oath of Allegiance, 102

Oatlands, royal estate, 131

O'Conner, an Irish priest, 120

Officers' plot, 124–125

Olivares, Count of, 18

O'Neill, Owen, 136, 189, 224

Orange, Prince of, Frederick Henry, 140, 147, 154, 164, 185, 215; negotiates for marriage, 119; opposes Henrietta's coming to Holland, 139; greets queen at Brill, 142; political policy in 1642, 146; reaction to Henrietta's appeals for aid, 151; offered English political alliance by Henrietta, 175; skeptical about employment of Lorraine's army, 180

Orange, Prince of, William, 126, 234; arrives in England, 125; death, 237

Order of the Visitation, 239

Orkney Islands, 163

Orleans, Duke of, brother of Louis XIV, 248

Ormonde, Earl of, James Butler, 182*n*, 184, 188, 192, 200, 210, 222, 226, 231, 233; as viceroy, hard pressed by Irish rebels, 182; goes to France, 224; travels to Paris in behalf of Gloucester, 242

Oxford, England, 44, 46, 155, 160, 162, 164, 166, 170

Oxford University, 97

Palatinate, German, 44, 95

Panzani, Gregorio, 99; sent as papal emissary to England, 89; ambitions exceed instructions, 90; and instrument of concord, 91; leaves England, 92

Paris, France, 35, 50, 206; welcomes exiled queen, 174

Parlement of Paris, 228

Parliament, Cavalier, 245

Parliament, English, 37, 112; demands recusancy laws be enforced, 20; hears report on Spanish marriage negotiations, 20; votes money for war against Spain, 20; war policy against Spain, 21; meeting postponed by James, 28; doubtful about Buckingham's foreign policy, 44; protests failure to enforce recusancy laws, 44; reconvenes in Oxford in 1625, 46; dissolved in 1625, 47; Charles's second parliament convenes, 52; in 1628, 66; dissolved in 1629, 69; Protestant attitude of members, 72; meeting of Short Parliament, 111–112

Parliament, Scottish: invites Charles II to Scotland, 234

Parliamentary army, 155, 162, 163, 170

Parliamentary navy, 148, 157, 158, 172, 180, 186

Parliament of 1640 (Long), 113, 119, 120, 131, 132, 134, 135, 138, 140, 144, 146, 154, 159, 160, 164, 168, 207, 227, 244; convenes, 115; hears grievances against popery, 116; and enforcement of laws against recusancy, 117; asks queen to dismiss Catholic servants, 118; reminds king of statutes against Catholic priests, 121; votes impeachment of Wentworth, 126; passes attainder of Wentworth, 127; opposes queen's trip to Continent, 129; informed of Irish rebellion, 133; asks for own corps of guards, 136; responds to king's charge of treason against several members, 136–137; addressed by king in Guildhall of London, 138; approves queen's leaving England, 139; presents declaration of grievances, 140; sends own ambassador to United Netherlands, 153; publishes Charles's intercepted letter, 160; members think queen obstructs understanding between king and Parliament, 160; lower house impeaches queen, 161; accepts Covenant, 167; recognized by Charles I as legal parliament, 177; publishes letters captured at Naseby, 187; differences among religious factions within, 217–218

Passions Calmed or the Settling of the Floating Island, play: presented at Oxford before Their Majesties, 98

Pendennis Castle, 172, 186

Pennington, Sir John, 140

Pepys, Samuel, 248; comments on Henrietta's return to London, 246

Percy, Algernon, Duke and Earl of Northumberland, 124, 227

Percy, Henry, Lord, 231

Perone, Madame, 171

Philip, Father, 87; allowed to remain in queen's service, 59; introduces Panzani to queen, 89; imprisoned, 133

Philipbaugh, battle at, 196

Pibrac, Seigneur de, Guy du Faur, 11

Plymouth, England, 64, 199

Poigny, Marquis de: receives instructions from Richelieu, 87

Pointoise, abbey of, 241

Porter, Sir Endymion, 214

Portland, Earl of. See Weston, Richard

Portsmouth, England, 49, 127, 154

Presbyterians in England, 73, 179, 194, 198, 207; fear Independents, 217

Presbyterians in Scotland, 107; and state of the faith, 105; and Assembly of the Kirk, 107

Preston, Thomas, General, 225

Protestants in England, 93, 100, 143; observe fast in November of 1640, 117

Providence, ship, 149

Prynne, William, 92; attacks stage plays, 83; alleged diatribe against queen, 84

Puritans in England, 48, 85, 92, 103, 117, 159; do not celebrate when prince is born, 73; rankled over admission of queen's Capuchins to England, 74

Pym, John, 129, 153, 157, 161; presses charges against Wentworth, 116; learns of officers' plot, 125; reveals officers' plot, 126; forewarned of king's intention to arrest five members of Parliament, 137

Ravaillac, François, 6

Retz, Cardinal de, Jean de Gondi, 227, 228n

Rhé, French island, 65, 70

Rich, Henry. *See* Holland, Earl of

Richelieu, Cardinal, 38, 50, 57, 92, 122, 152; appointed head of royal council, 26; insists recusancy laws in England be suspended, 26; opposes Buckingham's wish for military alliance, 33–34; sends Blainville to England, 47; prepares second set of instructions for Blainville, 48–49; opposes Buckingham's coming to France, 50; fears war with England, 51; relents on demands concerning Henrietta's household, 54; reaches accord with Spain over Valtelline, 55; continues to refuse military alliance with England directed against Spain, 55; rejects Buckingham's visit, 63; belittles Bassompierre's accomplishment, 63; does not wish war with England, 64; suggests mediation of Henrietta and her mother, 69; and plot to overthrow power, 79; illness, 81; strikes down enemies, 82; wants Henrietta's friendship, 87; wishes English alliance against Austria, 94; refuses to release de Jars, 94, 96; and agents in England, 113; discourages Henrietta's seeking asylum in France, 146; death, 155

Richmond, Duchess of, 141

Richmond, Duke of, James Stewart, 177

Richmond, palace of, 131

Rinuccini, Giovanni, Bishop of Fermo, 188, 204, 221–226 *passim*; sent to Ireland as pope's nuncio, 187; at Paris en route to Ireland, 189; on Irish aid for Charles, 190–191; leaves Paris for Ireland, 191; opposes Glamorgan's treaty, 193–194; opposes treaty with Ormonde, 200; excommunicates adherents of treaty with Ormonde, 211

Rochester, England, 141

Rome (papacy), 222

Rossetti, Count, 118; arrives in England, 111; encourages appeal to Rome, 112; leaves England, 128

Rouchefaucault, Cardinal: pronounces nuptial benediction at Henrietta's wedding, 32

Roxburgh, Countess of, 141

Royalist army, 144, 164, 201

Royalists, 161, 162, 165, 179, 225; at Oxford, charge queen obstructs peace between king and Parliament, 178

Royal Navy: salvo in welcome to new queen, 43

Royal Slave, The, drama, 98

Rue de la Ferronerie, Paris, 6

Rupert, Prince, 165, 177, 184, 225; receives degree at Oxford, 98; commands ships carrying military supplies from Netherlands, 148; lands at Newcastle-upon-Tyne, 148; surrenders Bristol, 196

Sabran, M. de, French envoy, 171

St. Denis, abbey church of, 6, 252

Saint-Georges, Madame, 10, 48; close to Princess Henrietta Maria, 14; disputes with Charles over travel accommodations, 42; Buckingham speaks to on personal relations between king and queen, 56

Saint-Germain-en-Laye, France, palace at, 188; as royal nursery, 8; description of, 9

St. Giles, Cathedral of, Edinburgh, 105

St. James's Palace, London, 57, 76

St. John's College, Oxford, 98

Saint Mary's, Scilly Islands, 203, 204

St. Patrick's Purgatory, shrine in Ireland, 106

Sales, St. Francis de, 239

Sancy, Father: in embassy of Blainville, 60; discovered to be spy, 62

Santerre, M. de, French ambassador: confers with Henrietta concerning political alliance, 95

Scampari, Father, 190

Scarborough, England, 159

Scheveningen, The United
Netherlands, 156

Scotland, 86, 111, 128, 159, 163, 168,
194, 223; National Covenant in,
105; rebellion in, 105, 107; Assembly
of the Kirk, 107; English invasion
of repelled, 111; meeting of
Parliament, 111

Scots, 117, 134, 139, 163, 198, 208;
occupy northern England, 112; join
Parliament in war against king, 167;
again deal with king, 219

Scottish army, 113, 201, 207; occupies
northern England, 112; invades
England to aid Parliament, 168

Seine, river, 8

Shepheard's Paradise, The, drama:
presented by queen, 83

Sherburn, battle at, 195

Shetland Islands, 163

Somerset House, London, 59, 61, 70,
103, 113, 245; residence for
Henrietta, 43

Southampton, Earl of, Thomas
Wriothesley, 177

Southampton, England, 49

Spain, 43, 55, 60, 195; concludes treaty
ending war with England, 71

Spanish Armada, 110

Spanish marriage negotiations: initial
terms of, 17; Charles and
Buckingham travel to Spain in
furtherance of, 17–18

Star Chamber, court of, 107; sentences
Prynne, 84

States General (United Netherlands),
154, 180; rebuked by Henrietta, 157

Strafford, Earl of. *See* Wentworth,
Thomas

Stratford-on-Avon, England, 165

Strickland, Agnes, 149

Strickland, Walter, 153, 154

Sully, Duke of, M. de Bethune, 4, 13

Supreme Council of the Confederate
Irish, 177, 183, 184, 187, 189, 192,
200, 201, 210, 221, 224, 225, 233;

concludes treaty with Glamorgan,
192–193; reaches agreement with
Ormonde, 201

Sweden, 181

Sword of Tyrone, 224

Thames, river, 43

Theobalds, country estate, 135

Thirty Years' War, 7, 16, 94

Tillières, Leveneur de: thinks
Henrietta obstinate, 42

Titchfield, country estate, 49

Tower of London, 116, 135

Traquair, Earl of, John Stewart, 111*n*;
consents to meeting of Scottish
parliament, 111

Tremouille, Duchesse de: visits
Henrietta, 78

Trexel, The United Netherlands, 148

Tromp, Admiral van, 142

Tyburn gallows, London, 57

Ulster (Ireland), 177, 222

Urban VIII, Pope: sends gift to
Henrietta, 99

Uxbridge: conferences at, 178

Vallot, M., physician, 250

Valtelline (Switzerland), 55; seized by
Spain, 24; success of French arms in,
33

Vane, Sir Henry, 129

Vantelet, Madame: permitted to
remain in queen's service, 59;
promised restoration of pension, 87

Verney, Sir Ralph: mocks king's
uxoriousness, 87

Vic, Sir Henry de, 181

Vieuville, Marquis La: pliant attitude
on terms of marriage treaty, 25;
dismissal from office, 26

Ville-aux-Clercs, M. de: recalled from
England, 48

Villiers, Eleanor: names Jermyn as her
lover, 85

Villiers, George. *See* Buckingham,
Duke of

Wakefield, England, 163

Wales, 196

Warburton, Bartholomew, 149

Wellingborough, England: queen takes the waters at, 64, 67

Wentworth, Thomas, Earl of Strafford, 29n, 97, 103, 106; letter to Sir George Calvert, 28; strikes against enemies, 106; advises king to call Parliament, 111; charged with high treason, 116; trial, 122; attainted, 126; death, 128

Westminster Abbey, 52

Westminster Hall, 52, 122

Weston, Jerome: takes letters from diplomatic mail pouch, 84

Weston, Richard, Earl of Portland: queen asks for money, 65; detested by both Protestants and Catholics, 76; disliked by queen, 77; cabal plots against, 79; opposes Marie de Medici, 81; survives attack of enemies, 82; informs king of duel, 84; death, 93

Westphalia, Peace of, 227

Whitehall Palace, 52, 53, 135, 136, 138

Wight, Isle of, 219

Williams, Sir Abraham, 85

Wilmot, Henry, 231; and officers' plot, 124

Windebank, Sir Francis, 90n, 104, 117, 150; talks of reconciliation with Rome, 90; thinks queen's Capuchins not safe, 113; flees to France, 113–114

Windsor Castle, 139, 141

Winter, Sir John, 136

Woodstock, country estate, 46

Woodstock, England, 165

Worcester, England: Charles II and his Scottish forces defeated at, 236

Wren, Matthew, Bishop of Norwich, 100

Wyatt, Sir Dudley, 204

York, Duke of, James, son of Henrietta, 126, 203, 224, 226, 234, 236; at odds with mother, 235; vain boasting, 236; joins Charles in Cologne, 237; amour with Anne Hyde, 245

York, England, 112, 135, 139, 158, 163

Yorkshire, 150, 156, 162, 164, 165; lost by Royalists, 177

Note on the Author

QUENTIN BONE is professor of history at Indiana State University at Terre Haute. He earned his B.A. (1940), M.A. (1941), and Ph.D. (1954) degrees from the University of Illinois. He has taught at both the secondary and college levels. *Henrietta Maria, Queen of the Cavaliers* is his first book.